Beyond the Wire

A Soldier's Perspective on the Iraq War

By Ross Bryan

Paperback Edition

ISBN: 9781983167515

To my father, a Vietnam vet. May he rest in peace.

A note from the author:

This book chronicles my two deployments to Iraq and my thoughts on the war. Mostly, it's a mix of combat stories interspersed with political commentary. I have added footnotes to clarify certain passages and provide readers with additional commentary. That said, I'd like to add that all stories herein are based on actual events, told exactly as I remember them. However, the names and identifying characteristics of certain individuals have been changed, minus our KIA (killed in action). I did this for obvious legal reasons, though also to protect the identities and privacy of those I served with.

Regards,
Ross Bryan

PS: Questions? I can be contacted at:
rossbryan.us@gmail.com

CONTENTS

People ask, *What's it like over there?* I'll tell you…

Prologue

Tal'Afar, Iraq
Jun 7, 2005

JUST A FEW minutes past sunup, a roaring column of armored vehicles floods into *Sarai*, cleverly slipping in through the southern bowels of the city. We've completely blindsided our enemy. Within minutes there's a tank on every street corner and Apaches buzzing overhead. Hundreds of American and Iraqi troops converge onto the scene, each squad pounding their way into the homes of known insurgents. Minus the occasional burst of gunfire, all remains calm. In war, the early bird gets the worm. With such a heavy concentration of force centered within a few square blocks, I assume little can go wrong. It seems the *Mujahedeen* are boxed in, if not just now waking up. The most activity I can see from behind my gunner's sights is a plump orange-feathered rooster whose crows are drowned out by the incessant rumbling of our diesel engines.

It's not until 0700 that the small arms fire begins to intensify. Suddenly, we have a real fight on our hands. As our dismounts bound from one property to the next, they're sniped at from rooftops and apartment windows. Battle lines start to merge, as friend and foe exchange fire with one another from just a few meters apart. Bullets ping around our vehicles, errantly ricocheting in every which direction. Periodic explosions rumble the city floor, each *boom* tearing at our nerves.

Soon enough, our air support begins taking fire as well. Within the hour, insurgents down two helicopters, forcing an Apache and Kiowa out of the sky with well-placed bursts of machinegun fire. The Apache is knocked out for the rest of the fight, having sustained damage to one of its engines. But the small Kiowa reconnaissance chopper is deemed still fit for flight following an emergency landing.

Meanwhile, the ground battle rages on into its fourth hour. Gunmen continue to slip from one alleyway to the next, popping up here and there like phantoms, only to shoot and vanish.

Then comes a panicked call for help I'll never forget.

"Officer down!"

When I hear those two words over the troop net, my heart skips a beat. It's Sergeant First Class Greggory Velasquez, our mortar platoon's top dog. Accompanied by American advisers from the 98th AST (Advisory Support Team), he was tasked with leading a platoon of Iraqi soldiers – or *jundis* – onto a cluster of enemy targets. While securing the objective, his team came under attack in a narrow alleyway. Trapped in a fusillade of bullets and exploding RPGs, Velasquez stood his ground, fully exposed, firing back like a madman. As the alleyway erupted in gunfire, only two jundis remained at his side; the rest cowered for safety, peeling off to their rear. With AK rounds snapping all around him, he lobbed a hand grenade in the path of his attackers, killing at least one and pushing back an onrush of enemy fighters.

At some point, an officer with the 98th was hit. Taking notice, Velasquez heroically thrust himself into a salvo of bullets, dragging the man to safety at risk to his own life.

Our crew immediately answers Velasquez's plea for backup, racing our Bradley to his aid. Getting there is no small task. Sarai is the most ancient subdivision in all of Tal'Afar – an architectural monstrosity of crazy labyrinthine streets and narrow back alleys. A place where modern building designs blend into the millennium-old constructs of Islam's Golden Age. From within, it's easy to defend, as there are incalculable ways through which one might lure his enemy into an ambush. Many of its backstreets are barricaded, if not altogether impassable because our vehicles are too wide. And from the rooftops above, one can easily shoot or firebomb his enemies below.

Unfortunately, we're blocked out of the only route of entry to Velasquez's position by some tank crew from another unit. They've completely buttoned themselves up, shutting their turret hatches while continuing to scan their sector. In doing so, they've unintentionally bottlenecked the alleyway we need to pass down in order to evacuate that casualty from the 98th. Even worse, because of the high magnification of their gunner's sights, they can't see us trying to flag them down, frantically begging them to remove themselves from the narrow passageway they've corkscrewed themselves into. Nor is there any way for us to reach them over the radio; not with the wild flurry of information pouring over our radio waves. Plus we have no clue as to which unit they even belong to.

This place is scary as hell. My surroundings look and feel almost post-apocalyptic, like we've entered some kind of dead zone. The sun is up, but the streets are empty. The main routes are filled with blackened craters. There isn't a building in sight that isn't either cut up with bullet holes or marred by the blistery splashes of impacted mortar rounds.

I begin to tense up. My throat is dry and my lips are quivering. Under my body armor I can feel my heart pulsating violently, like it's going to explode out of my chest. I clasp my gunner's hand station, scanning the turret back and forth. I scan down alleyways and scrutinize the uneven rooftops that dominate the city's skyline.

I've got an itchy trigger finger, yet there isn't much I can shoot at. I spot this one jihadi. He's dressed in all black, with a long beard and an AK-47. I see him dash across a back alley, between two buildings – way too fast for me to pick him off. It's like we're battling shadows or something. Bullets are pouring down on us from every angle, and yet the whole time I only spot one guy (and wouldn't ya know, I missed my chance to take him out). The other problem is that we're all bunched up and I can't see jack shit through my sights; not on this tight a city block. Peering through the sights of our main gun is like staring at a brick wall through a magnifying glass. So for now we're just a big target sitting out in the open.

A few minutes pass before that tank crew spots us and FINALLY moves, allowing us to squeeze through. In matters of life and death, five minutes can seem like an eternity (especially for someone who's rapidly bleeding out). Couple the several minutes it took for us to get there with the time lost in that alleyway, plus the minute or so that'll elapse before we're on site. By then, we can only hope that Sergeant Velasquez and his men are still alive, and that the Iraqi Army have taken to bandaging up that wounded officer – whoever he is.

The clock is ticking. After another minute or so we finally reach them. Our vehicle grinds to a halt and our driver lowers the back ramp. As the wounded officer is carried in through the rear of our vehicle, I lower myself off my seat, sliding open the turret shield door and swinging myself into the crew compartment below. I expect to find the man writhing in pain, begging me to save his life. That isn't the case. He's as stiff as a board and responding to neither touch nor sound. So I check his vital signs. No heart-beat. No pulse. He's dead.

I now have a real dilemma on my hands: Should I try to resuscitate this fellow, or get my ass back in the turret? This guy had long since given up the ghost, probably within a minute or two of being mowed down in that alleyway. He's pale and has already bled out, his body riddled with bullet holes. If I stick by his side, doing all I can to bring him back, just maybe he'll pull through. After all, greater miracles have been known to happen on the battlefield. If I can just get this man's heart pumping again, he'll pull through.

But the situation is grim and I have no reason to believe I'll witness a miracle – not today anyhow. The problem is that if I waste my time on the inevita-ble, doing so will deprive me of being in the turret, leaving our crew without someone on the main gun. If the guy commanding our Brad gets rubbed out while I'm stuck in the back, there'll be no way for me to climb back inside the turret to take command of the vehicle in his stead (because the turret will likely be canted at an angle, blocking the entranceway back inside). If that happens we're all screwed. Worst case scenario, I lose comms with my driver and have to exit the vehicle in order to access the turret, only to get left behind or picked off by a sniper. It's a tough choice, but I decide to err on the side of caution, climbing back into the turret, planting myself behind the 25mm. Besides, we're just a minute or two out from getting this man the attention he needs.

Before long, we arrive at the casualty evacuation point. As several Bradleys encircle us our driver low-ers the back ramp. I fly out of the turret, assisting one of our medics, Sergeant Kirk Tasi, in carrying the wounded officer out of our vehicle and laying him in the supine. He's a short Caucasian with a scruffy mustache. As I peel open his flak vest and glance down at his name and rank, I suddenly realize it's none other than Lieutenant Colonel Terrance Crowe – a Reservist who'd been heading up local efforts to mold the Iraqi Army into a more effective fighting force.

I scramble for a med bag and the two of us kneel down on the pavement and get right to work. Sergeant Tasi begins CPR (cardiopulmonary resuscitation) on Crowe while I snip away at his blood-soaked trousers. I locate each bullet wound by tracing it back to the dark profusions of blood gushing from each tear in the fabric. Crowe is in terrible shape. He's not breathing and remains as pale as a ghost, having taken a bullet to the femoral artery, in the upper half of his right leg, just beneath the thigh. In laymen's terms, the femoral artery regulates the flow of blood throughout the lower body. In Basic Training I was taught that if someone's shot there, they're pretty much a goner – especially if the wound isn't treated within a few minutes.

As several others race over to assist, a fellow "non-com" pinches off the head of the wound by fastening a tourniquet above the top – causing the skin around it to bubble up something fierce, half the size of a cantaloupe. The added help frees me up so I can move on to treating the next injury. Crowe's been shot at least half a dozen times, and in all the worst imaginable areas. I look down and notice he's taken a bullet to the left calf muscle. A large slab of flesh is dangling from the bone. I grab an Israeli bandage and reseal it to his leg.

He's been hit so many times it's like trying to plug a crumbling dam. As I feel around the back of his left leg, I briefly take notice of Sergeant Tasi, who's nearly exhausted himself in trying to resuscitate Crowe. He's on the verge of collapse. Forget the fact that Crowe's probably been dead for twenty minutes. Tasi is not giving up. Even as other medics start to back off, he's giving it his all, and I'm filled with a newfound respect for the man.

But I have work of my own to do, so I get back to it. But in the end it's all for naught. Crowe is loaded into the rear of an armored personnel carrier and pronounced dead somewhere between Sarai and our squadron's forward aid station.

As the med track speeds off I'm ordered to get back on the gun. This battle isn't over yet. We still have a fight on our hands. Our dismounts are still taking fire and another Apache has just been shot down. As I pile into the rear of our Brad, I look back, noticing crimson stains on the pavement. I see that Crowe's top has been left behind in a bloody heap of gauze wrappers and surgical gloves.

No, I tell myself. *They're not getting it.*

I grab a five-gallon jug of water and dash out of our Brad, scooping up Crowe's blouse and then washing down the scene. In less than twenty-four hours the whole world will know what happened here today, and Crowe's name will be running across the ticker on CNN and Fox News. I'm not giving the vermin who killed him the benefit of parading around on Al Jazeera with the uniform of a dead American officer — especially a man as high in stature as Lieutenant Colonel Crowe. I rinse over the scent of death with several gallons of water, refusing to leave behind so much as a shred of fabric from his trousers.

Now that my work is done, I climb back into our Brad.

Within the next two hours our squadron exfiltrates the city, having accomplished its objective. By mission's end, a third Apache is shot down and another soldier is wounded. But we've killed nearly two dozen insurgents; and of the 28 individuals we've just detained, 23 are registered on Squadron's blacklist, suspected of terrorism. The battle for Tal'Afar is some pretty ugly business, and though we've won this round, it doesn't feel like an astounding victory.

Our platoon makes it back just in time for lunch. Though I haven't eaten in nearly twenty-four hours, I'm as wired as a time bomb. My face is crusted over by an awful layer of muck, and a huge band of sweat runs across the midsection of my uniform. I dust myself off and march over to the chow hall with a buddy. The boot-licking *fobbits* in Regiment are notorious for barring dirtied soldiers from entering the inner sanctums of their precious chow hall. Especially if they're unshaven and caked in filth, as we are. I swear that if anyone jumps on my case over my appearance, I'll lose it right then and there. I'm simply in no mood to be lectured. Not today, and not by them.

Chapter One
SEPTEMBER 11

WHEN I TELL people I hail from the Rustbelt city of Ashtabula, Ohio, I'm not being totally honest. For "Trashtabula" is a mere reference point, a blip on the map orbited by the several small towns where I spent my youth. In the not so distant past, Ashtabula was a place where any John Q. Public could settle down, land a good-paying union job, buy a nice home, raise a family, and thus enjoy the fruits of his labor. As a small port city located on the southern shores of Lake Erie, our local economy thrived with booms in the steel industry, manufacturing, and trade. Sadly, much has changed since then. My hometown is now the second most prolific county in the Buckeye State for the production of illegal methamphetamines, and the Urban Dictionary describes it as "pretty much the shittiest place in Ohio," in which "there are no warning signs before entering, so make sure you are up on shots, have a gun and or mullet, and generally resemble lakeshore trash when in the vicinity."

Though I love bagging on where I grew up, in all reality, I love the place. To me it's home, and always will be. Nonetheless, I had plenty of reasons for wanting leave, and the Army was my ticket out of "Bula."

At the age of nineteen I considered joining the armed forces, but I wasn't sure what branch to enter or if I was even ready to take that plunge. The military offered what seemed to be endless perquisites, like free housing and healthcare, a fair salary, enlistment bonuses, and the alluring promise of tens of thousands of dollars in college money, should I wish to tap the GI Bill. Not to mention, I was turned on by the prospect of escaping Ashtabula, as its once great industry-driven economy seemed to be in an irreversible state of decline, and therefore offered little promise for an unskilled high school dropout like myself.

Though at first I wasn't easily sold on joining the military, the more I thought about it, the more I wanted to. I believed then, as I still do today, that military service is one of the highest measures of honor for any American. From the battles of Lexington and Concord, well up until this very day, our freedom has been paid for in the blood of fighting men. At present, less than one percent of our population serves in the military. My father had served in Vietnam in his time, enlisting into the Marines right out of high school. With so few from my generation capable of relating to our modern-day warrior class, I could think of no finer way to give back to my country.

Then September 11 happened, and I needed no further convincing.

I had been working the graveyard shift in a factory across town for the past several months. I had grown accustomed to coming home every morning, taking a cool shower, getting a quick bite to eat, and then plopping down on the couch, only to fall asleep to the morning news.

I first learned of the attacks shortly after Flight 175 was piloted into the South Tower of the World Trade Center. This unconscionable act of violence left me numb with grief, and I figured that no less than five hundred innocents must have perished in that first round of attacks; perhaps even a thousand. I wasn't sure how many were dead or wounded, but there wasn't much I could do about it, and I could no longer stomach the sight of smoke billowing from atop those mighty towers, so I proceeded about running a few errands, just as I had originally planned. When I returned home I went straight to bed, completely unaware of the Trade Center collapse, the attack on the Pentagon, and that a fourth plane, Flight 93, had crashed outside of Shanksville, Pennsylvania.

I remember awaking to what seemed like the end of the world. I couldn't believe what I was seeing, that all of this had happened in the space of a single morning. Unlike most, I didn't have to wait around for any White House press briefing to learn who'd do such a thing. I knew who to point my finger at. I knew this ghoulish act could only be the doing of one jihadist group or another. Probably bin Laden's. This much seemed evident, given the attacks in recent years on our embassies in East Africa, as well as the bombings of the USS Cole and the Khobar Towers in Saudi Arabia.

Hungry for vengeance and inspired by some of our earliest strategic successes in Afghanistan, I decided to join the fight. I couldn't let my generation's war pass me by while I sat around watching it on TV from the sidelines of my mother's living room. Three months after 9/11, I found myself at the Cleveland MEPS (Military Entrance Processing Station). I had never received such an extensive medical evaluation in my entire life. Then again, this wasn't a routine checkup. For the better part of eight hours I was shuffled around from one line to the next, only to be prodded and questioned by health specialists. I was practically put under a magnifying glass. They checked me from head to toe, molesting me with their vast assemblage of high-tech medical instruments; poking around in every orifice, drawing my blood, and feeling my balls.

After a full day of abuse, I was accepted into the Army. Now all I had left to do was choose an MOS (military occupational specialty) and sign the dotted line. Despite my surname ending in "B," I was the last recruit to pass through MEPS that day. I could tell that the military liaison who'd be handling the remainder of my enlistment paperwork was even more eager than me to be done for the afternoon.

I remember quite vividly what he said as he approached: "You look like someone who wants to blow shit up!"

Because I was looking at a three-year commitment, I wanted to thoroughly peruse all my enlistment options. However, I didn't want to leave the man waiting. So I simply replied with, "Uh, yeah...blow shit up. Actually, I'd love to blow shit up. But I also want a job that's mentally challenging. Basically, I want the best of both worlds. I'm looking for a happy medium between using my brain and all the action that comes with killing bad guys...and blowing shit up, of course."

"You know what, kid? I have just the job for you."

"Really?" I replied.

He came back a minute or so later with a single sheet of paper in his hand. It was a basic summary of what a "Cavalry Scout" does, what my overall function in the US Army would be:

> *The Cavalry Scout is the commander's eyes and ears on the battlefield. When information about the enemy is needed, they call on the Scouts. They are responsible for reconnaissance and you will learn about various weapons to include explosives and mines. Cavalry Scouts engage the enemy with anti-armor weapons and scout vehicles in the field, track and report enemy movement and activities, and will*

*direct the employment of various weapon
systems onto the enemy.*

My only response was, "Awwwesome! Is there a video, too?"

Naturally, there was. The short presentation on his computer included, among other things, soldiers blowing things to pieces and Bradley Fighting Vehicles aggressively maneuvering over rugged terrain, jumping huge mounds of dirt. I was even led to believe I'd be on a dune buggy at some point. *A freakin' dune buggy!* Oh, how I'd dreamt of such things. My wildest boyhood fantasies were finally coming true. This three-minute video clip was perhaps the coolest thing I had ever seen. I mean, what red-blooded, all-American, twenty-year-old male doesn't want to ride a dune buggy, or shoot an endless stream of bullets into the plastic bodies of human-shaped targets?

It never occurred to me that the liaison assigned with handling my paperwork only had a quota to meet. He probably didn't care whether or not I found my way into an occupational specialty that I was suited for, much less enjoyed. Given all that my new job entailed, I was initially under the impression that I had just been sworn into some elite, Spartan-like warrior society, and that soon enough I'd be camped out somewhere in the mountains of Tora Bora, Afghanistan, hunting down Osama bin Laden and Mullah Omar. My assumptions couldn't have been further from reality. I was about to get a taste of what it means to be a modern-day cavalryman. It's not all guns, guts, and glory.

I'd soon learn that slaving away in a motor pool isn't all that much fun, and that the US Army doesn't even use dune buggies. Or if it ever had, their use was now mostly obsolete, or limited in part to elite "spec-ops" (special operations) units, like the one that put the kibosh on bin Laden & Co. So, no dune buggies for Private Bryan.

Nonetheless, I was pleased with my decision then, and to this day have absolutely no qualms over signing up as a Scout. I craved adventure, and I was about to get it.

Chapter Two

112 DAYS OF SUCK

I LEFT HOME for Fort Knox, Kentucky two months later, starting Basic Training in the dead of winter. I was promptly assigned to Bravo Troop, 5/15 Cavalry. It was sixteen grueling weeks of misery, the days seeming to blur into one long, continuous training exercise.

On day one, our drill sergeants marched us out to a column of payphones that stood atop a concrete slab parallel to our barracks. *Phone time?* I thought. *I guess they're human after all.* Having taken the bait, our platoon eagerly lined up at the booths, with phone cards in hand. What I initially perceived to be an act of compassion on the part of our drill sergeants was really a cruel joke, a teaser meant to soften us up before breaking us down.

"Okay ladies, you've got one minute a piece! That's sixty seconds from your first 'hello' to say 'I miss and love you.' After that say your goodbyes and fall out. Got it? This will be the last time any of you use a phone until Family Day, eight weeks from now!"

They stood there with stop watches, as if they were clocking run times, hollering at us recruits with glee in their eyes as each newbie was cut off in mid-sentence. *You're done!* One after another:

"Hello?"

"Mom?"

"Ross, honey, is that you?"

"Hey, Mom, I've only got a minute to speak, but I want to let you know that I'm doing okay and that I love and miss everyone…"

"Time! You're done! Off the phone, Private Bryan!"

I hung up and peeled off out of line, racing back to the barracks with soggy eyes. For the record, I wasn't that much of a pansy, just a little homesick. Reality was setting in and I began to wonder, *Man, am I ready for all this?* Once upstairs, I found my bunkmate – a large, burly Southerner – with his face buried in the green wool blanket adorning his bed, desperately trying to hide his rosy, tear-stained cheeks. Here I thought I was the only one who had welled up; apparently not. Nor were we alone in our grief. There were others, too. It was quite a scene – a bunch of full-grown men all choked up, struggling to hold back their tears. And to think, in just a year's time some of these guys would be at the tip of the spear, charging into Iraq at full throttle.

Our drill sergeants kept us up all night, barking orders as we made our bunks and unpacked our duffel bags. At some point, I pissed one of them off by waltzing up to ask a question and failing to stand at the position of "parade rest," with my hands interlocked behind my back and legs spread shoulder-width apart.

"Private Bryan, beat your fuckin' face!"

Beat my face? The expression was new to me. Choking on a response, I stood there with blank eyes, confused by the order.

"Hey, dipshit, that means pushups!"

So I dropped to the ground and beat my face.

"You will never address me in person unless you are first at the position of parade rest," he said, staring down at me as though I were a pile of human excrement.

"Got it? Now recover, Private."

"Sir, yes Sir!" I hollered, springing to my feet.

I'd heard that line a thousand times before in movies like *Full Metal Jacket*, and thought he'd be wooed by this hearty show of respect. I had even practiced it in the mirror before boarding my flight to Fort Knox.

"What the fuck did you just call me, Private?!"

"Sir, I called you *Sir*!"

"Pushups! Now!!!"

I dropped to the cold tile beneath our feet, my chest nearly caving in on my bony triceps as I returned to beating my face.

"Damn it, I work for a living! Do I look like an officer? Do I have lieutenant bars on my collar? I'm an NCO – non-commissioned officer! We are the backbone of the Army! Without us, the machine doesn't run. Didn't they teach you that in reception, Private?! From here on, you will ONLY address me as Drill Sergeant! You got that, maggot?! Now recover!"

"Sir, yes Sir!" I replied, exhaustedly rising to my feet.

Oh, shit! I thought.

It was an honest slip of the tongue – a complete brain fart.

"Hey, shit-for-brains! What did I just tell you?! Back down," he gestured, pointing to the floor.

So I returned to the "front-leaning rest position." After a minute or so I sprung back to my feet at the command to recover. And again I repeated my mistake, accidentally calling him *Sir*. So I beat my face a little while longer.

That was day one. Already Fort Knox was beginning to feel like a Russian gulag, and I was antsy at the thought of what the remainder of my time there would be like. I could only hope and pray I'd have the cojones to stick it out another four months.

—

The training aside, it was 112 days of mind games. On one occasion, after a long day in the field, we came back to the barracks only to discover an ankle-high layer of mud spanning the full length of our hallway. While we were out, the cadre had hauled in a couple dozen wheelbarrow loads of topsoil, wetting it down and then stirring it up. We came home to a virtual pig pen. They told us, "You've got one hour to clean this shit up and make the floors sparkle again or none of you ladies are going to chow!" That's the Army's idea of a team building exercise. I'm not sure how we pulled it off in time, but we did. I guess we were that hungry.

On numerous other occasions we'd get woken up in the middle of the night, usually between midnight and 0500. They'd zoom through our barracks, flipping on ceiling lights and yanking the covers off us.

"Hey girls, who wants to go to the beach?!"

We'd form up along the wall in our hallway, on something called "Red Line," screaming in unison at the command to *Sound off!* From there, we were rushed out to a nearby sand pit known as "The Beach." As remedial training for various infractions, we'd be punished as one every time somebody screwed up – and occasionally for no reason at all.

"So, a little birdie told me that one of you decided to eat cake and ice cream on KP when we specifically said: 'Don't think twice about eating junk food!' Now, which one of you was it?"

They'd torture us in that sand pit to the point of vertigo, until somebody would either fess up to the crime or they felt content with our punishment. Then we'd have to clean up afterwards, leaving us under-rested the following day, as we'd barely get any sleep before having to wake up again and assemble on Red Line.

There's a reason "enlisted military" ranks third among the worst careers in America (all depending on who you ask), and this right here is one of them. It was no kind of life, and there seemed to be no end in sight. All I can say is that those first couple months felt like two years. Still, I have no right to complain. It's not like I was forced at gunpoint into joining the Army. It was my decision and now I had to live with it. Basic Training is not meant to be fun. It's a human blast furnace that transforms boys into men. Hence, 112 days of suck. As the son of a Marine, I knew exactly what to expect: lots of ruck marches and long hours in the field, coupled with sleep deprivation and a onetime trip to the gas chamber, where I'd turn peach-colored and vomit all over myself. Maybe that's why my dad advised me to join the Coast Guard.

We should have hated our drill sergeants for the misery they inflicted upon us, and yet we looked at them with great reverence. In our eyes, they were the personification of all we hoped to become. They were soldiers, and that was a title we hadn't yet earned. In time, we discovered they weren't the monsters we originally thought them to be. They were just passionate about whipping us into shape and readying us for combat. Very soon we'd understand why.

One downside to being penned in at Fort Knox was that I was starved of any tangible information about the impending war with Iraq, as well as our soon-to-be-forgotten expedition in Afghanistan. In an adjacent barracks facility, a separate unit was having its training schedule condensed into only twelve weeks. From what I gathered, it was purely experimental, but that didn't keep us recruits from starting new rumors. Guys would speculate that a preemptive invasion of Iraq was only several months away, and that this was a preparatory move to ensure that we'd have absolutely as many troops on the ground as possible, should such an event transpire. While there was no evidence of this, war with Iraq seemed to be in the cards, and our drill sergeants assured us it was inevitable. "You're all headed to the Sandbox," they'd tell us. "Each and every one of you!"

But my thoughts were elsewhere. I couldn't stop daydreaming about my first duty station: Fort Carson, Colorado. Had it in writing, right in my contract. That's where I was headed once I made it out of this shithole. For I was lucky enough to have been afforded the option of choosing my own duty assignment. I wanted more than anything to go to Europe, but since my father resided in the "Centennial State," both of us saw this as a prime opportunity to strengthen our father-son relationship. So I chose Colorado over Germany. It was a tough decision, but in hindsight I'm glad I did. I was just a toddler when my parents split up and didn't get to see my dad much when I was young. He'd make cameo appearances every now and again, but as a trucker living most of his days out of state, he was largely absent throughout my childhood. So this was our chance to make up for lost time. And believe me, we had a lot of catching up to do.

Earlier that year, while I was at Fort Knox, he booked a trip to Vietnam. Three decades had passed since he had last been there. Like many veterans of that war have done, I think he was hoping to find peace of mind and come to terms with the past. He had yearned to do so for some time now, and often spoke of wanting to visit there. But closure wasn't all he found. With the war long behind him, he took this sobering act of redemption to a whole new level and married a local. Apparently, the alluring mystique of

Vietnam's women remained as deeply seared into his memories of Southeast Asia as the war itself.

You can't image the stir this caused in our family. Especially for my aging grandma, whose last memory of Vietnam was probably watching Saigon fall to the Communists on the evening news three decades earlier.

But the joke was on me. I was standing on Red Line one evening, listening to the drill sergeant on duty call out the last name of each soldier who received mail. As he'd holler for us, we'd race up and snatch our letters out of his hand after he briefly inspected them for contraband. At mail call, there were a few guys who could always count on a huge stack of envelopes awaiting them. Not me. I rarely received anything, but that night I did.

"Jackson...Birmingham, Alabama!"

"Hernandez...Los Angeles, California!"

"Polanski...Chicago, Illinois!"

"Bryan...Ho Chi Minh City, Vietnam! What the...Ho Chi Minh City?! Is this some kind of a joke!?"

"No, Drill Sergeant!"

"Are you a communist subversive!?"

"No, Drill Sergeant!"

"Then why in the hell are you getting mail from Ho Chi Minh City?"

"It's from my dad, Drill Sergeant! He's a Vietnam vet. It's a long story..."

And through that letter I became acquainted with my new Vietnamese family, including my stepmother, Thuy, a daughter of Saigon.

—

Overall, I didn't find Basic Training as physically demanding as I thought it'd be. I saw my time there as more of an inward quest to prove to myself that I wasn't a complete failure in life, some "scrawny, gin-

ger-headed fuck" who'd washed out of training because he couldn't hack it. No, this was a test that I
swore I wouldn't fail. Until then, I had never been
good at anything – not at school or sports, nor setting
any kind of personal goals for myself. So I pledged to
give it my all. I swore up and down that I wouldn't let
our drill sergeants break me off.

Between what little sleep we got, pairs of us
would get woken up in the middle of the night for
one-hour guard shifts, during which time we'd clean
every square inch of our living quarters. I was quickly
imbued with a whole new appreciation for custodial
work, waxing floors and scrubbing pubic hair off of
piss-stained toilet seats well into the wee hours of the
morning.

To weaken company morale, our drill sergeants
would fill our heads with all kinds of debilitating non-
sense, like stories of how some recruits had lost their
minds there, or what percentage of us "pussies"
would likely get flushed out of Basic Training halfway through and sent home in shame.

One particularly famous urban legend known to
many recruits who've passed through the iron gates of
Fort Knox is the story of a young soldier who killed
himself in the barracks. This unfortunate soul didn't
have the wherewithal to keep up with the pack, so he
decided to end his life in the most gruesome fashion
possible. Early one morning, he went to one of the
utility closets and quietly removed a heavyweight
buffing machine, pushing it to the base of a nearby
window. Next, he wound the electrical cord around
his neck so that he and the clunky machine were fastened as tightly to one another as a ball and chain. He
then used all his strength to lift the awkwardly shaped
device and chuck it through the window, causing
himself to be violently yanked by the neck over
shards of jagged glass and pulled to his death some

three stories below. His skull was said to have split open like a watermelon thrown from the roof of a tall building. Of course, this story is pure myth, just like the hollow tales of new recruits getting locked away at Fort Leavenworth on twenty-year prison stints just for going AWOL (Absence Without Leave) from Basic Training.

Then every guy had to hear about how "Jody" was "balls-deep" in his wife or girlfriend. This nefarious Jody character is a devilish Casanova who'll swoop in on the wife or girlfriend of any soldier who's out of town for an extended period of time. He's not an actual person, per se. Rather, his existence is symptomatic of a much greater problem – like a whorish wife who isn't willing to stand by her man while he's gone. In theory, Jody could be just about anyone – a slick neighbor or mailman, some random guy she met at a nightclub, or even a fellow soldier if you're not careful. But one thing is for certain – Jody's a real homewrecker. He doesn't care if you have kids. He'll literally break your family in two, because his pleasure comes at your despair.

Sadly, this Jody epidemic brings us full circle to the all-too-common "Dear John" letter, which has been known to throw many a man into long bouts of depression or riotous conniption fits. Any would-be military spouse hoping to make a clean split from her boyfriend or fiancé will usually opt-out of telling him to his face. Instead, she'll wisely avail herself to letting him know while he's deployed overseas or safely penned-in at a well-guarded military installation, as to avoid serious confrontation. If she's courteous to his emotional state, she'll hold off on informing him of her intentions until his time in this faraway place nears its end, as sudden word of the split might push him over the edge. So, in other words, it's better to learn that your significant other has been getting railed by Jody a week before coming home from the "Sandbox" than two or three months into a year-long deployment.

By the time of our June 13 summer graduation, barely half of our original unit was left standing. But that's what Basic Training is all about – "no pain, no gain." Bravo Troop managed to weed through the weaklings and break off nearly half of its recruits, causing them to either be "recycled" into other units, or permanently discharged for insubordination or various medical issues. Some had sprained ankles, while others had blown out kneecaps or dislocated shoulders. A few had gone AWOL, and in my platoon, there was even a habitual bed-wetter who was booted out for soiling his sheets on a nightly basis. I was proud as hell to be among the one hundred or so who'd been tough enough to handle everything our drill sergeants had thrown at us.

There's a wealth of history behind the US Cavalry. We're essential on the battlefield and to the outcome of any major conflict involving American forces. For me, joining their ranks was an enormous personal feat. Doing so helped me build that stronger sense of self I had longed for. With this job came new responsibilities and big challenges. I'd now be entrusted to do things that would have been impossible for a hundred and fifty-pound weakling like myself just months earlier. It was a little daunting at first, but I had proven to myself that I had what it took to make it in the Army. But was I ready for war? Only time would tell…

Chapter Three
IRAQ FEVER

THAT JULY, I packed up my car and began a fifteen-hundred-mile journey to my new home, Fort Carson, Colorado. Carson rests at the base of Pikes Peak and is situated at the southernmost tip of Colorado Springs. I couldn't have been happier or more at peace with myself. I loved Colorado then, as I still do today. In terms of beauty, its mountainous landscape is practically beyond description. The exquisite natural scenery is even said to have inspired Katharine Lee Bates while penning America the Beautiful: *O beautiful for spacious skies, for amber waves of grain, for purple mountain majesties above the fruited plain.* With the evening sun having splashed the heavens with varying shades of gold, this is what I saw as I rolled into town. Yes, it would seem *God shed his grace on thee,* as the lyrics go.

By moving to Colorado to be closer to my pops, I had opened a new chapter in my life. That summer I spent most of my weekends at his cabin, up on Indian Mountain, near South Park. We had a great time, the two of us. My Army buddies loved him as well. He'd spend hours talking about his experiences in Vietnam as a young Marine, and I'd listen in pure awe, hoping that someday I might have a few war stories of my own to share.

However, when I wasn't up at his place or enjoying nightlife in the Springs, I was usually back in garrison, preparing for a newly opening front in the "War on Terror." I had just been assigned to 3rd Platoon, Fox Troop, 2/3 ACR (Armored Cavalry Regiment). I was Bravo Section's newest dismount, an entry-level position more commonly referred to as the "JAFO," or "Just Another Fucking Observer."

In an armored scout platoon, it's the lowest ranking spot on the totem pole. In battle, dismounts actually serve a purpose, observing enemy movement, clearing rooms, calling in artillery strikes – you know, the kind of stuff that gets your blood pumping. Otherwise, they're the Army's equivalent to an errand boy, pulling guard, fixing things, and fetching stuff for their superiors. It's the sort of job that requires little more than a strong back and a weak mind. But you have to start somewhere, and I was the JAFO for our new platoon leader, Lieutenant Jeremy Anderson. In the coming months, I'd be doing little more than refilling this guy's canteens during field training exercises.

The 3rd Armored Cavalry Regiment was established in 1846, during the Mexican-American War. It numbers around five thousand soldiers. In the 3rd ACR, we have a little saying known as the regimental accolade: *You've been baptized in blood and fire and have come out steel!* We're also the only unit in the entire U.S. Army that uses "Ai-ee-yah!" as our official battle cry instead of "Hooah!," which I'm told was adopted from the Lakota and Cheyenne.

Still young and naive, I was utterly enthralled by the idea of being marched off to war against another country. At the time, as Bush was staking out his case for "Operation Iraqi Freedom," I felt that not only was it a just cause, I was sure it'd be well worth the steep cost in blood and treasure. Not only would I get the chance to fight for my country, just as my father had, I'd play a frontline role in helping America settle its scores with Saddam Hussein. Though most important of all, we'd be smashing one axis in a "triad of evil" while simultaneously "liberating" over twenty million people.

What could go wrong? I thought.

Maybe I should have listened more closely to the political admonitions of my maternal grandfather, retired Air Force pilot Lieutenant Colonel Russell Heath, the most decent person I've ever known. He seemed bothered by the prospect of America being dragged to war by a bunch of Washington ideologues. He first expressed these concerns to me in a handwritten letter dated October 8, 2002: "Did you watch and listen to President Bush Monday evening?" he asked. "And what is your opinion? I dread the thought of another Vietnam scrap in the Middle East."

And he wrote me again, this time on February 19, exactly one month prior to the invasion: "Any word on your outfit's heading to the sands? Sure seems like there are lots of protests. I'm not in favor of a big war, plus it seems that there are already enough embargos and political pressure to slow things down. And there seems to be lots of trouble-spots around the world."

How right he was! Yet I shrugged off Grandpa's concerns, believing such ideas to be an overly simplistic take on a very complicated geopolitical matter. Somehow I thought myself wiser than he, and I was ready to follow George W. Bush to the far ends of the earth. Even if that meant dying in Iraq.

—

At Fort Carson there's a long and rolling stretch of foothills that span the eastern half of the base, overlooking the motor pools below that house every piece of equipment used by the men and women stationed there. At least once a week, our commander would divide our company into groups of three – from slowest to fastest – and take us on five-mile "fun runs" in the trails above.

At 0615 sharp, we'd start at "Sabre Field." From there, he'd lead us to the southeast tip of Fort Carson and up the side of a steep, gargantuan chunk of earth dubbed "Medal of Honor Hill." We'd charge up that slope in what felt like a big game of king of the mountain. Once at the top, he'd stand off to the side and read gloriously bloody accounts of American troops who'd been awarded the Medal of Honor:

> *Citation! Specialist Gary Wetzel distinguished himself by conspicuous gallantry and intrepidity at the risk of his life above and beyond the call of duty! Specialist Wetzel was serving as a door gunner aboard a helicopter which was part of an insertion force trapped in a landing zone by intense and deadly hostile fire! Specialist Wetzel was going to the aid of his aircraft commander when he was blown into a rice paddy and critically wounded by 2 enemy rockets that exploded just inches from his location! Although bleeding profusely due to the loss of his left arm and severe wounds in his right arm, chest, and left leg, Specialist Wetzel staggered back to his original position in his gun-well and took the enemy forces under fire...*

> *Now let me hear your war cry!!!!!!!!!!!!!!!*

That shit always got our blood pumping. As we'd scramble up the face of that rock, we'd learn of their bravery, wondering if someday one of our names might be on that list.

From there he'd lead us through a circuitous maze of long and winding foot trails, through a little area we'd come to know as "Togonon Hill," in those grassy highlands behind our motor pool.

"Specialist Togonon" was First Platoon's least stellar soldier. While some charged that he was a complete "shitbag," I just sensed he had chosen the wrong job. He was a portly Filipino-American with a Bachelor's degree in Graphic Design – you know, the quiet, nerdy type who stays in on a Friday night to play video games alone and watch the Star Wars trilogy. Though no ball of fire, he seemed like a nice kid. But he lacked the drive and natural dexterity that characterizes most fighting men, and struggled to fit in with the guys in his platoon.

So what do you do with somebody like that? I always thought it would have made sense to just stick him behind a desk somewhere (perhaps at Squadron or Regiment). There, his tech-savvy computer skills could have been put to good use, making pie charts or whatever.

But instead of just transferring him to another unit, First Platoon would work him like a plow mule; especially when they'd get reamed for him screwing up. Or they'd have him do torturous exercises for hours on end. I'd watch as he'd be forced to repeatedly run up and down those hills behind our motor pool in the dead of summer, dressed in "full battle rattle" while lugging heavy objects – tools, large stones, spare parts, what have you.

Hence, *Togonon Hill.*

But I can't say that I felt entirely sorry for the kid. For he was also a known thief and was caught red-handed one day pawning off another soldier's gear at a local Army surplus shop. In the "Cav" that shit doesn't fly. Whether or not you like the men you serve with is irrelevant. It all comes down to trust. So there's no room for "buddy-fucking" in the Army – not on that scale. When the bullets start flying, you have to trust the men to your right and left. If you can't do that, you're as good as dead.

Eventually, Specialist Togonon was demoted and then flushed out of the Army, receiving a general discharge in the months just before our deployment.

For those in Fox Troop, Togonon Hill was more than a mountain. It was a lesson for each man to absorb: Don't be a slug or screw over the guys in your platoon. Because if you do, we'll crush you!

As one of the strongest runners in Fox Troop, I was among the half-dozen or so who ran in the "Jackrabbits" group, along with Specialist Jacob Simpson and a few others. Simpson was a fellow Scout and the newest addition to Fox Troop. He had just come from Germany, where he served as a gunner in a similar unit. We hit it off right away. He was a tall, friendly, half-Jewish kid from Ashland, Oregon. I remember him being easy to spot in a crowd on account of his goofy trademark stride. He always traipsed around with his toes canted slightly inward, making me wonder if he had been born with webbed feet.

I remember this one time, we were trudging along on Togonon Hill through about six inches of mud. I trailed Simpson the whole time, who could run just a bit faster than me. He wouldn't have known it, but I had been intentionally kicking mud all over his backside as a joke. After our run, we stood at the base of Togonon Hill and cooled down with some light stretching exercises.

"Man, you're dirty as shit!" I said, holding back my laughter. "What'd you do, stop to roll in the mud or something?"

"Damn, you're right," he said. "It's all over me. I need a shower."

"Hell yeah, ya do!" I replied, biting my lip.

Yet it still hadn't dawned on him. That might sound like a terrible prank to play on a friend, but when you put a bunch of young dudes together, this is what happens. Just as in high school and college, she-nanigans are commonplace in the military. I've had much worse done to me by even closer friends, so I had no qualms doing the same to Simpson. Besides, we were drinking buddies, so no harm, no foul. I just figured if I didn't clue him in by the end of the day, I'd hold off until a few months into our upcoming deployment.[†]

———

In those first days after the March 19 invasion, my evenings were spent doing a variety of last-minute tasks, like stuffing my duffle bags and rucksack full of military equipment. I'd usually do so while listening to conservative talk radio, which I was quite the fan of back then. Like everyone else, I was subjected to routine equipment inspections – and lots of them. I got pretty good at laying all my stuff out, packing it up, then laying it all out again a day or two later. Sometimes these inspections were conducted at random, and sometimes not. Either way, I was expected to account for every item on that packing list – and God help me if I was missing so much as a single bootlace!

We were given very specific packing instructions. And believe me, with only x-amount of space for x-amount of items, this was no easy task. But somehow I managed to cram it all in there as best I could and make it fit. I even recall being ordered to place all my NBC (Nuclear, Biological, and Chemical) gear at the top of my "A bag." That way it'd be easily accessible once we got to Kuwait. After all,

---

[†] While most of the stories herein appear in chronological order, a couple do not. This is one of them. While "Togonon Hill" was certainly a place of legend to those in Fox Troop, the run I'm referring to happened in the summer of 2004, under a different commander – two years after my arrival to Fox.

Saddam was said to be in possession of enough chemical weapons to kill all of Planet Earth five times over, and had shielded himself by encircling Baghdad in a "chemical belt," or so we'd been told. Of course, it was all bullshit, just like the intel linking his regime to al Qaeda, but we didn't know that.

It was a truly strange time to be alive. I remember just as the invasion was kicking off, pro-war demonstrators across the country began tossing out their Dixie Chicks CDs in response to singer Natalie Maines speaking out against Bush's decision to attack Iraq; some radio stations stopped playing their music as well. Previously, I had always enjoyed hearing their stuff on the radio. Especially their cover of Fleetwood Mac's *Landslide*. But once they began publicly criticizing the war, I stopped listening to their music entirely. I'd just change the station and put on something different. I guess you could say I had come down with a bad case of Iraq fever, as had the rest of the country.

One evening I decided to go downtown with Simpson. We figured that pounding a few beers would be a great way to spend one of our last few nights of freedom. So we hit two of the most frequented spots on Tejon Street – first "Rum Bays," a twenty-one and up nightclub that some of its patrons had dubbed "Scum Bays," and then "The Ritz," a laidback taproom just down the street. Later that evening we sat in The Ritz's spruced up basement, sipping our beers as we watched gritty footage of the 3rd Infantry Division pouring into Iraq and maneuvering over its southern desert terrain. A whole bunch of us – all soldiers – were crowded around those TVs, wanting a glimpse of the action. Unlike me, Simpson had mixed views of the war and didn't share my initial support for Operation Iraqi Freedom. All these years later, I wish I had been as skeptical of the war as Simpson was. But my mind was set, and I was all for the United States opening a big can of whoop-ass on Saddam Hussein.

Chapter Four
KUWAIT

Two WEEKS INTO the invasion, various elements of the 3rd ACR began trickling into Kuwait. Fox Troop, to which I belonged, was among the first of those units to arrive.

Our entire squadron spent its first day or so at a transitional base just outside the airport. Then we were bused all the way out to Camp Victory, and eventually given our own set of tents located smack dab in the middle of Who-Gives-A-Shit, Kuwait. Camp Victory was a massively disorganized garrison tent-city that had been thrown together as hastily as the war itself. Once there, we were forced to wait…and wait…and wait. The anticipation was killing me. Anything would have beat sitting around on our asses all day, doing nothing. Our equipment, which we were useless without, was stuck on a massive flotilla somewhere in the Atlantic Ocean. The last time I had seen any of it, tanks or otherwise, was a month or two earlier. We had loaded it all onto freight carts at the Fort Carson rail station. No one could seem to give us a general date as to when it would reach Kuwait. I remember hoping our war toys would arrive in time for us to catch the tail end of the invasion.

Maybe we'll even get to see a little action, I thought.

Nearly three weeks passed before it finally made its way to port. In the meantime, we did what soldiers do best when there's nothing at all for soldiers to do – play cards, listen to music, write our loved ones, read books and magazines, swap stories, reminisce amongst ourselves, etc.

War is hell alright, but in your downtime it's also boring. In times like these, one really gets to know the men he serves with. At least half of my downtime was spent listening to guys cook up exaggerated tales of conquest over the opposite sex. It was like a huge dick-measuring contest in which everyone claimed they were Don Juan before joining the Army. One dude would be talking about how just months earlier he had banged some girl who looked just like Mila Kunis. Then some other braggadocio would chime in, one-upping his story with a tale of how he'd recently done the slam dance with a pair of blonde co-eds. More often than not, I found some of these narratives just a little hard to swallow. But the Army is a bull-shitter's paradise, so I expected nothing less. In reality, the only woman half of these guys had hooked up with in the last few months was "Leftie," a booze-begotten, one-armed barracks rat who used to sleep around with a bunch of the guys in Building 2551. God only knows how many diseases that woman had, or how many were passed on to the men of Fox Troop.

At Camp Victory our resources were scarce, especially fresh water. We were only allotted three bottles a piece per day, which didn't go far at all in the heat of the Kuwaiti desert. The camp's guidelines for showering were quite similar: use only what you must and not a drop more. Our bathing facilities were nothing more than supped up trailers with multiple shower stalls inside, run quite similar to a military firing range. Showering at Camp Victory consisted of little more than disrobing before some grouchy NCO, standing naked under the showerhead, and upon his command, turning the faucet on just long enough to lather up our filthy sand-covered bodies with soap.

Then as we'd scour ourselves clean, he'd briefly allow us to turn the water back on so we could quickly rinse ourselves off.

Before deploying, my section sergeant, Lucas Dupéré, advised each of us to bring a roll or two of what he dubbed "white gold," or what the average civilian back home might call "toilet paper." He warned us that this was a commodity he could not guarantee the Army would provide us enough of. And was he ever right! Along with the dearth of fresh water, in the earliest days of our deployment, there was a massive shortage of toilet paper. Only in the U.S. Army is one provided with overpriced "porta-shitters," but no rolls of toilet paper to wipe their ass. Fortunately, I had taken heed to his advice and brought a personal supply of this cheap, but much-desired good. Six rolls of double ply Angel Soft. My ass never felt better.

As for the rickety tents we were assigned to, they seemed to resemble something you'd suspect of having once been used to house a clan of Bedouins, not US soldiers. But they served their purpose all the same. In the military, you make do with what you're given and try not to complain too much about it. To quote then Secretary of Defense Donald Rumsfeld, "You go to war with the army you have, not the army you might want or wish to have at a later time." Fox Troop understood this all too well. When we deployed, some guys didn't have body armor or even an M4/M16 rifle, but ironically, we had all been issued bayonets. You might say it wasn't the gear we wanted or wished to have, but it was the gear had. Yet nobody complained. We had a mission to do, and we were ready to get it done.

—

After grounding our gear and sweeping the sand out of our tent, we embarked on our first march to the chow hall.

The only question was, "Where is it?"

"I'm told it's about half a mile that way," said one of our NCOs, pointing at the sun-baked horizon with a trace of uncertainty in his voice.

After twenty minutes of trudging through sand, we spotted a blocky set of rectangular structures way off in the distance. There was an enormous line of human-shaped figures curled around the largest one. I almost wondered if it was a mirage. As we approached, I squinted some and noticed a building marked with an iconic AAFES (Army and Air Force Exchange Service) sign, as well as several fast-food trailers that were under construction. We were definitely in the right place. I was just shocked to discover that Hardee's had beaten us to the desert.

Every army marches on its stomach, and Fox Troop was no exception. I had only been in Kuwait for two days now and already I would have traded my left testicle for an icy cold soda.

I entered the chow hall and stood patiently in line with my tray in hand and my M16 slung at a downward angle over my right shoulder. As I approached our server, I quickly realized that it wasn't an Army cook who'd be serving me, as I would have assumed, but instead, a swarthy-looking civilian with greasy, jet-black hair. I assumed he was a Kuwaiti worker. We had just been issued an Iraqi deployment guidebook. It featured some key words and phrases of the Arabic language. Wanting to put the only Arabic word I knew to good use, I looked at my server and said in a friendly tone, "marhaba," which in Arabic means "hello." Yet in return I only received an empty gaze.

I knew I had read the word correctly. So I repeated myself in an even clearer voice, looking him dead in the eyes: *Marhaba!* And once again I received that same blank stare in return.

Turns out I wasn't speaking with an Arab. I didn't know it then, but Kuwaitis are about the last people you'll ever find working on an American base. That kind of work is beneath them, they believe. From cradle to grave the Kuwaiti citizen is coddled by their government, and as of 1990, defended by ours. Being a petroleum-rich Gulf state has benefited Kuwait to the extent that it can afford to spread its vast wealth far and wide amongst its relatively small population. They're like the ultimate welfare state. Healthcare and education are free. Gasoline is subsidized; so is food. Even housing is free in certain instances. It gives the people little incentive to work hard, and even fewer reasons to plot against their government, despite its authoritarian nature.

The little brown men who had faithfully served us our meals three times a day, constructed our tents, and even scrubbed clean the dried specks of piss and shit from inside our porta-potties weren't in fact Kuwaiti civilians eager to serve their American guests. They were unskilled workers brought in from some of the poorest countries on the Asian continent – the Philippines, India, Bangladesh, and Pakistan. I can only assume these men were hired through Kellogg, Brown & Root (KBR), a subsidiary of Vice President Dick Cheney's Halliburton.

In retrospect, I knew very little about Iraq – or the Middle East. For starters, I didn't know the first thing about the Arabic language or Muslim culture. I knew that in itself would be problematic and would likely inhibit our ability to assist the Iraqis in rebuilding their country. Nor did I know much about the great historical battles that have shaped the modern political landscape of that region. A few months after joining the Army, I made an earnest attempt to beef-up my knowledge of that subject as well, but still found the whole mess over there rather perplexing. I even bought *The Complete Idiot's Guide to World Conflicts* at a local bookstore, but still struggled to understand the great schism between Iraq's Sunnis and Shiites. Reading up on this stuff, it seemed the whole damn Middle East had been awash in blood since Cane slayed Abel.

This should have raised a host of serious questions, like whether or not our military was up to the monumental task of bringing democracy to a people whose way of life had changed so little in the past one thousand years. Well, facts be damned! None of that deterred Bush. The very title of this mission, "Operation Iraqi Freedom," inferred that we'd be doing far more than just toppling Saddam Hussein and searching for weapons of mass destruction (WMDs). We'd be bringing the Iraqi people "freedom." However, what they'd choose to do with it was up to them.

—

I found serenity in the chow hall. I had come to regard the place as my own personal desert oasis. It was somewhere special I could slip away each day to splurge on lukewarm soda while feasting my eyes on around-the-clock war coverage.

On April 9, I awoke from a short nap and fought my way through a sandstorm just to be there, taking a seat in a dimly lit corner of the tent. On TV, something caught my eye as I was biting into my ice cream sandwich. It was a young Marine, later identified as Lance Corporal Edward Chin. He had an American flag in hand and was scaling an enormous bronze statue of Saddam Hussein in Baghdad's Firdous Square. Upon summiting the grand structure, he draped Old Glory over Uncle Saddam's head. The symbolism here was unmistakable. Iraq's aging despot had been tried and convicted in absentia and was now being dragged to the gallows, courtesy of the USA. It appeared as though young Chin was not only being cheered on by his fellow Marines, but the Iraqi people, too. I couldn't believe my eyes. Baghdad had fallen in only three weeks. This was history in the making, and I had been fortunate enough to catch it live on Fox News.

Is the war over?, I naively pondered.

These were extremely powerful images, and they were being broadcasted in real time throughout the greater Middle East and to every corner of every nation, not just the United States. And our message was crystal clear: *If you defy us, you'll be next. Any questions?* At that very hour, the entire civilized world saw America tout its power in the face of the Arabs. Though at the time I could have cared less what foreign audiences made of this. My country could do no wrong, I believed. I was swelling with patriotism and prouder to be an American than at any time in my adult life. My only wish was that it had been me atop that statue instead of Corporal Chin.

Chapter Five
ENTER MESOPOTAMIA

WE IN THE Armored Cavalry are not as swift on our feet as the Infantry, and unlike the Special Forces, there's no air of mystery to our job. But when it comes to good ole' fashioned battlefield warfare, we stand head and shoulders above everyone else. We can level damn near anything in our path, and we take tremendous pride in doing so. The Cav demonstrated its might during the first Gulf War, flattening entire enemy tank divisions. Iraqi military vehicles were reduced to blackened hunks of twisted steel, with the charred bodies of dead Republican Guard soldiers melted to the interior walls of their Russian-made T-72 tanks.

It's not simply that we're the best at what we do. Though well trained in the expertise of killing, we come to battle equipped to destroy anything that gets in our way.

Our scout platoons are mounted on Bradley Fighting Vehicles, or "Brads" for short. They're 30-ton beasts with caterpillar-like suspension systems, allowing each crew to operate in the most unimaginably harsh terrain. Protruding from the nose of the turret is its main weapon system, a belt-fed 25mm cannon that can alternate between firing high-explosive rounds that gnarl human flesh, and the even more lethal armor-piercing rounds that are tipped with depleted uranium, enabling the gunner to cut through enemy vehicles as if they're made of cardboard. Just left of the main gun are two even nastier 120mm TOW (tube-launched, optically-tracked, wire-guided) missiles, which can destroy practically anything on the battlefield at up to around four thousand meters. And right of the 25mm is a vicious chain gun known as the M240-Charlie. It's fed by a nearly two thousand round belt of 7.62mm ammunition, and can spray over 900 rounds per minute.

In case you're not salivating by now, strapped down elsewhere in the rear crew compartment is the M240-Bravo, a virtually identical weapon system to that of the Charlie, only it can be carried by hand, easily moved, and if need be, mounted on a static fighting position.

You could say the Bradley's a real-life killing machine.

And our tank platoons are even meaner! Each squad of four men is outfitted with a gargantuan M1 Abrams tank. It's like the Army's version of a monster truck. Weighing in at nearly seventy tons, it's more than twice as heavy as a Bradley Fighting Vehicle. With armor made of depleted uranium plates encased in steel, it's nearly impenetrable from the side. Its main gun is a 120mm cannon that could probably blow a reasonably-sized hole through the side of a small mountain, as many Iraqis had the misfortune of learning twelve years earlier. I pity any foe who's ever found himself stared down by its mighty barrel. In fact, in a hypothetical showdown between Transformer's Megatron and an Abrams tank, provided the guys in the turret know what they're doing, I'd give the upper hand to that tank crew (I'm just not sure Megatron could withstand a heat round to the chest).

So when I say we're pretty badass, it's no exaggeration. Bar none, we're the toughest force any army will ever encounter on the battlefield.

—

It's the third week of April and all of Sabre Squadron (to which my unit, Fox Troop, belongs) is amassed just a few kilometers south of the Iraqi border, not far from our designated crossing point. It's crunch time. In preparation for the mission at hand, there's a multitude of crucial tasks that still need to be taken care of, from zeroing our weapons and the divvying out of ammo, to our commander, Captain Michael Reinhardt, receiving the OPORD (Operation Order) from higher up.

Dispersing and properly stowing the vast array of ammunition and weaponry in our arsenal takes the better part of a day. Our platoon has been issued everything imaginable – gazillions of bullets, claymore mines, hand grenades, smoke grenades, thermite grenades, upwards to a hundred TOW missiles, dozens of AT-4s (single-use, 84mm anti-tank rocket launchers), and a massive supply of banana-sized 25mm HE (high explosive) and AP (armor piercing) rounds. We have enough weaponry on hand to conquer the entire Middle East, it seems, and just gazing at it all is a very sobering reminder of what we're about to find ourselves in.

I'm seized by mixed feelings. As I rake my eyes over this massive arsenal of destruction, I'm comforted some. I feel safer knowing that we have a tactical advantage over the Iraqis. But at the same time, this feels way too real. I'm heading off to war. I just wonder if any of this stuff will be necessary by the time all is said and done. This is a subject of major debate in Fox Troop. No one can say with any level of certainty whether we'll see action, or when for that matter we'll finally come home. We're told that most of Saddam's army has already surrendered, and that except for a few enemy units that haven't yet gotten the memo, Bush's "Coalition of the Willing" is now in firm control of Iraq.

"Those camel jockeys ain't got shit on us," declares one of the privates in Alpha Section, as he packs a huge wad of chewing tobacco behind his lower lip. "We own this bitch now. This is gonna be just like Kosovo. We show up, kick their asses, and give 'em food. The war's over…It's a humanitarian mission now. After we find the WMDs, we'll be back home by summer's end."

I wonder if he's right.

A couple days earlier we were trucked out to a shoot house somewhere in the middle of the desert for a refresher course in MOUT (Military Operations in Urban Terrain). We're there to brush up on our warrior skills, in the event we find ourselves ensnared in door-to-door combat. Our instructors are well-paid civilian contractors drawn from the ranks of the Army's legendary Special Forces, or "Green Berets," our branch's equivalent of the Navy SEALs. Today's training consists of several dry runs, followed by a live fire exercise involving the use of actual bullets. In small dismounted squads, we tactically file into empty rooms, all guns blazing as we clear each objective of imaginary enemy personnel. With the instructors watching our every move, we're assessed on our ability as a team to safely and efficiently annihilate anatomically correct wooden targets.

The training is intense. Our newly issued body armor, known as the "flak vest," is not the least bit comfortable and presents added challenges as we maneuver through doors and hallways. I feel like I'm sandwiched between two sheets of plywood and lugging steel plates on both sides of my upper body. Many begin complaining about how bulky their flak vests are, some claiming that if given the option, they'd prefer to not even wear them at all.

"Hey, don't take these things for granted!" barks one of our instructors. "I know they're a pain in the ass to wear, especially in this weather. But up north, they're saving people's lives. So if ya got 'em, wear 'em, and wear 'em right. Believe me, nothing ruins your day like a sucking chest wound. So, man up and stop whining. Got it?"

Our bitching quickly stops. His advice strikes a nerve in each of us, and then everyone sort of pipes down.

With little time to spare before our big move north, my gunner/immediate supervisor also tries to squeeze in as much applicable training as possible. He wants to make sure our squad has its A-game on the minute we hit the ground in Iraq. One afternoon, he gives a few others and me a crash course on how a properly functioning checkpoint ought to be run. Using small stones, an empty pack of cigarettes, and whatever else he can find, he builds a sand table beside our vehicle. Like a mad genius lost in his work, he etches lines into the ground while fastidiously organizing the props, placing them here and there, pointed off in every which direction. They're to serve as make-believe vehicles in a mock checkpoint.

Class begins. Having twice deployed to the Balkans, he seems to know what he's talking about. He presents a host of challenging scenarios we'll likely encounter, stating he's certain that we'll be tasked with searching vehicles and homes for weapons, money, and high value targets affiliated with Saddam's regime. He's the expert, not me, so I just listen.

As his subordinate, I respect him immensely, but otherwise hate this man with a passion. Or at least for the first few months I had known him, before he loosened up some. From here on, he'll be referred to only as "Kublai Khan." That was the nickname he had earned from his underlings in the platoon – a revealing comparison to Genghis Khan's brutal grandson. Like the actual Kublai Khan who ruled over the Mongol Empire during the final half of the thirteenth century, I'm convinced Fox Troop's Sergeant Kublai Khan is every bit as much of a tyrant. Only he has no legions to enforce his will, just the rank on his collar.

Remarkably handsome and built like a professional cage fighter, he's got a neatly faded crop of brown hair that complements his marble chin and penetrating blue eyes. His mere presence commands respect. He stands little taller than I, though is made of pure muscle. He's basically what soldiers look like in the movies.

Kublai Khan came to Fox only two months behind me. From the onset of his arrival, he maintained a policy of absolute control over our squad. Dealing with his overblown tirades and unwarranted outbursts became the hallmark of life under Kublai Khan. As a young soldier, he had been a little on the rowdy side while stationed in Germany, and it had taken the heavy-handed discipline of his superiors to get him under control (or so I'd heard). He came to our platoon with a firm conviction that I needed a dose of the same medicine, and in no uncertain terms, he set out to make my life a living hell.

"This isn't a democracy!" he'd remind me, flailing his arms about while handing down orders.

Granted, the guy was under a ton of pressure, but I found his methods to be extreme. Had I been a disciplinary problem, his hyper-repressive leadership style would have been the perfect antidote. But I had always kept out of trouble, did what I was told, and, for the most part, was a fairly decent soldier. In fact, before Kublai Khan showed up, I liked Army life so much that I began considering a twenty-year career. I guess I liked how structured the military is. This job didn't come as naturally for me as it did for others, but I enjoyed it all the same and seemed to have a pretty decent grasp of what I was doing. I knew there was absolutely no way I'd ever be interested in spending twenty years in the Cav, but after this three-year stint was up, if I didn't get out and go to college, I'd consider a career track more up my alley. Perhaps something in Military Intelligence. But after my first few encounters with Kublai Khan, I wanted nothing more than to do my time and get the hell out. I quickly realized that if I had to spend the next nineteen years of my life dealing with people like him, I'd probably lose my mind.

Every company has a Kublai Khan, and ours just happened to be my immediate supervisor. I sensed he was extra hard on me because we couldn't relate, what with our vast differences in personality. After six months or so, I became fully acclimated to his veritably explosive temper and regular flare-ups. Still, I found it extraordinarily difficult to focus in his presence. Though I tried to hide it, the guy was making me a nervous wreck. Whenever he was around, I felt like I was walking on eggshells. It was like he lived to ride my ass, inventing things to bitch about. It was unfortunate, too, because outside work, he seemed like a genuinely cool guy, or at least that was my impression the couple times I ran into him downtown.

But aside from his glaring personality flaws, Kublai Khan was the best at what he did, and could always be counted on when the shit hit the fan. Even in the worst imaginable situations, he always maintained the outwardly appearance of someone who was in complete control. For that, he deserves credit.

And to this day, I haven't forgotten something he told me on the eve of our deployment: "Listen…I'm going to do everything I possibly can to bring us all back alive."

I seriously admired him for that, and it was a promise I was eager to hold him to. Besides, I couldn't let the worst of Kublai Khan get the best of me. Not at this stage in the game.

If you ask any person who's ever served in the military, they'll tell you it's filled with people who, for better or worse, you'll never forget. Kublai Khan was one of them. So was Simpson. However, at the top of my list is David Beckett, a "battle buddy" of mine, who, though equal to me in rank, treated me as if I were his idiot kid brother the whole time we served together.

"Beck" was the oldest private in our platoon, and though he was five years my senior, he tended to act as if he had just turned twenty-one. In a way, he was my alter ego. Maybe that's why I liked him. Whereas I was a tad introverted and usually had my face buried in a history book, Beck was the life of the party everywhere he went. He was always pushing the boundaries; always doing some wild shit that, back then, I'd never be caught doing in a million years (allow your imagination to fill in the gaps). With the party habits of John Belushi, I was never quite sure how he even made it in to work for morning formation, but he did. It was like he operated by his own self-styled code of conduct, and our chain of command was perfectly fine with it because they adored him.

Beck was a gorilla-sized Floridian who resembled a cross between Walt Disney's Shrek and HBO's Tony Soprano. As we climbed the ranks together, I noticed that his soldiers really looked up to him, that he had an enviable way of commanding their respect. He was well-liked by his peers and admired by our superiors. A true man's man, he had acquired his people skills through his years of bartending, prior to joining the Army. Though new to our platoon from a recent hardship tour in Korea, our leadership had already taken to him. Even as a private he was being groomed to become one of our next buck sergeants; it was pretty obvious. That angered some of us peons because we'd get put on all sorts of shitty work details while he'd drink and play poker with the NCOs. In a way, I envied him for this. But some people are born to lead, and that was Beck's specialty – not mine.

Though a friend, he was also my chief tormenter – something I haven't forgotten. I was usually at the brunt of most of his jokes, and more often than I would have preferred, unprovoked, he'd wrestle me to the ground in front of our peers, twisting one of my arms behind my back until I was in blood curdling pain. Then, as a condition to being released, I'd have to tap out (typical Army roughhousing). On a separate occasion, he once borrowed my car without asking permission. When I found it in the barracks parking lot, it was sitting halfway up on the curb in the farthest row back, with his NWA CD still in the CD player – that way I'd know it was him. When I turned the stereo on, *Fuck the Police* was blaring at maximum decibel level.

Ah, the memories…

Needless to say, I wasn't always a fan of his comedic stylings. But it was all in good fun, so I never took it personally. Though much to his credit, Beck made Army life survivable for the rest of us. Even when coming off the most horrible missions, when most guys were at their tipping point, he always had something amusing to say, as though he was unfazed by war. For that, he earns a special place in my memories of our time overseas.

—

We eventually get our OPORD. We're told that we'll be holding "a little place called Fallujah," just west of Baghdad, and home to around half a million Iraqis. Until now, it's virtually unheard of. For CENTCOM (Central Command), it's not a major strategic objective, and as far as the media is concerned, this place doesn't exist.

Where's Fallujah? Right now that's the million dollar question.

"And all I wanted was to see a little action," I pout. "We could have gone to Baghdad or Mosul or Basra…where the action's at. But nooooooo, we get *Fallujah*…which nobody's even heard of!

"Well, at least we'll be getting a humanitarian badge out of this mission, because that's about all we'll be doin'…passing out foodstuffs."

Lieutenant Anderson warns us not to get too complacent. He says there's no telling for sure what we'll be doing, and that we might even be "kickin' in a few doors and doing some raids."

I hope he's right, I tell myself.

I've just spent a year of my life training for this war, so part of me wants a good fight. We've already missed the invasion. Having beaten our unit to Iraq, right now the 3rd Infantry Division is basking in endless media coverage. Back home, their heroics are all over the news. So I'm eager to mop up whatever they've left behind.

It's like there's some primitive force within me that desires a slight taste of combat. I can't really explain it. Maybe it's because I grew up on war movies and *G.I. Joe*. Or perhaps I desire to be looked upon by my father as equal in terms of manliness. I'm twenty-one. By my age, my pops was already married, had fathered two little girls, and was wrapping up his second tour of Vietnam. So there's that. Either way, I feel a need to get this out of my system before I can call myself a man.

—

It's our last evening in Kuwait. We all sprawl out in different areas of our vehicle, with each man hoping to get as much shuteye as possible. After tonight, none of us will be getting more than four or five hours of pure sleep anytime soon. Our Brads are more to us than just a means of transportation and defense. They serve as our cramped, short-term living quarters, drawing together each member of our squad. We're like a big dysfunctional family that's been forced to live under the same roof. Only we eat, fart, sleep, piss, and shit within just feet of each other.

The softly cushioned bench in the vehicle's crew compartment is the most coveted spot in the entire Bradley, followed by the mattress-sized back ramp, which can be lowered ninety degrees, parallel to the desert floor. Kublai Khan and Anderson have dibs on those areas. The driver's hull can get a bit stuffy at night, but is generally suitable for long periods of rest and guarantees maximum privacy (if you know what I mean). That's our driver Preston Parker's domain, and I'm not sure I'd want to sleep there even if I could. Alas, there's my spot – balled up in the fetal position on the floor of the turret, the least comfortable place in the entire vehicle. Of course, I can always bed down outside on the engine deck, but at risk of rolling off the side of our vehicle. So for now the turret will have to do.

In many ways, I feel this is symbolic of my low-standing within the platoon. Like a dog that sleeps at the foot of his master's bed, I'm forced to lay my head where others rest their feet. That may come as a blow to my pride, but this is the Army. Don't like it? Too bad. Suck it up and soldier on!

—

It turns out Fox Troop will not be stampeding over the Iraqi border with sand grinding between our tracks, as I had long imagined. Somebody heads above me has had the common sense to coordinate the movement of our vehicles into war via the use of HETSs (Heavy Equipment Transporter Systems).

HETs are enormous wheeled vehicles with truck cabs in the front end and long metal platforms in the rear, allowing slower tracked vehicles like ours to be loaded up and rapidly transported from one location to another. They're an asset in any land war. They'll get us to our destination in about three or four days, well ahead of how long it had taken the 3rd ID to close in on Baghdad.

After a thorough headcount, we pile into our vehicles, which are tightly fastened down by thick chains affixed to the truck beds of each cab. With all our personnel accounted for, our convoy begins snaking over the border on an empty stretch of highway that's littered with trash. I've anticipated this moment for a while, with some degree of anxiety. I'm hoping to get the same adrenaline rush as those brave souls who poured into Normandy six decades earlier for the liberation of Paris. Instead, this feels more like my first time on a rollercoaster ride. I'm overcome by the rousing sensation of being at war, even though we're unlikely to see any combat on our way to Fallujah. So in a way, this isn't war. I mean, we're at war alright, though not really. This is more like going on a well-armed desert safari.

Crossing into Mesopotamia is like being magically whisked to a bygone era, and though it doesn't resemble something out of *Arabian Nights*, as I assumed it would, it's like nothing I've ever seen. The best way to describe southern Iraq is to say that it's hot, flat, brown, and dry. There isn't much to see. We pass a camel or two every now and again, but nothing too noteworthy – no desert caravans, no crowded bazaars, no lush stretches of palm groves. Just the occasional sandstorm.

Small brick huts line both sides of the highway. Since we're no longer bound to the "no-littering" policies of our host-country, Kuwait, our invading army has left a trail of garbage strewn about in its path. The children greet us with big ear-to-ear smiles, ecstatically waving as our convoy rolls by. In protest, the men, some with sandals in hand, choose instead to show us the bottom of their soles – the Middle Eastern equivalent of "Fuck you!"

Of course, back then I didn't know what that meant. I thought it was their culturally peppy way of greeting outsiders; or perhaps a way of displaying gratitude for us having liberated them from Saddam. Well aren't I naive? I would have never guessed that it literally means you're the scum beneath our feet. By waving their sandals at us, they might as well have been saying "Eat shit and die!"

In the Middle East, it's considered to be in poor taste to expose the bottom of one's feet to others, which explains why people there rarely sit with their legs crossed. But I don't know that yet because I'm from Ohio. Each time I see the bottom of somebody's sandal waved at me, I try to spread some love, returning the act by giving that person a thumbs-up. I innocently assume this gesture is universal in meaning. But what I also don't know is that in Iraq "thumbs-up" really means "thumbs-down," or at least it used to before we showed up. Though not as offensive as slapping an Arab male on the back of the neck or calling him an *ibn kalb* (son of a dog), a skyward thumb is on par with giving someone the middle finger. The folks we pass along the side of that highway weren't raised in America, and therefore don't realize that what I really mean to say is, "We're the good guys and we mean you no harm." Instead, I'm sending the opposite message. What I perceive to be a positive exchange between our people and theirs is really little more than a massive exchange of insults.

But not all of them wish us ill will. In fact, most seem relieved to be free of Saddam. To those who wave, we reward their allegiance with edible goodies thrown from both sides of our northbound convoy. We toss them an assortment of discarded items from our MREs (Meals Ready-to-Eat). The MRE is a 1,200 calorie "self-contained, individual field ration." Each case contains a choice of twelve separate meals, with each one packaged in a thick brown plastic bag. Intentionally low in dietary fiber, shitting them out is about as pleasant as passing a kidney stone. We'll be eating a lot of these in the months to come. As for the less desirable options on the menu, we toss those ones to the hungry children lining the highway.

Of course, that's not all we're chucking off the side of this convoy. There are at least one hundred fifty of us and not enough rest stops to please everyone. It's hot out and we're all drinking a ton of water. What we don't sweat off, we piss out. Plus this new all-MRE diet is killing our asses, literally. Many of us are horribly constipated. I typically spend a day or two all backed up, and when I finally have to go, the sudden release in my bowels feels like I've just passed a cannonball.

There's nowhere for us to deposit our waste but onto the side of the highway. So out the hatch it goes. Much like the Native Americans are said to have used every part of the buffalo after slaughter, we do the same with our empty water bottles and MRE packaging. We fill our empty water bottles with urine almost as quickly as we guzzle down the next, and use the empty food packaging as bags for disposable waste. We then hurl them just beyond the margins of the highway.

As our convoy passes each village, children race from the sand-swept mud huts they live in, eager to see what the Americans have left. At times, it must be disappointing. At the head of our convoy, I see one soldier lob a huge bag of shit from his vehicle. A small mob of children spot it, with one particularly agile little girl having outpaced several others to get her hands on it. As she picks it up and looks inside, expecting candy, a look of horror comes upon her face. I doubt she saw that coming. Likewise, these kids are quick to realize that the plastic bottles we've littered the highway with are not filled with sweet-tasting lemonade made from powdered concentrate. Still, it's not as bad as the few occasions in which I spot fellow soldiers deliberately throwing "non-halal" pork MREs to Muslim villagers (not that they can even read the labeling on the packages, which are written in English).

Right about now, I feel like Indiana Jones. In the twenty-one years I've inhabited this Earth, I've traveled little and have only been outside of the United States once in my life, and that's when my family drove to Canada for a day to visit Niagara Falls in the early Nineties. So for me, this is the adventure of a lifetime. I'm utterly intrigued by the people we encounter. Their lives remain largely untouched by the technological modernizations of the last century. Maybe that has something to do with the embargo. I'm not sure. But I'm trying to gain as much from this experience as possible. We're in the Cradle of Civilization. Five thousand years earlier, this area was home to the ancient Sumerians. These people invented writing, irrigation, the wheel, were governed by the earliest laws known to man, and were among the first people to brew beer. Now it's a lonely hellscape bearing few signs of life.

As we continue north, I'm ecstatic upon first sight of the Euphrates River. I whip out my camera and snap a photo or two. At the time, I had been reading the Old Testament in its entirety and had guesstimated our position to be only one or two hundred kilometers from Ur, the biblical stomping grounds of

Abraham, the great patriarch of Judaism, Christianity, and Islam.

"What a shithole!" somebody says over the radio.

"Yeah, it looks like Mexico," jokes another, hoping to get a rise out of Sergeant Fernando Gomez, one of Bravo Section's Mexican-American NCOs.

Along the way, we pass through many solidly Shia territories that I assume had once been occupied by the Marsh Arabs. For generations they had acted as stewards of the land until Saddam's rise to power and the advent of up-steam damming, which brought about irreparable ecological and cultural ruin to the entire area. Once upon a time, hundreds of thousands of fishermen lived in these marshes, in small dwellings made of compressed reeds that sat atop thousands of miniature islands dotting the landscape. The marshlands were to southern Iraq what the Everglades are to Florida. These wetlands, once abound with thousands of unique species of plant and animal life, were reduced to a sprawling desert wasteland incapable of sustaining life. Fresh water was diverted away from these areas and channeled to Baghdad and its neighboring suburbs, and with no concern for how it would impact life in the marshes. The prolonged continuation of this policy was also a way for the Iraqi government to punish the Shiites for their 1991 uprising, which the US had encouraged though failed to back, allowing thousands of rebels to get slaughtered.

As we endure, somewhere in the back of my head I begin to vaguely recall the first Gulf War, remembering talk of Saddam Hussein and the footage of his army plundering Kuwait. These are long-obscured memories that rise to the surface amid the backdrop of my own experience. I was about to enter the third grade when the Butcher of Baghdad plowed headlong into Kuwait, forever sealing the fate of his nation.

My stepfather, Ralph, was a Green Beret in 11th Special Forces Group (an elite though now defunct unit of the Army Reserves), but otherwise worked a pretty typical nine-to-five job at a local power plant in Ashtabula. Between episodes of *Rosanne* and *The Simpsons*, the evening news was usually on in our household. I remember being terrified by the thought that he'd get called up to go overseas, and that maybe he wouldn't return. During the start of that war, initial estimates indicated there might be as many as twenty thousand American casualties. So I was pretty relieved when the fighting ended. Now here I am a decade later, where it all began.

—

At some point, I wonder if we're traveling along Highway 80, better known as the "Highway of Death."

As the first Gulf War drew to an end some twelve years earlier, Highway 80 was a scene of mass carnage. After a swift and crippling defeat, on the evening of February 26, 1991, Iraqi ground forces began pulling out of Kuwait under orders from Baghdad. The Iraqis began their panicked retreat by commandeering thousands of civilian vehicles, stuffing them full of ransacked merchandise before exiting the country. After a mad dash across the border of Iraq, the vehicular exodus was stopped in its tracks by American aircraft. Fighter jets began strafing the lead vehicles, bringing the convoy to an immediate standstill. Nor was escape from the rear possible; all vehicles at the tail end of the caravan were bombarded as well. Like a candle burning from two ends, everything in between was consumed by an awesome display of American airpower as fire rained down from above.

As the bombing commenced, thousands clawed their way out of cars, trucks, vans, and buses, racing beyond the fiery edges of the highway to take refuge in the surrounding desert. Hundreds were burnt alive, many completely incinerated. So intense were the flames that some who didn't escape the attack seemed frozen in time, their bodies perfectly intact and encrusted with ash.

The aerial assault lasted the better of a day, until every means of transportation on that three-mile stretch of highway was completely obliterated. Under the Geneva Convention, armies are strictly prohibited from targeting "soldiers out of combat." But General "Stormin' Norman" Schwarzkopf Jr. deemed it necessary, citing the "great deal of military equipment on that highway" as his justification for the strike, as well as the horrific atrocities committed by Iraqi troops against Kuwaiti civilians. However, among the tangled mess of smoking debris and melted flesh stood only two dozen or so Iraqi tanks and armored personnel carriers; the rest were hijacked civilian vehicles.

What that meant for us twelve years later, I wasn't sure. But something told me it wasn't good.

—

Several days into our long journey north, we finally reach the outer ring of that "little place called Fallujah." In typical Army fashion, there's a bit of a holdup. We're left waiting some before we can download our vehicles from the wheeled transports they're fastened to. As the suspense grows and grows, large swarms of children begin circling our convoy, greeting us with big adorable smiles and lots of *hellos*. They cheer us on as though we're rock stars, leading me to believe that what we've done in Iraq is a good thing.

In a way, I feel like a hero (as cheesy as that might sound). For once in my life, I have a purpose. I'm on the cusp of history and believe this to be my generation's liberation of Paris. Flush with cash and yearning for souvenirs to mail home, I lean over the left side of our Brad and begin bartering with a pair of teenagers over the price of a red and white checkered headscarf. Kublai Khan quickly spoils my fun with his abrupt command to "Get the fuck back in the vehicle!" He's right. I'm already becoming way too complacent. This isn't a trip to the Pyramids of Giza. This is Iraq. There's still a war going on, and though we haven't seen a trace of enemy contact, people are dying, and by month's end, 138 American troops will have been killed in action.

I'm inundated by the scenery. Iraq looks nothing like I had imagined. I assumed it'd resemble the arid deserts of Saudi Arabia, which stretch farther than the eyes can see. Instead, its dense boscage of greenery looks more like something out of Southeast Asia than the hot and sandy badlands of the Arabian Peninsula. I suppose that's why this area of Iraq is known as the Fertile Crescent. There are lots of rivers and canals, and lining the horizon, long swaths of palm groves with thick, bushy canopy. In the nearby pasturelands, shepherds can be seen herding large flocks of sheep through the fields, watching over them as they nibble on grass.

In the countryside, most of the people lead very simple lives, dwelling in boxy rectangular-shaped homes made of concrete and baked brick. The more affluent Ba'thists, however, reside in villas and beautifully adorned two-story mansions, with large Roman-esque pillars in front and an aging Mercedes Benz parked in the driveway. It's a very traditional society. The people who live here have farmed this land for generations. The men walk in pairs, some holding hands (which is not uncommon in the Middle East, nor an indication of one's sexual preference). While many sport blue jeans and t-shirts, most are decked out in Muslim attire, carrying *sibhas*, or Islamic prayer beads. They eye us with great suspicion, showing no signs of being as thrilled by our presence as the animated throngs of children lining both sides of our convoy.

There's an unfamiliar sound blaring over a pair of loudspeakers bolted atop the minarets of a nearby mosque. It's their call to prayer, known as the "adhān," which is commonly heard five times a day throughout most corners of the Islamic world, at prescribed hours. God is great, it says, summarizing the entirety of their creed in a few simple words: "I bear witness that there is no god but Allah, and Muhammad is his prophet." It's not a declaration of faith that I personally embrace. Though having spent much of my twenties in the Middle East, it's one that I've certainly come to respect.

We haven't the slightest clue what the *muezzin* is chanting. From the rear bench of our crew compartment I offer my own interpretation: "Fuuuuuuuuuck Israel, and fuuuuuuuuuck America, too…you stinking infidels!" Kublai Khan finds it so amusing that he demands an encore performance over the platoon radio. So I pick up the hand mic and begin chanting something along the same lines. I score hoots of laughter from the guys in my platoon. For the moment, I feel like a real comedian. But looking back, it was exactly that sort of arrogance that would prove to be America's Achilles' heal. Especially in Fallujah.

Once given the order to rock 'n' roll, we carefully maneuver our vehicles off the long metal platforms they're chained to. From there, we relocate to a temporary encampment somewhere on the outskirts of the city. As more information becomes available, we learn that a small contingent of US ground forces from the 82nd Airborne is holding several government buildings in downtown Fallujah, and that we'll be relieving them bright and early the next day.

Already Fallujah is proving to be wilder than we had earlier thought. It's April 28 and the sky is alight with celebratory gunfire in observance of an important Iraqi national holiday: Saddam Hussein's birthday. He just turned sixty-six. Downtown there was a violent anti-American demonstration just outside the walls of some building that had been recently commandeered by the 82nd Airborne – a schoolhouse or something. An angry mob of Iraqis amassed out of nowhere, hollering slurs at these troops while pelting them with stones. A few even brandished AK-47s and fired them into the air. It was ballsy, but stupid. As could be expected, a couple of those soldiers got spooked and responded by unleashing a wave of gunfire on the crowd, killing an untold number of unarmed civilians.

I have to admit, when I first heard what happened, I was rather cavalier about the whole incident.

"Oh, well..." I said. "Don't get me wrong, that sucks and all...It really does. But if they think we can be driven out of here with sticks and stones, they've got another thing coming."

But so far I only know half the story.

A dozen and a half civilians were just killed, and dozens more wounded. I wasn't there when it happened, so it's not my place to judge whether or not those paratroopers from the 82nd Airborne had shown proper restraint. Talk to any of them, and they'll claim they were fired on; the demonstrators claim otherwise. In a way, I empathize with the soldiers who fired on that mob. Like them, I know what it means to be scared for my life. In war, sometimes your eyes play tricks on you, as the shadows toy with your mind in the heat of battle. You're forced to shoot and ask questions later. Anything to save your life and the lives of your buddies. Though I didn't know it yet, this tragedy was a mere foreshadowing of the bloodshed that was soon to come. For a welcoming party bent on vengeance was now eagerly awaiting our arrival. We'd learn the hard way that blowback's a bitch.

Chapter Six
FALLUJAH

THE FOLLOWING DAY we venture into the heart of Fallujah and relieve the 82nd Airborne from the local Ba'th Party headquarters. As for our mission, we're not given much in the way of specifics. All we know is that we'll be establishing something called a "FOB," or "Forward Operating Base."

We carefully maneuver our Brads into the rear courtyard, barely squeezing in through the back gate without destroying everything in our path. It's a large two-story compound planted smack dab in the middle of the city, on the northwest corner of the busiest intersection in town. Like most architectural structures in Iraq, it's a gated facility with high concrete walls and thick metal gates. The westernmost half of the building is directly interlinked with the mayor's cell. Until now, it would appear the headquarters of the local Ba'th Party has dually served as Fallujah's version of city hall. I find this hardly surprising. It epitomizes the totalitarian concept of one-party rule and speaks volumes as to the sheer level of control the Ba'thists have held over every facet of Iraqi political life. And surrounding the other three sides of the party headquarters are several mosques of astonishing beauty, with towering minarets and enormous blue domes that are embellished with Arabic calligraphy and colorful mosaic patterns. It's a spectacular sight to behold.

The 82nd is relieved to see us. They've had a rough past couple of days. In ones and twos, we begin to fan out, inspecting every square inch of our new living quarters. A tight, narrow courtyard stretches around three-quarters of the premises. The palm trees and tall concrete walls shade us from the blistering wrath of the sun, also providing us with cover from those curious spectators outside who're eyeballing our every move. Great caution must be applied when moseying around the compound, and not due to the threat of unexploded ordinance. Those slobs in the 82nd have shat all over the place like barnyard animals. Apparently it hadn't dawned on them to simply burn or bury their droppings. Instead, the grounds remain booby trapped with huge piles of shit that blend in with the sun-scorched patches of brown grass.

Over the years, this particular facility has been poorly maintained. It's also recently been gutted of all useful construction materials by local thieves. Next to the rear entrance on the first floor, there's a room filled with party propaganda, military armaments, and an old broken dirt bike that no one had bothered to steal when the government collapsed two weeks earlier, on April 9. Both floors are stacked from top-to-bottom with Ba'thist literature and shredded wall posters paying homage to the greatness of Saddam Hussein. One such poster depicts a far more youthful Saddam nobly strolling through an Iraqi village, with heavenly rays of sunshine beaming all around him as he passes out loaves of bread to hordes of smiling children. And on the building's second level there are children's desks scattered about, leaving me to conclude that this place had also served as some kind of brainwashing camp for Iraqi youngsters.

We quickly implement a host of security measures, establishing a guard roster and mounting several M240B machineguns atop the roof. For added fortification, we also park one of our Brads in the southeast courtyard, giving whoever's in the turret clear visibility over the front gate, which runs parallel to the city's most heavily trafficked intersection. We've just been assigned the most laborious guard shifts imaginable – eighteen hours up, divided equally three ways, with each "swinging dick" having to man a different guard station every six hours. But that's what "force protection" is all about, and we take it seriously.

In the meantime, as others set up makeshift toilets and plastic, crotch-level urination tubes that have been pounded into the ground at 45° angles, a couple of our NCOs begin mounting high-powered radio antennas atop the building's apex. This way we're able to maintain comms with the rest of Fox Troop, which has been tasked out on several other missions. *Now this is what I signed up for*, I tell myself. I'm utterly thrilled, and begin snapping pictures of everything and everyone, as though I'm a photographer for *National Geographic*. This is shaping up to be exactly the kind of mission I had hoped for. A year earlier, I was working a dead-end factory job, manufacturing porch columns in Conneaut, Ohio. Now I'm halfway across the globe, making history.

Our presence invokes a mixed reaction from the locals. While on guard, I wave and smile at everyone I see, wanting them to know that we're *the good guys*, here to rid them of tyranny. As Mother Teresa once said, "Peace begins with a smile." I understand we're at war, but I'm trying to be diplomatic. As I see it, we have few options. If we fail to win the Iraqis over to our cause, there'll be hell to pay later on. So if that means acting like a door greeter at Wal-Mart, I'll do so. Besides, I don't want these people to hate America. I want them to view us as liberators, not occupiers.

Some wave in return, while others outright ignore me, or just stop to wave the soles of their footwear. It's just now that I'm beginning to realize that this isn't exactly a welcoming gesture. But I don't let it dampen my spirits. Instead, I just keep waving till my arm tires.

Still, there are others who pass by, eyeing us with looks of ambiguity. They're not sure what to make of our presence. They stand there, thumbing their prayer beads and analyzing our behavior, wondering just what our true intentions are. I can't say I blame them. A day or two earlier, the 82nd painted these streets with the blood of their youth. Now here we are, smiling at them, passing out candy to their children as though nothing had ever happened.

—

It's high noon and sweltering outside. I'm just an hour or so into my second guard shift, and I can tell it's going to be a long, miserable day. In fact, it's so hot out that I've completely forgone wearing underwear. It's called "freeballing." Since arriving in Kuwait a month earlier, I've learned that it's one of the best ways to stay cool (that and a smidgen of Johnson's baby powder). Not to mention, in this sort of climate, tighty-whities cause baby rash, and boxers just ride up the inner-thigh, causing extreme discomfort. So freeballing's the way to go!

While standing in the commander's hatch of the Bradley that's parked on the southeast corner of our property, I smile at a beautiful young woman who's accompanied by her aging mother. She's simply stunning, this girl. She has long and silky black hair, dark, mysterious eyes, glistening olive skin, and a captivating smile that's charming enough to be in a toothpaste commercial. As I wave, her face lights up like a Christmas tree. She giggles some and waves back, exchanging glances. Then, out of nowhere, her mother's arm swoops down like a predatory bird, slapping her in the back of the head. That's what she gets for attempting to interact with me. As her daughter stiffens up and keeps marching, the old woman looks back and gives me the evil eye, her cold and wrinkly stare forever burned into my memory.

Perhaps she didn't like the idea of her daughter flirting with a grown man in public, especially an American soldier/infidel. After all, such taboos have been known to get women killed in certain parts of the Middle East. Or maybe her actions were more indicative of local resentment for America – for originally propping up Saddam to our benefit during the Cold War, then flattening their military in under one hundred hours in 1991, then slapping a twelve-year economic embargo on their country, thus denying them the ability to import even the most basic items, then turning their world upside down by invading their country under false pretenses. I bet that's why she gave me the evil eye. Either way, I can sense a lot of the people don't want us here.

Later that evening, Sergeant Dupéré spots a tiny street-side grocery shop through his binoculars, just a few blocks north of our base. He gets the nod from higher up to take several of us on a short foot patrol so we can grab some cold sodas. Within minutes our small squad has geared up and is cautiously marching up the street, locked and loaded. The owner, along with several customers, is shocked to see half a dozen American soldiers come streaming into the shop, waiting patiently in line with cash in hand as those in front of us check out. Bound by tradition, the men receive us with the utmost hospitably, shaking our hands and offering us cigarettes. It seems like a good sign, but upon exiting the shop, I'm left to wonder if this show of kindness was little more than a front.

Waiting outside is our "fan club," the small army of neighborhood children who regularly congregate around the gates of our base and trail us everywhere we go. They've just followed our squad all the way to the grocery store, and they'll be following us all the way back, blatantly defying their parents' demands to stay away from the Americans. As loyal as dogs, they eagerly wait for us to finish up, hoping to practice their elementary-level English and perhaps even finagle a little cash out of us.

Stomping on a 250 dinar bill bearing the image of Saddam Hussein's face, they emphatically chant, "Bush good! Bush good! Saddam bad! Saddam bad!"

After mingling with the locals, we begin our march back down the street. We're trailed the whole time by a legion of neighborhood kids who keep cheering us on. Along the way, passersby toot their horns at us, and one gentleman even pulls over in his white Toyota pickup, signaling for us to hop in the back so he can drop us off at the FOB, several hundred meters down the road. Dupéré wisely declines the offer, but thanks him anyway, and with a smile on his face, he gestures for the man to keep driving.

"Well, at least we're making *some* headway in terms of winning people over," I say. "They'll catch on soon enough and realize we're not so bad."

Unfortunately, the battle for "hearts and minds" was a fight that we had no strategy for winning. If ever there was a chance to convince the Iraqis that us being in their country was in their best national interest (and knowing what I do now, I doubt there ever was), it would have been in those pivotal days immediately following the collapse of Saddam's regime. Instead, we holed ourselves up in our little fortress, guarding over the place as though it were the Alamo. We completely neglected to engage the local citizenry on any level, political or otherwise. All we did was gawk at them from behind our machineguns, rousing their every suspicion as to what our actual intentions were and what sort twisted ulterior motives were really driving us.

I'm reminded of one morning in which we found our compound surrounded by the usual droves of children. One of my buddies stepped out onto the northern balcony with an issue of *Maxim* in his right hand. With a huge grin plastered across his face, he held up the centerfold and bellowed out, "I bet ya never saw tits like this before!" Without the slightest clue what he just said, the boys laughed and clapped their hands in excitement. This was exactly the kind of attention we *didn't* need. It was bad enough Squadron thought it a good idea to position our company betwixt and between three mosques; the passersby didn't find our buffoonery as amusing as these kids, who would have otherwise been in school if not for us having invaded their country.

While part of me laughed at my friend's antics, as well as those of my own, I knew that with each passing day our window of opportunity was quickly shutting on any real chance of us winning over the local populace. I guess we lacked the diplomacy skills necessary for this mission. After all, we're not the Peace Corps. We had come to do our government's dirty business. That's why soldiers make horrible peacekeepers. We're trained to kill, not keep the peace.

—

On April 30, just two days after our arrival, the shit really hit the fan.

While pulling guard on the roof of our FOB, I was halfway through my shift, scanning a pie-shaped sector of Fallujah from behind an M240B, which was perched on the northwest ledge of our compound. I heard a loud commotion up the street, just a few blocks to the west, and noticed several dozen protesters marching toward us. They were carrying homemade placards and tapestries bearing anti-American slogans, some written in English. They continued our way, with one man at the head of their column screaming through a bullhorn until they reached our compound. Without even stopping to face us and air their grievances, they continued marching, circling the block just south of us and returning in the direction from which they had just come.

It was enough to briefly pique my interest, though not enough of a scene for me to really give a shit.

Well, half an hour or so has passed, and I've returned to fantasizing about Katana Baker and Tanya Ballinger, the busty Miller Lite girls who're featured in this month's issue of *Stuff*. I can't say I like Miller Lite – in fact, I think it tastes like piss – but I sure like these two. Personally, I've got a thing for brunettes and think Katana is way hotter. But it would seem a couple of the guys in my platoon beg to differ, claiming that Tanya – the blonde – is way more seductive.

I'm guzzling down a bottle of water when, all of a sudden, something grabs my attention. I hear this growing noise up the street. I shift my head to the left and see what looks like half the city descending upon us.

"Oh, fuck." I tell myself, gulping nervously, knowing blood will be shed before the day is through. Time to put on my warface...

They continue marching our way, a thousand advancing fearlessly toward our position. Some are waiving Iraqi flags, others chanting murderous threats in Arabic. We aren't exactly sure what to make of this. Or, for that matter, what to do. The ball is entirely in their court. With their numbers having multiplied and their fists raised in the air, I can tell that dispersing the crowd will be no easy job. They inch closer and closer, then suddenly charge our gates. As the masses squeeze up against it, several of them drape cloth banners over the front wall of our base.

"Sooner or Later U.S. Killers we'll Kick you out," reads one.

They pelt us with anything they can get their filthy hands on. Some even throw their sandals. The loudspeakers from a nearby mosque ring out simultaneously, blaring angry messages that further incite the crowd. Not wanting a repeat of what happened two days earlier, we show a tremendous amount of restraint. But if they come over that wall, we'll stack 'em ten feet high if we need to. It's that simple – their lives or ours, and I'm not looking to die anytime soon.

I abandon my machinegunner's nest and take up position on the southern edge of the roof, watching the mayhem below unravel from behind a huge stack of sandbags and metal railing. There's a cluster of us just standing there on the edge of the roof, watching them, awaiting their next move. It suddenly dawns on me what those guys in the 82nd were up against two days earlier.

I notice Old Glory in the crowd. She's being stomped on and riven to shreds. I feel like racing into that mob and pulling her from their clutches, but right now that isn't exactly an option. So I keep watching.

Then the situation takes an ugly turn. The main route cutting through Fallujah and past the front gates of our base is one frequented by a loose collection of military units operating within Iraq. At that very moment, a string of American Humvees just happens to be passing through town.

The convoy slowly maneuvers into the crowd, parting it like the Red Sea. For a minute or so, it takes the focus off us. The soldiers hunker down into their vehicles, ducking from the barrage of spit and stones flying their way – all while the angry mob presses on, absolutely fearless of the consequences of doing so. Having snaked through the demonstration largely unscathed, the tail end of the convoy is nearly out of the crowd. Then one of them suddenly fires several bursts of gunfire directly into the angry stream of people lining the road. His bullets tear into the crowd, killing some and maiming others. The demonstrators scatter like cockroaches, some limping away covered in their own blood.

It all happened so fast that it's sort of a blur for me now. My most poignant recollection from that day was the sight of a man who had collapsed at the nearby intersection after being shot in the face at near point-blank range. Most of his head was gone. His body lay there in a plash of blood until it was ferried away in a white and orange taxicab that soon pulled up. I couldn't believe what I had just witnessed. Until then, it was the single most gruesome thing I had ever seen.

The shooting fills the remaining demonstrators with a level of animalistic rage unlike anything I have ever seen in humans. Unable to storm our base and bludgeon us to death, they begin destroying everything in sight. It's like a scene from the L.A. riots. Some even vent their anger on the media people covering the whole ordeal. From about fifty meters away, I see two or three of them start pushing a cameraman, violently prying the camera from his hands and smashing it to the ground, knocking him down as well. I place the iron sights of my M16 on one of them, half-tempted to squeeze the trigger if they lay another finger on him. We've been issued a "rules of engagement" card, briefly detailing under what circumstances we're permitted to use deadly force. Not wanting to create an international incident or add fuel to the fire, I refrain. Looking back, I'm glad I did. I'm not sure I would have been entirely justified in doing so, and if I had pulled the trigger I'd have to live with that decision the rest of my life.

For reasons unknown, some dude on the roof begins firing on the remaining demonstrators with his M16, as though their unruly but fading presence is enough of a threat to warrant such action. Not sure if he's shooting at them or near them, but he's definitely squeezing off a few rounds. It's not anyone from my platoon, but instead, some guy from some random unit that's sharing the compound with us.

"Ceasefire! Ceasefire! Stop fuckin' shooting!" one guy yells at the top of his lungs.

Within a few minutes, the rest of the crowd disperses and traffic picks back up, and oddly enough, everything returns to normal as though nothing at all had even happened.

Footage of the protest-turned-bloodbath can be seen in the PBS documentary *Truth, War & Consequences*.

With the camera steadied on our base, you can hear gunshots emanating from the roof and see my platoon – with me sandwiched in somewhere in the middle – gazing into the crowd, shocked by the horror unfolding before our very eyes. Then, as the camera is panned 180 degrees to the left, you'll see a dead Iraqi man lying in the streets, his white garbs soaked in blood as he's scooped up and thrown into the back of a taxicab.

With an Al Jazeera microphone pushed in his face, one man, screaming at the top of his lungs as he stands in the victim's puddle of blood, leans down and runs his fingers through it, stands back up, and then begins pounding his chest and tearing his garbs:

"Is this the freedom they want to bring us?! How do you like this freedom?! This freedom is for the dogs!"

That was our first taste of Fallujah, the "City of Mosques," as it's known by the locals. We had only been there a couple days, and already the rage of its people had manifested itself in two violent clashes that ended each time in the killing of unarmed civilians. Now that we had let the genie out of its bottle, there was no stuffing it back in.

—

About twelve hours or so after the shooting, it's pushing midnight, and many of us are bedding down for the evening. With less than an hour to go before I relieve Parker from his guard shift, I decide to take a catnap near his position on the roof. This way, I don't create too much of a stir when it's time to get up. I'm lying there on my back, gazing up at the stars. As I begin wondering what sort of craziness the following day will bring, I soon doze off.

Almost as quickly as my consciousness leaves me, I'm awoken by thunderous explosions and the earsplitting machinegun fire of Parker's M240B. Smoking hot brass cartridges spray everywhere. I roll over onto my stomach and into a pile of fresh shell casings, the brass searing into my forearms. As I drag my M16 by its sling and low-crawl to my helmet, it's like I'm inching my way through a fiery pit of smoking embers. I look up and see others doing the same. It's total chaos. Everyone's running everywhere, scrambling for safety. My heart is pounding. Every sinew in my body tightens up. I cling to my rifle and take cover behind the nearest concrete bulwark. I brace my weapon over the ledge of the building, scanning from left to right. But I can't see anything, or anyone.

Lurking in the alleyways and moving stealthily under the cover of night, the assailants had lobbed hand grenades over the walls of our base. Parker had spotted one of the perpetrators trying to flee the scene, diving over a fence or something. He engaged the man, though barely missed.

A few guys sustain mild flesh wounds; none from our platoon. As we regain our composure, flares are shot off in every direction over nearby rooftops and alleyways, lighting the storied buildings that surround us. Packs of stray dogs begin to howl, and people all throughout the city begin flipping their porch lights on, knowing full well what has just gone down. It's pretty obvious we've been hit in retaliation for what happened earlier. I wonder if the locals are celebrating the attack in the privacy of their living rooms, chanting "God is great!" in Arabic while debating how many infidels have just been blown to smithereens.

Then, standing at the farthest corner of the intersection near our compound, is a man appearing almost frozen. Nobody has any idea where he came from or what he's doing out past curfew. We're thinking he's not one of the attackers, as he didn't hightail it out of there. But we don't know that for certain. The situation requires further investigation. Captain Reinhardt orders us to ready a vehicle with two dismounts, saying he and the XO (executive officer) will personally check it out. I'm one of the guys ordered to go, along with someone from Charlie Section.

The four of us pile into the back of someone's Brad. Our vehicle creeps out the rear gate, slowly rolling towards him. We're not sure if he's just a scared old man who's lost and frazzled, or if he's wired to blow, so when the ramp comes down, we cautiously approach. Reinhardt and the XO train their M4s on the man, as me and my fellow dismount guard their right and left flanks. He orders him to raise his hands; instead the guy panics and begins slowly backing up into a dimly lit corner. He fires a warning shot or two at close range, demanding compliance.

Just then bullets come raining down on our position. "Ambush!" I yell, feeling tiny bits of asphalt pepper my face as 7.62 tears into the ground near my feet. I scan the nearby rooftops, expecting a second burst to hit us. Just as I assume it's about to come, we learn it's friendly fire. That's right – one of our own guys! Somebody in Alpha Section assumed Captain Reinhardt was trying to shoot the guy; figured he'd lend a helping hand. Never mind the fact he almost took out our command, along with two guys from his own damn platoon. In a failed attempt to hit the man, he used an M240B to neutralize a precision target in dangerous proximity to four comrades who had the situation perfectly under control. His so-called "help" was completely unneeded.

We. Almost. Died. No exaggeration!

As for the mysterious figure we had come to investigate, he fled, disappearing into the shadows. Can't say I blame him. Meanwhile, we can only imagine who pulled the trigger, nearly causing an act of fratricide. *Probably some dipshit private*, I remember thinking. Nope! It was a buck sergeant, marking the SECOND TIME in just as many days that an E-5 almost killed fellow soldiers. The first time, a gunner from one of our tank platoons accidentally shot one of his guys in the foot while clearing his 9mm. Miraculously, it only grazed his boot. This time, it was some jackass from Alpha Section who made rank just before we deployed. I can still remember the scene on that roof when we got back: Kublah Khan was up in his grill, flipping out on the guy, along with our platoon sergeant. In the Army, it's not every day you see an E-5 roast a fellow E-5 in front of his soldiers, but when you do, it might be because he almost killed your only dismount.

Nobody goes back to sleep.

At the end of my shift the following morning, I drag myself off the roof to a room on the second floor, hoping to get at least three or four hours of solid shuteye. I've just finished brushing my teeth when a distinctively metallic *ting-ting-ting* sound comes in through the window behind me. I look up, only to hear my buddy Hector Hernandez shout "GRE-NADE!" Our instinctual sense of self-preservation kicks in as both of us dive for cover. I press my chest to the floor, hoping to block my innards from shrapnel, also smashing my face to the ground and covering the sides of my head.

One final thought races through my mind: *So this is it?*

A second or two elapses, then three or four. And still nothing. We cautiously look up, eyeballing each other, then, gazing about the room, wonder if we've just been spared by God Almighty Himself. *A miracle?* Perhaps. Though probably not. We stand upright and dust ourselves off, both shocked to still be alive and in one piece. We look around in hopes of finding what it was that had given us such a scare. Lying in the corner of the room is an empty 40mm casing to a flare, one shot off the night before.

We angrily dash out onto the balcony, looking upward.

"Who the fuck threw this down here?!"

Turns out one of the guys above us had kicked it off the roof. From there, it hit the windowsill and bounced in, giving Hernandez and I a bit of a jolt.

But here's the best part. Several hours later, President Bush donned an unworn flight suit and put his training in the Texas Air National Guard on full display, safely piloting a Lockheed S3 Viking onto the deck of the USS Abraham Lincoln, just a few miles or so off the coast of San Diego, California. It was there he triumphantly declared "Mission Accomplished" in Iraq.

Mission Accomplished? I thought. *My ass...*

Chapter Seven
THE OCCUPATION BEGINS

IN THE DAYS after that first attack, we relocated our base of operations to a sleepy little resort town known as "Dreamland." Tucked away behind tall, fortress-like concrete walls on the eastern outskirts of the city, it was once a getaway spot for Iraq's well-heeled ruling elite. Squadron allotted us our very own lakeside bungalows, three to each platoon. Like the Ba'th Party headquarters in downtown Fallujah, all the buildings there had been ransacked by the locals and stripped of any salvageable construction materials – copper wiring, toilets, air conditioners, bathroom tiling, windows, etc. All that remained was their bare skeletal framework, nothing else. With no air-conditioning, these bungalows were like oversized hotboxes, roasting in the sun by day and emitting a steady wave of heat at night. Yet, this was still a major improvement over being forced to live out of our vehicles.

Like many of the Iraqi people, I often slept outside on the roof, under the stars. It allowed me to catch an occasional breeze or two. Though even on our nights off, I still had difficulty sleeping. The temperatures were simply unbearable. If that wasn't enough, I could feel mosquitoes and sand fleas feasting on my skin. Our bodies were so badly marred by insect bites that we all looked like smallpox victims, with horrendous rashes and bug pecks running up and down our necks and forearms. Bad as the insects were, they weren't half as unnerving as the camel spiders. Those things are as large as sea crabs and they bite, too. Just the thought of them crawling over me at night was enough to keep me from falling asleep.

We ran a variety of missions from Dreamland. Mostly checkpoint operations and routine patrols through key areas of interest. Occasionally, we'd participate in a raid or two, but our main function was to guard over three areas of relative importance in Fallujah: (1) The mayor's cell, located downtown. (2) A large dam on the Euphrates River, to the west. (3) And last but not least, a huge cluster of storage facilities on the eastern periphery of the city. That's where we spent most of our time. Otherwise, there wasn't too much else for us to do.

During these missions, we'd often get to interface with the locals, proving we weren't the monsters certain anti-American propagandists in the Middle East would have liked them to believe we were. Our biggest fan was some fourteen-year-old named Za'id, who used to hang out around our Bradley whenever we'd guard the mayor's cell.

Arabs are extremely hospitable; they pride themselves on it. He'd always find a way to bring us something, be it a cold Pepsi or a bag of market-fresh vegetables. One day, he even went to the effort of making each member of our crew a handmade notepad, with each one composed of about three dozen pieces of blank paper that'd been sewn together at two ends. The covers were penciled-in with colorful patterns and designs. And on the back, our names were emblazoned in Arabic and English, encircled by a heart-shaped outline (in fact, I still have mine).

While some of the guys in my platoon thought it was "fucking gay," I was moved by Za'id's act of goodwill. I used to wonder how much better off Iraq would be if only there were more kids like him, and that maybe this world would be a slightly kinder place if only the people living in it could lay aside their differences from time to time. It was wishful thinking like that which carried me through my first tour of duty, allowing me to believe against all reason that the war was morally justifiable. You could say I was living in a fool's paradise.

In a May 20 letter written to my father, I announced with great optimism:

> *Most of what we do anymore consists of patrolling the city and running traffic control points. We've been getting the chance to bullshit with some of the locals. Quite a few of the Iraqis really like us. Yesterday I got my picture taken with a couple Iraqi teenagers named Mohammad and Zaid. Really cool kids. They even bought us some cold Pepsis while we were watching over the former Ba'th Party compound (which will be turned into a community center).*

Even in Fallujah, quite a few of the Iraqis liked us. At our traffic control points, folks would offer us everything from freshly baked pita bread to free cigarettes. Others would smile, graciously shake our hands, and tell us their stories of life under the brutal oppression of Saddam Hussein. At the dam, we mingled with local fishermen, learning that some net their biggest catches by using hand grenades. And at a nearby hospital, we'd have our pictures taken with the guards, with them holding our M16s and us holding their Kalashnikovs (AK-47s). Children of all ages flocked to us as though we were celebrities, and at the storage facilities to the east, some family there used to bring us hearty servings of deliciously seasoned grilled chicken. It was some of the best cooking I'd ever had. I wasn't sure how these people felt about the occupation, but they didn't seem to mind us.

But we also had our fair share of enemies, too. Nor did they make any attempt to hide their hatred of us. Occasionally, we'd cross into certain corners of the city only to be pelted with stones by the children and receive an unwelcoming thumbs-down from everyone else. In most neighborhoods, it seemed we were universally despised. And the longer I was there, I noticed that an insidious breed of Islamic extremism was beginning to rear its ugly head.

On one occasion, while guarding the mayor's cell, a scholarly-looking gentleman in traditional garb approached our vehicle and began speaking to us in surprisingly crisp English. He was a kindly old fellow with a frail build and calm demeanor. In a soft and gentle tone, he demanded some form of financial compensation for his vehicle having been clipped by one of our tanks a week or two earlier. Apparently, his bumper had been dinged up pretty bad. We politely explained to him that we didn't handle matters of this nature, and that if he preferred, he could file a complaint with the mayor's office. Though he seemed a bit dismayed by our response, he wasn't particularly angry.

Eager to brush up on his English, he proceeded to hang around for a while, making small talk. When asked about the regime, he voiced contempt for Saddam Hussein and the Ba'thists. My first assumption was to lump him into the generically black-and-white category of "pro-American" Iraqi nationals.

Then Kublai Khan asked him what he thought of Osama bin Laden.

To our utter amazement, he told us that this homicidal maniac "is a very good man."

Hearing that, Kublai Khan fired back: "Wait, wait, wait…I just want to make sure I'm hearing you correctly. He killed three thousand Americans, and you're saying he's a *good man*?"

"Yes," he replied without hesitation, pushing his wire-framed glasses up the slope of his nose. "A righteous man. A warrior of God."

Astonished by his reply, and now taking the safety of our crew into consideration, Kublai Khan told him, "Ok…you need to get the fuck outta here right now! Go! Get!" shooing him away like a dog.

This is what decades of US meddling in the Arab world has wrought, albeit unintentionally. For that very reason, we had been advised to steer clear of discussing politics with the locals. Especially any topic centered on the never-ending Israeli-Palestinian conflict. There were many Fallujans who'd try their best to gauge our views on this matter, but in all truthfulness, most of our rank-and-file were far more consumed by simple worldly diversions like beer, football, and chasing women.

Decades of strategic setbacks in their on-and-off wars with Israel have left many Arabs in that corner of the world simmering with hatred for this tiny, New Jersey-sized nation-state. The Iraqis are no exception, and the odious views *some* hold of the Jewish race are just as appalling. Whenever I'd hear such talk, I'd do my best to keep from being dragged into longwinded discussions on the American-Israeli alliance, choosing instead to quietly listen. I'd just stand there every time, nodding my head while pretending to have no clear opinion on the subject.

Until the founding of Israel in 1948, Baghdad was actually home to an enormous Jewish minority. For centuries they lived side-by-side with the Arabs in relative peace. The Jews had flocked to Mesopotamia en masse as a result of the Diaspora, after the Romans had all but flattened Jerusalem in 70 AD. There were also many Iraqi Jews who, I assume, had remained there since the sixth-century BC, after King Nebuchadnezzar's conquest of Jerusalem, which left many Israelites marooned in Babylon for the better part of a century (as chronicled in the Old Testament).

Jews and Muslims aren't natural enemies. Nor is the Koran innately anti-Semitic. After all, Islam regards both Christians and Jews as "people of the book." However, this previous arrangement was soured by the lingering impact of colonialism and the upheavals of war and anti-Semitism in Europe, helping to foster widespread ethnic strife between two peoples who share the same bloodline. It's like all the crazies in that corner of the world doubled-down on their fanaticism after World War II. Hence the morally depraved manner by which Arabs and Israelis are constantly at each other's throats, fighting over land and religion.

I'm reminded of a story Simpson once told me, in which he was engaged in a polite conversation with a groundskeeper at the storage facilitates in eastern Fallujah. He offhandedly mentioned something about being half-Jewish. Upon hearing this, the man turned pale in disgust and withdrew from the scene, as though he wished he had known this irrelevant tidbit of information beforehand.

"The whole time, he had been laughing and shaking hands with a Jew and didn't even know it!" Simpson joked.

On a separate occasion, our crew was parked somewhere downtown, pulling security. A university student approached the rear of our vehicle, wanting, like so many others, to practice his English. What started off as a pleasant conversation about the weather quickly evolved into a hateful spiel rife with conspiratorial claims about Israel and the Jewish people (his thoughts, not mine).

Though seldom discussed in American politics, it's a well-established reality that the Israeli lobby has tremendous leverage in Washington, D.C. – certainly more so than I'm comfortable with at times, despite my fondness of Israel. However, the ideas this young man espoused were just plain sickening, and disturbingly akin to something out of *Mein Kampf.* In short, he claimed that America is a tool of Israel – one wholly owned and operated by maniacal billionaire Jews who are bent on ruling over the Arabs, stealing their oil, and ultimately creating a "Greater Israel" that stretches clear from the eastern shoreline of the Mediterranean Sea, all the way to the muddy banks of the Euphrates River.

Then, just when I thought I had heard it all, he also tried to convince me that it was Israel who brought down the World Trade Center, and Jewish bankers who controlled the world economy. I could no longer keep a straight face during this hate-filled diatribe, so I tried defusing the situation with more small talk, alluding to the number of Jews who work in Hollywood. When forced to admit being a fan of American cinema, I reminded him that a good number of Jews work in the film industry, making him a de facto admirer of Hollywood Jewry. That shut him up real quick.

It was a real-life education in the utterly dysfunctional nature of politics on the Arab street. One of the hallmarks of a failed society is when its people begin blaming Jews for most of their problems; another is when conspiracy theories run amuck, unchallenged by the media. Both were very common in Iraq. So common, in fact, that some of the people I spoke with actually believed Saddam Hussein had conspired with America and Israel, making the invasion possible. Nobody had much to say about where they thought the WMDs might be located, but they'd talk your ear off on this subject. I remember speaking to a guy who claimed Saddam was not hiding out somewhere in Iraq, but instead, at Bush's ranch in Crawford, Texas. Not a suburb of Baghdad or his birthplace, Tikrit, where he'd surface later that year following a military raid, but the Lone Star State? I'd heard some bull in my life, but never on this scale!

Of course, many Iraqis also believed we had x-ray vision. A week or two before deploying, Supply issued every guy in our unit a pair of Wiley X's – a slick brand of ultra-flexible sunglasses with interchangeable lenses. Their brand logo, "X," is stamped onto both sides of the frame, similar to a pair of Oakley's. Some of the locals interpreted this as meaning we could see through homes, clothing, and automobiles. What bothered them most wasn't the thought of us invading their privacy per se, but the idea that we might see their women in the nude. In smaller villages, this really bothered the elders. On one occasion, we had to let them inspect our sunglasses just to prove they didn't have such capabilities. Earlier in the occupation, it was a real concern. It also seemed to underscore the challenges of policing Iraq.

—

By the second week of May, the search for Saddam Hussein's alleged stockpile of WMDs hadn't turned up so much as a single canister of mustard gas. We personally investigated many of the sites where it was believed some of these weapons might be located. Yet the most we ever found was conventional weaponry, completely unguarded, there for the taking. That being the case, a lot of the guys began talking about redeployment. It was an issue on everyone's mind. After all, we couldn't occupy Iraq indefinitely, not under the current pretenses – or so we thought.

Fueling much of this chatter was none other than Private Michael Calvin, our platoon rumor mill. The more he spoke of home, the more we all missed it. Built like the Brawny Man, Calvin was tall, strong as an ox, and had the countenance of a drill sergeant. He generally fit the mold of what you'd expect a soldier to look like. Months earlier, he sounded like a modern-day Rambo, carrying on at length about how he wanted to "get over there" and earn his "combat stripes" kicking the snot out of Saddam's Republican Guard. But once we were in the thick of it all, he began singing a much different tune. He was not at all cut out for these long deployments. Now, like everyone else, he just wanted to go home.

It wasn't uncommon to hear Calvin carrying on from afar, spreading unconfirmed news: "Guys, you're not gonna believe this! I just heard from the chaplain's assistant, who overheard the chaplain tell some officer that he heard from the squadron commander himself that Bush wants *all* tracked vehicles off the streets of Iraq by August!"

Panting and nearly out of breath, he had just enough oxygen in his lungs to make the following proclamation: "You know what that means?! Redeployment, baby! WE'RE GOING HOME!"

This was the fantasy world he lived in.

I liked Calvin, but at times, listening to all this hearsay was a bit much. But it wasn't entirely his fault. All of us were becoming a little stir crazy. The uncertainty of redeployment, as well as our general lack of cause, was felt throughout the entire regiment.

To pass time, we held wrestling competitions in the dirt. Or we'd don our body armor and take turns kicking each other square in the chest, watching one another tumble to the ground. Our colleagues would stare on in amusement, howling and stamping their feet like cavemen in clear approval of these random acts of stupidity.

Some played water sports in the bacteria-infested lake, only to come down with the runs after learning it wasn't recreationally safe. Others would go fishing, it never crossing their minds that just beneath the surface of these murky waters rest the corpses of Saddam Hussein's political opponents, fastened by chain to concrete blocks.‡ But command put the brakes on us playing in that lake real fast. After the guys in CHEM sampled the water, it tested positive for a "blister agent precursor," indicating that at some point the regime *might* have used the lake to dispose of chemical weapons. Still, despite all warnings, every so often I'd see some guy from another unit with a fishing rod in the water; I just hope he never filleted any of those fish he caught.

One day, a soldier in Alpha Section got so bored that he charged his M16, placed the weapon on "safe," put the barrel in his mouth, and began squeezing the trigger. It was the most reckless stunt I had ever seen, and yet kind of funny in a dark sort of way. When asked what might have happened had the rifle's safety mechanism failed, he didn't seem to care, joking, "Well, I guess I wouldn't be stuck in this shithole any longer, now would I?"

---

‡ How do I know opponents of Saddam's regime were sent to sleep with the fish at Dreamland? A decade later, Beckett was deployed to Afghanistan. One day he randomly struck up a conversation with another soldier on base. They got to exchanging war stories about Iraq, and this guy claimed to have also been stationed at Dreamland, just at a much later date. He claimed that while he was there the lake was drained by a team of engineers. At the bottom were human skeletons, chained to concrete blocks. He didn't specify how many, but I have no reason to believe the story is false given the lack of respect for human rights under Saddam Hussein.

On another occasion, I remember sitting peacefully by myself in our bungalow, reading a magazine. I felt the presence of someone creep up from behind, practically brushing me. It was Lieutenant Anderson.

"Bryan, did you check the fluids on the track?" he asked, wanting to know if the engine and transmission had been topped off with oil.

"Yes, Sir," I replied, not even raising so much as an eyebrow.

"Damn it, Bryan!" he snapped. "You look at me when I talk to you!"

As I turned my head, I was nearly blindsided by a huge, untrimmed mane of pubic hair as he stood there towering over me, still wet after having just taken a shower. I'd been had. Everyone in the room exploded in laughter.

I would have expected this sort of buffoonery from Beckett or maybe even Kublai Khan, but not our well-mannered, church-going platoon leader. But this is the sort of stuff guys do on a deployment when they're bored out of their minds. It sustains them. It's all part of the greatest "bromance" that ever was.

Fortunately, I can say I never fell for the "atomic sit-up," which is perhaps the ugliest prank of all. This one is commonly reserved for rookie soldiers fresh out of Basic Training. The idea is that you challenge some unwitting private to do one full sit-up while somebody else holds a neatly folded towel over his face, with a bunch of guys telling him he doesn't have the muscle to pull it off. Having accepted that bet, with his eyes blindfolded, the poor bastard doesn't realize that another man has just pulled down his trousers and squatted in the general trajectory of his face. Struggling to keep the volunteer's upper body pinned to the floor, the person(s) holding that towel suddenly lets go, causing the victim's head to sling forward into the other man's ass crack. It's pretty disgusting, though always good for a laugh!

All things considered, we made the best of our time, keeping ourselves well-entertained. The Iraqis, however, didn't find us as amusing.

Adding to the growing dissatisfaction with our presence was the fact that all our on-base antics were beginning to spill over into the streets for all of Fallujah to see. There was a period of relative tranquility in those first three weeks following our arrival. The streets were quiet and the evenings calm. Because of this, we grew very complacent, allowing our sense of professionalism to slip a notch or two. We started clowning around a lot during missions. In doing so, we had taken our eyes off the ball, inadvertently sabotaging our chances of success in Iraq. On the streets and in the mosques, there were malevolent forces at work, seeking to do us grave harm. They were in the backdrop of Fallujah this whole time, galvanizing the masses, recruiting, conspiring, disseminating propaganda, plotting against us, capitalizing on our tactical shortcomings, feeding on local antipathy for the occupation. And we only made it worse.

I recall one evening in which one of our NCOs ran up to a vehicle full of young men and threw a glow-stick in through the passenger's window, making them think he had just dropped a fragmentary grenade inside. Expecting their car to erupt in a huge ball of fire, they all dove from the vehicle in horror, only to realize the good sergeant had just been kidding with them. Needless to say, this sort of behavior didn't win us all too many friends.

On another occasion, two sections from our platoon were paired up for a mission way out in the countryside, doing curfew enforcement in the hours past dark. As cars and trucks would approach our traffic control point, we'd throw on our headlights and blind them, thus stopping the drivers dead in their tracks so we could search their automobiles for weapons and large sums of cash, then inform them that they weren't permitted to be driving around late at night. A few of the guys got bored and decided it'd be a real hoot to toy around with those in the next car to come rolling up.

Well, lo and behold, as some poor family approaches our checkpoint and slows to a halt, two of our guys – both privates – charge their vehicle with M16s, hollering as loudly as they can. As the family tenses up, a third soldier appears to their front, doing cartwheels. He stops just short of their bumper and draws a pistol on them, aiming it directly at their windshield. They're completely freaked out. Startled by the animal-like howling, the family begins screaming as well. Now everyone on the ground is wailing in perfect blood-curdling harmony. My peers hastily extract each of the passengers, frisking the males and performing a cursory inspection of the car while continuing to sound off. Then, as quickly as they were pulled over and yanked from their automobile, the family is ushered back to the car. With all our guys still howling, one soldier, using hand and arm signals, gestures for them to leave as quickly as possible, yelling "Go, go, go!"

Now, does such behavior constitute a violation of the Geneva Convention? No. But is it in poor taste? Absolutely. It does more than reinforce the stereotype of the ugly American, it emboldens our enemies. Still, I can't say I didn't laugh my ass off. After all, I am only human, and at the time it seemed pretty funny.

With boredom at an all-time high, nothing happening on the streets, and no one in the upper-echelons of our chain of command having yet clarified what exactly our mission in Iraq was, these sorts of shenanigans were commonplace. Occasionally, some Fallujans shared in on our laughter, finding our odd sense of humor very entertaining. Still, the majority weren't as amused by our fatuous stunts. They'd glare back at us with utter contempt. It was from the ranks of these aggrieved masses that our enemies would soon emerge, confronting us with more than just stones and picket signs.

It wasn't merely the sight of U.S. troops on Arab soil that drove some Iraqis to violence; or even extreme interpretations of the Koran. I think it had more to do with our whole approach to managing their country. Earlier that month, Bush appointed Paul Bremer III to head the newly established Coalition Provisional Authority (CPA), Iraq's American-run transitional government. Much to his credit, Bremer is an enormously talented individual with decades of experience at the State Department as a diplomat and Foreign Service Officer. Among other professional achievements, he's a counterterrorism expert and served as an ambassador to the Netherlands under Reagan. The guy even speaks several languages. However, as impressive as his credentials may be, at the time of his appointment he had zero diplomatic experience in the Middle East and little knowledge of the Islamic World or Arab culture. Yet he was given full dictatorial control over Iraq's future, leaving many to question why Bush appointed him of all people to head the CPA, and furthermore, why Bremer would even accept this position knowing full well he was unqualified to run a country he knew so little about. It defies all logic. Yet this is exactly what happened.

As chief administrator of the CPA, his first order of business was disbanding Iraq's army, leaving just under half a million Iraqi soldiers without a job. Whereas they could've been put to good use, providing security and labor in the post-Saddam era, just the opposite happened. Instead, they were turned loose on the streets for us to deal with. Along with a slew of other irreparable gaffes, he also pursued radical "de-Ba'thification" measures, which effectively prohibited former members of the Ba'th Party from having any future in Iraqi public life. This would have been a reasonable policy had it been crafted in a way that barred Saddam's henchmen from infiltrating the new government, but what it really did was block low-ranking party members from having any future in the public sector, where they had spent their entire lives. This shafted everyone from bureaucrats to school teachers – of whom many had probably never had any genuine allegiance to Saddam or the Party, but joined out of necessity for the sake of having a decent job. Now, they too, were without a paycheck and angry as hell. Well, guess who paid for the mistakes of Paul Bremer and his elite clique of white-collared puppeteers? That's right – us! Us and the Iraqi people.

Team Bush had no strategy for keeping the peace because they hadn't anticipated an insurrection, revealing a gross lack of contingency planning on their part. As the days passed, our chain of command was forced to shoot from the hip, formulating a course of action as ambiguous as the administration's post-invasion strategy for rebuilding Iraq and transforming it into a semi-functional democracy. The mission at hand didn't make a lick of sense. I understood the rationale behind guarding the mayor's cell and conducting random presence patrols, as well as having to interface with the city's inhabitants. But I couldn't see the utility in other assignments, especially those which seemed to further alienate the locals and erode any chances we may have had at winning them over to this newfound cause of ours.

Among other things, we were expected to help stem the smuggling of gasoline and confiscate any automobiles that were believed to have been stolen in the aftermath of the regime's collapse. At first, I thought many of these orders sounded halfway reasonable, and that maybe the residents of Fallujah would appreciate our efforts to restore the rule of law to their city. I regret to say that wasn't the case.

Siphoning off fuel from the oil-beating veins of Iraq's crippled petro industry had long been a lucrative means through which common thieves could make a quick buck. However, with no security apparatus in place, smugglers were now free to sell this hot commodity from the side of the road, where they'd stand by with plastic jugs of gasoline in wait of passing customers. These weren't large-scale smuggling operations either, just kids struggling to make ends meet in a country wrecked by war. I'd say they probably raked in just enough cash to keep food on the table, if that. We were given orders to shut down these operations by crushing their fuel cans and informing them of our new protocol banning the roadside distribution of gasoline. So that's what we did. As a result, what the residents of Fallujah saw on the outer edges of their city were American tanks flattening the gas cans of street children trying to eke out a living. A buddy in Green Platoon told me they'd routinely dismount their tanks, fix bayonets on the ends of their rifles, and then jam holes into these plastic fuel containers, letting the contents drizzle out onto the side of the road.

In short, there was no way for us to enforce this measure without appearing like oppressive colonial overlords. Bystanders would glare at us with pure hatred in their eyes as we'd flatten these kids' gas cans, as puzzled by our actions as they were angered. We might as well have been detaining children for operating lemonade stands without a permit. It all seemed pretty asinine to me.

During some of these missions, I was forced to wonder: *How, in a country where oil is more plentiful than clean drinking water, and there's no standing government, can we impose our will on these people as we are? Moreover, what do we stand to gain by meddling in trivial affairs of this nature?* The whole notion was just plain absurd.

Nor did we stop there. We were also given the easier-said-than-done task of confiscating stolen automobiles – a job better suited for Iraqi security forces, had Bremer not dissolved their whole damn government. Aside from the obvious difficulties associated with determining which vehicles had actually been "stolen," only one interpreter had been assigned to our entire company. Regardless, with each passing day, we'd conduct traffic control points, requiring the individuals in every passing automobile to either show us their vehicle registration or provide some proof of ownership. Our soldiers, who aren't schooled in how to read Arabic, would stare at their documentation, utterly baffled at what they were looking at, and then use their own discretion to determine whether the vehicle registration was legit. If the drivers were thought to be in possession of a stolen vehicle, we'd simply confiscate their automobile.

I specifically remember one instance in which some poor fellow couldn't prove he owned the pickup truck he was driving, as he lacked the required documentation. As the man stood off to the side of our checkpoint, speaking with our interpreter, he seemed frantic at the thought of us confiscating his vehicle.

As we searched the inside of his truck high and low, our interpreter spotted a children's book lying under the front seat. He casually picked it up, noticing a child's name written in crayon on the backside of the front cover. He then looked back at the man and asked him in Arabic if he had children. "Na'm," the gentleman replied, answering in the affirmative. With that response, he then asked him their names. When none matched the one written in that children's book, he was accused of being a liar and a thief. A couple of our guys even compared him to "Ali Baba" of *Ali Baba and the Forty Thieves*. He was then turned away and told to go elsewhere.

As he walked off into the distance, I could tell he was struggling to hold back his anger. He looked as though he wanted to murder each of us.

This policy proved highly unpopular with the locals. Especially when random individuals were left stranded on the side of the road, either forced to walk home or flag someone down for a ride. In the States, I've seen people go absolutely berserk on city workers when issued a small fine for letting their parking meters expire. Now, just image how angry you'd be if, while driving home from work, a group of foreign soldiers commandeered your automobile. Imagine they couldn't tell you where they're taking it or how to get it back. Well, that's exactly what we did in Fallujah.

What's more, Parker and I began to notice an emerging trend. Each platoon was beginning to amass a small hoard of luxury vehicles, seized in all probability from the more affluent residents of Fallujah. From the back patio of our lakeside bungalow, no matter where I looked, I'd see American soldiers driving around in cars and trucks confiscated during routine traffic control points. Parked in our driveway was a white SUV with air-conditioning and a CD player, and next door, a Mercedes Benz. Up the road a ways, I'd see others driving around in BMWs. To put it nicely, we had become a bunch of marauders.

To quote one of my peers who'll remain anonymous, "Man, where I'm from, this shit's called carjackin'!"

From what I understood, the only way for the locals to contest the seizure of their automobiles was to submit a written inquiry to the mayor's office. I somehow doubt these poor folks ever got their vehicles back. If those crooks at the mayor's office didn't keep them for their own use, they probably sold them to a chop shop in Baghdad.

—

The situation in Fallujah was also paradigmatic of the greater power struggle playing out in the heartland of Iraq. We had promised the Iraqis "democracy." This terrified the Sunnis, and rightfully so. For democracy is, as Benjamin Franklin once put it, "two wolves and a lamb arguing over what to eat for lunch."

Iraqi public life had been dominated by the Sunnis for the last eight decades, leaving the Shia without a voice. Though Sunni Arabs are well within the majority in a few parts of Iraq, nationwide, they're a minority, accounting for just a fifth of the population. Therefore, they were bound to lose considerable influence – especially under a system of government dominated by a spiteful Shia majority.

Conversely, Iraq's Shiites were fairly cooperative with American ground forces. They had every reason to be. Though widely reviled for occupying their country, we had unwittingly laid the groundwork for their ascension to power. For the Shia, this short-term alliance with the "Great Satan" was but a necessary step in a gradual path to gaining control of Iraq. See, in the West, we perceive the Sunni and Shia as tearing their countries apart over religion – and maybe there's some truth to that viewpoint. But it's also an oversimplification of reality. While much of the fighting over there does occur along religious lines, what it all boils down to is *power*. Nothing more, nothing less.

Many of the Sunnis, still reeling over the invasion and subsequent occupation of their homeland, began to identify with the battle-hardened Islamic cadre who were pouring into their country to combat us infidels – i.e., the long-bearded Salafist guerrillas who had come from as far away as Chechnya just to shoot at Americans. And that's what we'd soon be up against – a tireless Islamic militancy with so little appreciation for human life that they had no qualms over giving theirs just to take ours.

Chapter Eight
MUSLIMS GONE WILD

OUR USUAL FUN and games come to an abrupt end on May 22. It's Bravo Section's turn to guard the mayor's cell. Before heading out, Parker and I conduct our usual pre-mission vehicle inspection, making sure our crew will be ready for anything, even though the likelihood of something bad happening is pretty slim. As my driver tinkers around under the hood of our Bradley, checking oil levels and what not, I make sure our radios are working and that we have enough water on board.

This is a pretty typical mission on a not so typical day. In the springtime, sandstorms are a daily occurrence in Iraq. During the big push to Baghdad, it's said the weather was unusually intense that year. Many Iraqis held that God had sent these winds upon us to stymie Coalition forces from advancing as quickly as they would have liked.

But today the weather is off pattern. Instead of punishing gusts of sand-laden wind hammering us down, we're enveloped by a smothering cloud of silt that's been swept up off the plains of the Fertile Crescent. The sun is blotted out by a reddish-brown haze that's hovering in the atmosphere, dirtying my goggles. I'm not superstitious, but it feels like some ghostly forewarning – like a sign from the heavens that something bad is going to happen.

We mount up on our Bradleys and maneuver out the front gates of Dreamland, en route for the heart of the city – all to guard over a bunch of crooks from

Saddam's regime. The mayor is shady as hell and we don't trust him, but he's our only intermediary to the people of Fallujah. So we have to protect this guy no matter what.

Instead of our usual medic, we have "Doc Cochran" riding along as a special guest. Cochran is Sabre Squadron's physician's assistant. Though he isn't required to go out on these sorts of missions, he got bored hanging around the aid station and decided to hit the streets with us for an evening. Twice my age and pushing retirement, Doc Cochran is a complete badass. Years earlier, he was in the Special Forces, but had severely injured his back during a training exercise gone awry, or so I'd heard. Whereas an accident of that nature would have left most crippled for life, defying all odds, he stayed in the Army, got better, transitioned out of the Special Forces, and started anew as a commissioned officer in the Medical Corps.

Sewn atop the unit patch on his left shoulder is a bow-shaped Special Forces tab, and on the right, an SF combat patch – a clear indication of his service during the first Gulf War, back when he was a Green Beret, or as they're also known, "the quiet professionals." In Sabre, he's as much a legend as he is a mystery. Though he rarely, if ever, speaks of his time in the Special Forces, many prate about all of the things he's *supposedly* done. I once heard he was grazed by a bullet while exchanging gunfire with coke-trafficking narco-rebels in the jungles of Colombia. On another occasion, I was told that he had single-handedly slain dozens of elite Iraqi soldiers during Operation Desert Storm. He was said to have done so from behind the scope of a well-trained sniper's rifle. I'm not even sure where half of these stories came from. Fellow soldiers, I suppose. With all these unsubstantiated tales of gallantry, it's hard separating fact from fiction. Out of respect, I don't bother asking him how much of it's true. Either way, I'm thrilled to have him along for the ride. I like Doc Cochran. As far as I'm concerned, I might as well be sitting next to Chuck Norris.

Within minutes, we arrive on site and position ourselves directly outside the mayor's office. We dutifully stand watch outside, getting sandblasted by high winds while his entourage of armed guards lounge around inside, reading porno mags and sipping cardamom-flavored chai. As neighborhood kids begin crowding around the rear of our vehicle, Cochran warily shoos them away. It's a smart move. After all, we were attacked in this very spot just three weeks earlier. The last thing we need is a hand grenade tossed in at us through the back ramp.

As dusk sets in, Lieutenant Anderson and I climb atop our vehicle, both of us sitting nonchalantly on the turret hatches, which have been tipped back and locked into place. I'm not the avid sports fan that he is, but in the ten months we've gotten to know each other, there's never any shortage of things for us to talk about. In our downtime, we spend a lot of time discussing politics and religion. Anderson is a superb young leader, and I admire him greatly. Like most of our officers, he strikes me as one of those all-American types who comes from a good family; a real straight shooter. His father is a brigadier general, and though he's but several years older than me, already he's married, has kids, has completed college, earned his commission, and led a scout platoon into war. I'm lucky to be a part of his crew.

Aside from a howling pack of wild dogs roaming the city, it's shaping up to be an otherwise calm evening. We can hear what sounds like children playing with firecrackers behind the building directly across the street. Though it's nothing that would warrant us leaving our post to investigate. So we stay put. By now, the winds have died down and the streets have already cleared out for curfew, as not a soul can be found wandering about. Our guard shift is almost over, and next up in the turret is Kublai Khan and Parker, the latter of whom is pestering Cochran with questions about entry into the Special Forces.

Adjacent to our position is a mobile element from Red Platoon. They're just wrapping up a routine patrol through the city.

"Blue, you got anything that needs checked out before we return, over?"

"Red 2, this is Blue 1," Anderson replies over our troop radio. "A little while ago it sounded like some kids were messin' around behind that building across the street, directly south of our position. You mind checking it out, over?"

They acknowledge our transmission, and without a trace of hesitation, the lead vehicle, Red 2, which my buddy Simpson is a gunner on, peels off around the corner of the building to our south. For the most part, this has been a pretty quiet neighborhood, save those two demonstrations and that one grenade attack on the Ba'th Party compound.

Just a block southeast of the intersection we're on, there's a small, wheat-colored mosque with a blue-tipped minaret. Spiraling upward around it are several ribbons of brown and turquoise-shaded diamond patterns. East of the mosque is a three-story apartment building with an old Mercedes billboard on top, and beneath that, dozens of short concrete arches demarcating each door of each apartment on the upper two levels. And just west of the street Simpson's crew has turned down, there's a pocket of residential buildings tightly clustered together; one that's notoriously ugly because it's still under construction and has rebar spiking out of the top. Though hardly a portrait of beauty by day, in the twilight it all looks rather picturesque.

Silhouetted by short, bushy palm trees, the two Brads creep along between a pair of brick and mortar walls that line both sides of the road. Meanwhile, as Anderson and I climb out of the turret, Kublai Khan and Parker step in, assuming watch as the two of us remove our helmets and take a seat on the padded bench in our rear crew compartment.

"Ahhhhhhhhhhhh," I yawn, flexing my back while stretching my arms outward. I'm as stiff as a board, as my flak vest is killing me.

"Man, I'm really getting tired of wearing this thing," I tell the lieutenant.

Out of nowhere, there's a thunderous explosion, followed milliseconds apart by the ear-piercing resonance of something big getting rocked. *BOOM!!!* The flash is so bright that it lights the walls of every building in the area, begetting tall, statuesque shadows that loom over us like evil spirits.

Then our troop radio comes to life: "Red 2 is hit! Red 2 is hit!"

The dual explosions we heard were from the back-blast of an anti-tank rocket propelled grenade (RPG) that just slammed into the right side of Simpson's Bradley. It penetrated their armor, rendering the vehicle inoperable, with a gaping hole torn through the engine compartment and transmission fluid spraying everywhere.

As Lieutenant Anderson flies into his commander's hatch, the rest of us instinctively assume each of our given positions in the vehicle. Calls for help are sent out to our headquarters unit at Dreamland, summoning all of Fox Troop. There's so much panic and confusion over the radio that nobody's really sure whether or not there are casualties. In the spur of the moment, the ambushed crew has just fled their Bradley, loading up into their wingman's vehicle and leaving theirs behind. In addition to all the sensitive equipment that's been left behind, like radios, maps, and night-vision goggles, there's a whole bunch of weapons that mustn't fall into enemy hands. Our crew races to the scene to recover these items. This way the vehicle won't get looted by some random street mob, or its weapons used against us at a later date.

We arrive on site only to find Red 2 just sitting there, with all hatches open and a long slick of oil beneath it. Doc Cochran and I dive from our vehicle into theirs, grabbing everything we can while making sure to account for all the gadgetry typically found on a Bradley Fighting Vehicle. Cochran isn't fooling around. He even cuts their GPS system out of the turret, slicing through the power cable with a sharp knife as he stealthily moves through Red 2, schlepping armfuls of weapons from their vehicle to ours.

Talk about living close to danger! For the second time in three weeks, I've gotten close enough to the fire to feel the heat, though not the burn. While clearly shaken by the evening's turn of events, part of me finds this extremely invigorating. I mean, I'm working side-by-side with an actual Green Beret in what feels like a scene right out of *Black Hawk Down*. How cool is that?!

Within minutes, the rest of Fox Troop joins the party. Together, we set a cordon around the scene of the attack and recover Red 2. With the added manpower, we're now able to get things under control. Or at least that's the plan. But instead, the situation takes a turn for the worse.

At some point, a white Nissan pickup tears around the corner of a nearby building, blowing through our cordon and darting straight into the area we're trying to secure. Not wanting our platoon to get blown to pieces by a suicide bomber, one of our gunners engages the truck. The young soldier fixes the sights of his M240C on the lone vehicle and blasts away at it, cutting through the front windshield and killing whoever's inside. The driver is torn to shreds by short, cyclic bursts of rapid machinegun fire, and soon after loses control of his pickup, plowing head-on into one of our Bradleys. The unyielding might of this thirty-ton beast stops the lightweight Nissan in its tracks, crumpling in the front half of the truck and violently launching its owner through the windshield. The sheer force of the collision heaves the man's body several feet in front of the vehicle, his contorted frame sprawled out facedown in a gooey pool of blood.

At the moment, I'm getting jostled back and forth in the rear of our Bradley. It whips around street corners and alleyways, pivoting in one direction, then another, tossing me to the floor of our crew compartment with each nauseating turn. Suddenly, our back ramp comes down and I'm commanded from the vehicle.

"Bryan, go search the truck for weapons!"

It's a simple order. I nod my head and run toward the battered pickup, carefully stepping over puddles of splattered blood to verify whether we've just killed a "terrorist," or some poor bastard who just happened to be in the wrong place at the wrong time. I peep into the truck, cautiously raising my M16 as I peer inside. The cab is dark. I've got my glasses on but can't see much due to the greasy film of sweat and dirt that's smudged all over my lenses. I'm struggling to get the driver's door open but can't. So I reach in through the window and attempt to shimmy it open from the inside.

As my vision comes into focus, I'm shocked to discover a second body. He too is riddled with bullets from the chest up, but unlike his buddy sprawled out on the pavement, his entire upper half has been violently crushed under the dashboard. I scuttle back to our Brad and yell up to Anderson, reporting my find and pronouncing the vehicle to be clear of weapons.

"There's a second body and no weapons!" I shout, knowing he probably can't hear me over the vehicle's engine exhaust and the flurry of radio traffic.

"What?!" he shouts back, as if he's not sure he heard me right.

He soon catches on to what I'm trying to say. Kublai Khan dismounts the vehicle to have a look-see for himself. It's a mess. The man is pinned under the dashboard. Half of his intestines are hanging out, and blood is dripping from every orifice.

"Sergeant, how ya suppose we're gonna get him outta there?" I ask. "I'm not touching him."

My question goes unanswered because we're not trained for this. We're soldiers, not first responders. The Army's done a great job of training us how to kill. Now we're just not sure what to do with the bodies afterward.

Before long, the local fire department comes screeching onto the scene, unannounced. It's like a gift from above. When it comes to handling the dead, Iraqis seem to share none of our finicky hygienic concerns. After all, if you're to catch some blood-borne disease, then *Allah wills it*. So it's of little concern to them.

They borrow a metal pry bar and use it to force the man's body from out of the truck cab. As they do so, his corpse makes gross and revolting sounds; a snap or two here, some squirting there. Upon untangling his twisted remains from under the dashboard, they grab the man's wallet, pull out a meager sum of cash, and then offer it to us, gesturing for us to take it.

Kublai Khan and I just stand there, mouths open, staring at them and then looking back at one another in complete disbelief, unsure of how to respond to such a gratuity. Taking that as a *no*, one of their crew members greedily stuffs the bloodied wad of cash into his back pocket and then throws down the wallet, not even bothering to check the man's identity.

It's been a crazy night. Even though one of our Brads was taken out and two more Fallujans are dead, we've been very fortunate. None of our guys were killed or seriously wounded. And right now, that's about all that matters. Simpson's driver sustained a mild concussion – one that earned him a Purple Heart, but nothing that left him scarred for life (or at least not physically).

The whole ordeal proved to be a confidence-shattering setback, erasing any notion that we – or our machinery – were somehow invincible. It also signified the beginning of a new phase in the war. Whoever was behind the attack knew exactly what they were doing. The sight of a destroyed American vehicle in the middle of their streets filled the people of Fallujah with a newfound sense of pride. They saw it as their David vs. Goliath moment. From then on, there wasn't a single night that we weren't attacked. They'd never hit us in the light of day, but after curfew, we Americans were fair game. Whenever we'd be out conducting our usual patrols, there was a noticeable rise in the level of anti-American sentiment, to the point that virtually everyone in the city stopped waving at us.

Instead, they'd glare upon our unit with smoldering hatred in their eyes, shaking their fists at us. Others made throat-slitting gesticulations as we'd drive by, staring at us while dragging their fingertips from one end of their neck to the other. When our convoys would approach, young boys raced from out of their homes with 2x4s and metal pipes, cupping them be-tween both hands and balancing them on their right shoulders, as if to imitate terrorists launching RPGs at our vehicles. Their elders would just laugh, cheering them on. The tide had turned, and not in our favor, as even the adorable children who played in the vicinity of our checkpoints were now to be looked upon with great suspicion. And that was sad, because Iraq's children were its only saving grace.

—

On the morning of May 27, I got yanked from the lieutenant's track and permanently transferred to Sergeant Dupéré's crew. Dupéré was on the verge of killing his dismount, who had thus far failed to pull his own weight in Bravo Section. New to our platoon, this kid had spent the last two years twiddling his thumbs in Supply, and therefore lacked the traditional work ethic and tactical know-how of the average grunt. You'd give him a small project, and no matter how simple the task, he'd find a way to screw it up. Not to mention, he didn't have his shit together. By choice, he lived like a slob, his hygienic practices rivaling those of Pig Pen. A trail of stench like you never spelt followed his every move, and that's all it took to set Dupéré off.

On the other hand, I had passed the litmus test for Third Platoon, proving myself to have enough grit to hack it in the Cav. I lived by a very simple motto: *embrace the suck*. In the Army, it's not like you have any other choice. For the last year I had stuck to that principle, and it kept me off Dupéré's shit list. Now I was the only thing that stood between him and a dead soldier.

When it came to dishing out punishment, Dupéré was an old-school disciplinarian who didn't waste much time on paperwork. He had spent half of his career in the Infantry, before the Army had gone soft.

If somebody screwed up once or twice, their transgressions were usually forgiven. But after that, he'd crush them, physically and mentally. That's how order was maintained in Bravo Section. Though I never minded his leadership style, because unlike Kublai Khan, he was always fair.

In the case of this particularly slothful soldier, Dupéré removed the firing bolt from his rifle, preferring instead to leave him behind on missions to guard over our bungbalows – not with a loaded M16 – but a wooden stick. I believe it was a broom handle. In a way, I felt bad that he had been made a spectacle for all to see. But at the same time, I was relieved to finally be out from under the yoke of Sergeant Kublai Khan. *Now he can ride this kid's ass instead of mine,* I thought.

Bravo is scheduled for another late-night mission. This time to relieve Alpha Section, who'd been posted at the dam for the last eight hours or so (to keep potential saboteurs from blowing it up, Squadron decided to maintain a constant presence there).

Per usual, we're set to move out in the midst of another sandstorm, only this one all the more intense. It's so bad out that we can't see more than a few meters in front of us. So we sit there at the gates of Dreamland, hunkered down in our vehicles, with few options but to ride out the storm until it's safe for us to resume our mission.

We soon get word that a scout platoon from Eagle Troop has just been ambushed during a traffic control point, and that two of their guys are in critical condition. One with a sucking chest wound. My heart sinks into the pit of my chest.

There aren't a lot of details, but enough to get a gist of what's just happened. Apparently a vehicle full of men pulled up in front of their checkpoint. As they casually exited their truck, they lobbed a couple hand grenades at our guys and began spraying them with Kalashnikovs. It was a suicide mission. These men wanted to die. Each of them desired to become a *shaheed*, or "martyr." The guys in Eagle Troop stood their ground as best they could, but were reportedly outflanked by heavy machinegun fire in the adjacent fields. They managed to kill some of the attackers, but like ghosts, the rest disappeared into the thick of night. That's how I heard it. Either way, it was quite a blood bath. At least half of their guys were wounded. And those two we'd heard about, the ones in "critical condition," eventually died.

By now the weather has lightened up some, to the point we can pick back up where we left off. In order to avoid certain death, we're forced to race as quickly as possible from one end of the city to the other, all to sit on a dam. Since getting attacked has become a nightly episode, we hope the same won't happen to us the moment we leave the gates of Dreamland. The medic and I are seated in the rear of Dupéré's vehicle. As we roll past the guards and hang a sharp left onto the main road, I can't stop thinking about what happened earlier. I pray under my breath. I pray for our comrades in Eagle. I pray for the safety of our crew. And above all, I pray that I'll make it through the night unscathed, asking God to redeem my soul if I don't. Spectacles, testicles, wallet, and watch. I trace the sign of a cross over my body armor and recite the Lord's Prayer, as though it's some magical incantation that'll protect me from harm.

As we pass through the downtown area, rolling through one neighborhood after another, I feel a powerful thud on the right side of our Brad, across from where the medic and I are seated. "RPG!" I hear over the internal comms system. We're hit. I feel the turret whip violently to the right as Dupéré returns fire, neutralizing the threat. Our retaliation is swift. The man crumbles, having made the fatal mistake of sticking around to admire the accuracy of his shot.[§] Miraculously, our vehicle seems unhindered by the attack, so we keep rolling. But Dupéré's legs go numb from the blast. He's freaking out and thinks he's hit. That, in turn, freaks all of us out. But after patting himself down, he quickly realizes he's alive and in one piece. It was just a scare. He initiates a head count. All respond, and nobody's injured.

Talk about a close call! It seems my prayers have been answered. I've lived to die another day.

Minutes later, we arrive at the dam. Our buddies in Alpha Section are there awaiting us. They're overjoyed to see that we're all okay. They pour out of their Bradleys to greet our squad as if it's some kind of family reunion, even though it's only been less than ten hours since we last saw each other. At the platoon level, there are well-established rivalries between certain members of their section and ours, but right now there's so much brotherly love going on that none of that seems to matter. I'm so grateful to be alive that I could've hugged Calvin, who still believes in his heart of hearts that we'll be home by mid-summer.

Everyone's eager to see what kind of damage our vehicle sustained, especially me. It takes a moment, but after examining the right side of our Bradley, we discover that one of our road wheels has been penetrated. The armor-piercing warhead melted through it

---

[§] This was an "unconfirmed" kill, based on a report I heard the next day. It was said that an Iraqi male turned up at the local hospital having sustained multiple gunshot wounds after attacking American forces. It's impossible to say whether he was involved in the attack on Eagle Troop or the one targeting Fox Blue 5, but I have no reason to believe Dupéré missed his target.

like nothing. I gently take a knee, poke my right index finger through the hole, then gulp, realizing that if only that jihadi had aimed just a tad higher, hitting our crew compartment instead of the suspension system, he would've made mincemeat out of the medic and me.

At first glimpse, the Bradley Fighting Vehicle appears invincible. But as we had the misfortune of learning just five days earlier, quite the opposite is true. It's no tank, that's for sure. For added mobility, it's lightly armored. About the only thing shielding the crew compartment I was riding in is a thin wall of Kevlar boarding that's bolted to the rear side of the vehicle's not-so-well-armored exterior.

That morning we returned to Dreamland, having survived the hellish events of the previous evening. Atop our list of things to do is change out our badly damaged road wheel. While banging away at our vehicle, we learn the names of Eagle's KIA: Staff Sergeant Michael Quinn, 37, and Sergeant Thomas Broomhead, 34. Think what you want about the war; each had given his life defending his men. That takes courage and warrants a great deal of respect. While I hadn't personally known them, I knew of them, and had seen them enough times to spot them in a crowd. That morning had a very solemn feel, with everyone in our squadron torn up over the news. I could only imagine how Eagle Troop was handling it, having just lost two of their brothers.

Days later, a beautiful memorial service was held beside the lake at Dreamland, commemorating the lives of these gentlemen. Nearly everyone from Sabre was in attendance that afternoon, along with the regimental commander. The chaplain led us in prayer, and several others delivered a very moving eulogy, sharing their fondest memories of Broomhead and Quinn. The service concluded with a ceremonial playing of "Taps" and a formal twenty-one gun salute. As that first volley of gunfire pierced the sky, the entire squadron was moved to tears, realizing the fragility of human life. At first, I tried to fight it. I tried my damnedest to hold back, but my eyes welled up and I started to sob. Until that day, I thought soldiers didn't cry. I was wrong.

—

A few days later, our squadron welcomes a boon of good news: Our time in the City of Mosques is coming to an end, as our presence is needed elsewhere. This time in a place called "Ramadi," fifty kilometers to the west. All we need to do is survive another week in Fallujah.

Early one morning, while returning to base from another mission to secure the dam, our crew is targeted yet again by another RPG-wielding jihadist. As we race down "RPG Alley," a big, gleaming fireball soars past our vehicle, barely missing the turret and giving everyone in our crew another unsought adrenaline rush.

"You missed, cocksucker!" Dupéré resiliently bellows out over our internal comms system. "I swear, it's like we have a bullseye painted on the side of this thing!"

It happens so fast that Dupéré doesn't even have time to return fire. Nor is he going to risk getting our crew killed trying to do so. We're not exactly in the mood for a game of cat and mouse. We just want to get back to base and get some shuteye. That's all. Is that so much to ask for? But now we're keyed up and on high alert.

Armed with an eclectic mix of racially-tinged ethnic slurs, Dupéré is cursing these unruly people whose land we inhabit. This in itself is ironic because Dupéré, though every bit a Southerner and self-professed redneck, is actually of Lebanese descent.

Between his accent and French last name, I initially assumed he was of Cajun upbringing. But no, he bears closer physical resemblance to the Iraqis shooting at us than any Caucasian in our platoon – and believe me, so far he's been called out on this a few times. In fact, even the Iraqis tell him he looks like an Iraqi. But the man's thick-skinned and doesn't get bent out of shape whenever he's called an Arab. He'll just remind you that he's an American above all else and...*not a Muslim!*

We get back around sunrise. Everyone else from my crew has gone inside, and all that's left for me to do is tidy up our vehicle. While sweeping out the back of our Brad, I begin airing my frustrations aloud, asking another guy in my platoon:

"What are we doing here? Seriously, can anybody tell me what in the hell we're doing here?! Don't get me wrong, I support the President. I support what we're doin' in Iraq, but this 'guard the dam' mission makes absolutely no sense at all!

"I mean, what are they gonna tell my mom when I get shredded to pieces in the back of this thing? 'Miss Heath, your son fought valorously in defense of a dam.'

"It's bullshit!" I continue, staring him in the face. "Every time we leave the wire, I feel like I'm riding around in my own coffin...

"Dreamland...what a crock of shit! This place is a nightmare!"

In the midst of my tirade, I notice one of our NCOs stop and prick up his head. It's Charlie's section sergeant. He follows my every word, during which I suggest our squadron commander has his head up his ass. As I continue, he casually approaches me. I sense I'm about to get reamed for slandering a senior officer.

Instead, he seems to agree.

"Bryan, ya know what? You're right. This is a load of shit. But what you need to do is stay focused on the mission and keep your head screwed on straight. This way everyone will make it outta' here alive and come home in one piece. Capeesh?"

"Roger, Sergeant." I nod.

A few days later, we transition to a small airbase in Habbaniyah. It's a geographical midpoint between Fallujah and Ramadi. We spend the next couple days parked on a bombed-out tarmac. It's a pleasant respite from dodging gunfire on a nightly basis, and a rare chance to get caught up on sleep. We have to make the best of our time there because after that, we'll be getting thrown back into the fight, to defend what Paul Bremer is now calling "Free Iraq."

One afternoon at mail call, I'm resting under the shade of a tarpaulin I've just propped up behind our vehicle. Dupéré strolls up and hands me a newspaper clipping that his family just sent him. In it, there's a picture of a smashed up, bullet-ridden Nissan pickup truck. It's the same one we shot up a couple weeks earlier. Apparently bad news travels fast. Alongside this disturbing image is a short article delving into the other half of the story. I quickly learn that the two gentlemen we shot to death had names: Hadi Jabar and Jassim Mohammed Aggar. As it turned out, Jabar was just hours away from being joined in marriage with his fiancée. While returning home from visiting his soon-to-be-wife, he and Aggar unknowingly drove through our cordon and were killed. It may not have been cold-blooded murder on our part, but I still felt like shit after reading this. I wished Dupéré's family hadn't stumbled upon this snippet.

In Iraq, I had seen my fair share of death. But there was something about this story that really tugged at my heartstrings. It's said there are only six degrees of separation between all of humanity. That means each of us are just six acquaintances removed from the other seven billion people inhabiting Planet Earth. These men weren't faceless "towelheads," out roaming the streets past curfew to prey on American soldiers. They were ordinary people, like us, made of flesh and bone. They had friends and family who, I'm sure, were just as devastated by the news of their loss as any spouse or parent of an American serviceman is when they find out their loved one has just made the ultimate sacrifice.

But there was no undoing what we'd done. And there was no use crying over spilt milk.

Chapter Nine
RAMADI

OUR DOWNTIME AT the Habbaniyah Airfield is over. We begin a tactical road march toward the city of Ramadi, where our new base, FOB Mallard, awaits us. As we approach the outer-limits of the city, I spring up from the back hatch of our crew compartment to provide an extra set of eyes as we roll into our newest destination. The butt stock of my M16 is nestled firmly into the pit of my right shoulder and my barrel is roosted over the commander's side of the vehicle, scanning everything from our 3 to 5 o'clock.

For a second, I glance toward the front of our convoy. As a big, smoky gust of engine exhaust hits me in the face, I chuckle some, noticing our old road wheel, which is strapped to the upper-right half of our Brad. The morning after we were hit by that RPG, Dupéré got a wild hair up his ass and decided to keep the damaged wheel as a memento to his time served in Iraq. So there it is up top, reminding me every time I see it of the night I almost got killed. I can only imagine where he'll place it once he gets it back to Fort Carson.

Now what the hell ya suppose he's gonna do with that thing? I wonder. *Mount it in his garage or above the fireplace? Or maybe during the Super Bowl he'll set it out on the living room table and people can eat Doritos out of it. No way I'd want that thing in my house...*

Halfway into the city, we round the corner of an old Iraqi military base and venture up the road a ways to a filthy, vacant, two-story barracks facility that'll now serve as Fox Troop's primary base of operations. It's not much, but it has potential. With time, we can spruce it up. But until then, we'll just have to make do with what we have and try not to bitch about it. "Hey, it may be a shithole, but at least it's not Fallujah!" Right now that's the general consensus in Fox Troop: At least it's not Fallujah!

We dismount our vehicles and perform a cursory inspection of the premises, making sure it's clear before settling in. I walk upstairs to our quarter slice of the barracks, where I find a wide-open room and lanky balcony that extends clear across the upper-half of the building.

"Hey everyone, listen up! First things first -- this place needs swept out! Got it? Now make it happen!" commands Dupéré.

By early summer, most of those big sandstorms we encountered back in April and May had come to an end, leaving the billets at this deserted army post covered in a thick stratum of fine dust. Even worse, because the Iraqi Army abandoned it, every building here – just like our bungalows at Dreamland – has been gutted by looters who're preoccupied with plundering their own cities, assuring that Iraq's reconstruction will be even more of a challenge than previously thought. As we sweep out our room, I notice that right where I've been ordered to place my cot, there's graffiti all over the wall and a huge dried out pile of shit that was left behind by someone who had relieved himself in this very spot a few weeks earlier. But not a soul in Fox Troop is complaining, *'cause at least this ain't Fallujah!*

Meanwhile, just a few kilometers down the road, our friends in Sabre HQ are settling into a luxurious, marble-floored palace that rests just off the banks of a sparkling manmade lake. The outside is like a caption from the Garden of Eden. It's beautified with shrubbery, blossoming gardens, and tall shade trees that weave throughout the palace grounds, adding to the grandeur of its magnificent landscape. This place is beyond remarkable; it's a genuine testament of architectural genius. Only on TV and in the pages of books and magazines have I seen such opulence. Not only is there one palace, but many, with each seeming to compliment the most lavish one of all. Though some of these structures have been demolished by American stealth bombers, this one remains standing. Like the centerpiece in a row of shiny sports trophies, it towers into the sky, symbolizing the eternal resilience of Iraq and her people. I can only assume this is where our squadron commander sleeps, probably taking up quarters in what had once been Saddam Hussein's bedroom.

This is how *fobbits* (a bastardized term derived from the acronym "FOB") typically spend their time in Iraq – living in style while doing less "romantic" things, like filing paperwork and typing up endless piles of Army memoranda. Unlike us grunts, they rarely step "outside the wire" and always seem well-rested, like they've been getting more than the recommended eight hours of sleep per day. In my father's time, they were known as "REMFs" (Rear Echelon Motherfuckers). Nonetheless, they're an intricate part of our military, though sometimes looked down on by those who do the fighting.

Later that evening, after settling in, we're all hanging around our room, playing cards and listening to music. As the thick of night blankets Ramadi, several RPGs are launched at our FOB, rocking the entire base and giving everyone in Fox Troop somewhat of a jolt.

Whoosh...boom!!! One after the next.

We pile into our Brads and race down the same dusty path we had driven in on just a few hours earlier. We spend a few minutes surveying the area, but with no leads and nothing left to investigate, we pivot back around and return to base. All of a sudden, Anderson's Brad gets snarled up in a large uncoiled roll of barbed wire, halting him in his tracks. So there five or six of us are, some without body armor, standing outside with flashlights and bolt cutters in hand, struggling to untangle a rusty ball of wire from his suspension system. It's all wadded up between two shocks and a road wheel. And we have to be quick about it or we'll get caught by the enemy with our pants down.

At this stage in the war, there's no greater threat to our being than an RPG. When aimed with reasonable accuracy from a short distance, they can slice through just about anything short of an Abrams tank. We've already seen the kind of damage they can do. Like this, we're sitting ducks. That's why each of us dreads the thought of getting trapped up in concertina wire outside base. We had all heard the story of some poor MP who had recently been struck dead in the chest by an RPG, killing him instantly. However, because the warhead had failed to detonate, and the risk of un-wedging it from his chest and suddenly exploding was too high, an EOD (Explosive Ordinance Disposal) team had to be called in to blow his body in place. Maybe the story was bullshit, maybe not. Either way, none of us want to be that guy.

As we free up Anderson's vehicle from the mess of wire he's driven into, I suddenly feel naive for thinking Ramadi would be any safer than Fallujah. But this is the life I chose, and I don't regret it. Not for a second. It's this job that sets me apart from all the kids I grew up with, and I'm damn proud of what I do. We all should be in my honest opinion.

—

Shortly before leaving Fallujah, we received word of a routine change of command that'd soon yield our entire company a fresh crop of rookie officers. Anderson's replacement was a young first lieutenant by the name of Bryan Keegan. As someone who's vertically challenged, you might say that he had a lot to prove – what with his sharp tongue and ball-busting demeanor. But he was smart as hell and had the heart of a lion. It took us a few weeks to get used to him, but in time he fit right in. Though Keegan differed in nearly every respect from his predecessor, he was definitely Third Platoon material, and we were lucky to have him.

And taking over Fox Troop from Captain Reinhardt was Captain Joshua T. Byers – an Airborne Ranger and graduate of West Point. Many of us were already familiar with Byers, who, just days before our deployment, had worked tirelessly at the squadron level to make sure that all our dismounted teams were adequately trained in the proper methodology of Military Operations in Urban Terrain and Close Quarters Combat. In fact, he personally oversaw every aspect of our training regimen, running us through multiple wartime scenarios while critiquing our performances.

Byers was a tall, lanky, red-headed Southerner with a handsome smile and down-to-Earth genuineness to him. He was also a man of strong faith. Though raised in the Bible Belt, he never came off as holier-than-thou. We liked him immediately. Upon coming to Fox Troop, he put meeting each platoon at the top of his list of things-to-do. He wanted to know who each of us was and where we were from. Like most guys below the rank of sergeant, I had come to accept that my name was synonymous with "Fuck Face," "Sperm Breath," "Dick Wad," "Hey, you!"

and "Shit-For-Brains." The fact Byers actually knew my name and called me by it said a lot.

He'd saunter through our billets in an almost shepherdly fashion, checking up on each of his men. I got pretty used to him strolling up to my cot and greeting me with the catchphrase, "What's up, Stud?!"

He seemed to respect the fact that I usually had a Bible lying out, resting atop a huge stack of history books. It's not always easy for officers to connect with their men, especially while handing down orders during the mid-point of a long and miserable deployment, but for Byers it came naturally. Even Dupéré liked him, and he rarely had anything good to say about officers, regarding most of them as little more than over-privileged frat boys. But Captain Byers was different. He had all the qualities of a great leader, and for that, he had earned our respect.

—

Just a week or so after our leadership's passing of the torch ceremony, we're out on a late-night patrol in the countryside, with Keegan at the helms of our platoon. It's another sleepy evening in the backwaters of rural Ramadi. Nothing's stirring as far as we can see. If I hadn't downed several cans of "Bebsi" prior to rolling out of FOB Mallard, I would've had to have pinched myself just to keep from dozing off in the back of Dupéré's vehicle.[**]

Suddenly, the calm is shattered.

[**] In Arabic, there is no phonetic equivalent to the letter "P," so foreign words with a *p* in them are pronounced as if they're a *b*. Hence, the "Bebsi" we used to buy from local street vendors.

An RPG sizzles over one of our Brads, narrowly missing it – followed by another that zips just a couple feet over Keegan's head. *Oh, shit! Not again!*

Whoever these guys are they just picked a fight with the wrong platoon. Some units might have responded by simply returning fire and attempting to break contact, not risking it all to give the enemy the benefit of getting another shot off. Well, not us! This is Fox Troop, and we're crazy as hell! There's a reason our company motto is "Relentless violence!" We're the unit of Buffalo Bill and George S. Patton (the latter of whom served as the twentieth colonel of our regiment). As Patton once said, "No bastard ever won a war by dying for his country. He won it by making the other poor bastard die for his." Our unit has a long, bloody history of armed combat on foreign soil, making other poor bastards the world over die miserable deaths. We've done this in Iraq before, and now we'll do it again.

Their first mistake was engaging us from an open field, where there's little cover and thus few places to hide. After all, this isn't downtown Ramadi. There are no frightened crowds of women and children to hide behind, just vast acreage of secluded farmland. These guys are no better off than the plastic targets we shoot at during gunnery. At the range, we average a ninety percent kill rate. So the odds aren't in their favor. Of course, those targets at the training grounds in Fort Carson don't scurry for cover, nor do they ever shoot back. So this could be interesting!

As our gunners fire back, Keegan begins rattling off orders. He seems pretty determined to win this fight. Then, in one bold and cunning move, he methodically checkmates our attackers. After the initial barrage of rocket fire is through, he assembles each crew around the origin of fire in a sort of L-shaped formation – enabling our platoon to corner them in while avoiding any possibility of fratricidal crossfire. It's a cunning move. Suddenly, the tables are turned. Every piece is lying in our favor like it's some kind of gigantic chessboard. We know where they're hiding, and now it's our move.

A firestorm of 25mm rounds tear through the field, lighting the sky and sending tiny chunks of hot, twisted shrapnel in every direction. *Thud! Thud! Thud!* Over and over again.

This goes on for a while, and we're just getting started. I would've hated to be in their shoes. The sound alone must be deafening. They're toast. They've got to be. There's just no way they'll crawl out of here alive. I consider it payback for May 27. Nobody's sure as to the number of enemy personnel, but we're not taking any chances. With each squeeze of the trigger, our gunners continue pounding away at them.

Thud! Thud! Thud!

Then Kublai Khan spots one of them, picking up on the man's heat signature through his sights. After slithering around in the grass for a while, the man gets up and dashes for cover. Kublai Khan lights his ass up and he drops into the waist-high foliage. Is he dead? He must be. There's no movement and we don't hear anybody wailing in pain.

By now it's nearing daybreak. We've shredded every square inch of that field. The likelihood that our attackers are still alive is pretty slim. Dismounted squads form up and begin sifting ever-so-carefully through the thickets. However, by 0500 there's still no trace of them. Everyone's thinking, *Where the hell are they? They aren't magicians. They couldn't have just up and vanished.* So we continue combing the fields.

Our doggedness soon pays off. Just before sunrise, Beckett stumbles upon a man buried face-down in the mud. There's an RPG launcher and several warheads lying beside him.

"Holy shit! I got one of 'em right here…alive!"

This is huge. I mean, it's not every day you catch one of these guys red handed. But when you do, you feel like beating them to a pulp – but aren't allowed to.

Soon enough, another is found hiding out in a nearby farmhouse, bleeding from a nasty gunshot wound to his upper frame. It's the guy Kublai Khan shot. We round them up and interrogate them on the scene. Through an interpreter, one frazzled detainee tries to claim they're merely "farmers," tending their crops in the dead of night. He says that's how they got caught up in our little early morning skirmish with the Mujahadeen. He adds that it was merely coincidental that he dove onto that pile of RPG warheads.

The gall of this man is unbelievable, but if I were in his shoes I guess I'd do the same thing. I'd just prefer that he spit in our faces and call us all infidels. After all, that's what he's thinking. But that'd require just a little more courage than he's got at the moment.

Looking back, I remember wishing that I had been at the initial interrogation, but I wasn't. My section got stuck setting the outer-cordon for the search; the guys in Alpha and Charlie did the rest. After hearing the news, I could only imagine the rush that must have come with finding that one guy who had buried himself in the mud.

I wanted a piece of them. But would I have had the personal strength of character to do the right thing, to conduct myself in accordance with the moral guidelines of war? Or at first chance would I have laid into one with the butt stock of my rifle, then cracked the other's skull open with a Maglight? I'd be lying if I said it didn't cross my mind. After all, they did try to kill us.

War can bring out the absolute worst in people. Even good men do things they wouldn't normally do if they weren't on the battlefield. Believe me, I've seen it all too often. But apart from the larger issue of ethical conduct, it wouldn't have been worth it. These two were far more valuable to us alive than dead.

But getting rubbed out in an RPG attack wasn't the only threat that weighed on our minds. Iraq's armed malcontents were beginning to widen their methodology of attacks – to now include artillery strikes on our bases. At night, they'd drive within striking distance of FOB Mallard, then pound us with mortars aimed from the backs of their pickup trucks, which served as mobile launch pads – allowing them to make a speedy getaway. Artillery isn't used to shred large numbers of enemy combatants on the battlefield. More often than not, it's simply used to "impede and harass." And harass us they did, every couple nights or so, with meteoric explosions that echoed clear from one end of the city to the other.

Before the attacks, I used to sleep outside under the stars, where it was cooler. But that came to an end after it started raining artillery every other night. Now I couldn't even get up to take a shit without having to throw on my flak vest and "brain bucket."

The attacks were causing me to lose sleep, too. I'd roll back and forth, practically scratching myself until I'd bleed. There are guys who can snooze through that; I'm not one of them. Rarely did I get more than a couple hours of pure sleep. There were times I'd go days without rest, and not because we'd get shelled every other night. Rather, I couldn't stand being trapped on the second floor of that stuffy-ass building. The heat was unbearable. I thought for sure I'd lose my mind by summer's end. I'd lie in my cot at night, wondering how my peers managed to doze off in these conditions, with mosquitoes and sand fleas feasting on them.

One evening, I crawled on my elbows over to a friend's cot, and with a shake or two woke him up. As he lifted his head, I whispered a few lines from one of my favorite war movies into his ear, drawing a simile between the petty personal squabbles that existed within our own unit and those in Oliver Stone's *Platoon*. "The only thing that can kill Barnes is Barnes," I said, pivoting myself around and returning to my corner of the balcony.

"Bryan, go to sleep!"

"I wish I could," I said, sighing as I crept elbows-first into my hot and sweaty cot, which I had soused with insect repellant.

But there was still some hope to be had – the fading illusion that we'd be home in August. Calvin continued to nourish this idea. But he wasn't alone. There were others, too. In the room adjacent to ours, somebody in Red Platoon claimed that "God" had told him in a dream that we'd be home in two months.

Common sense told me otherwise. Our enemies were gaining ground with each passing day. No matter how many doors we kicked in, there was no ebb in the number of attacks on Coalition forces. Regardless of the number of individuals we detained or the amount of enemy weapons that were unearthed, the threat level went unabated. It seemed to defy logic. So we turned up the heat a notch. Our patrols grew longer and more frequent. We aggressively enforced curfew polices. We raided more homes, detained more people, killed more "terrorists." But nothing we did seemed to yield any positive results.

On at least one or two occasions, we even had some of our Hispanic NCOs don Islamic "man dresses" and roll out of FOB Mallard in confiscated vehicles while disguised as Iraqi nationals. They'd scope out certain properties before we'd raid them, providing us with additional intel. With his bushy mustache, not only did White's Latino platoon sergeant look every bit the part of a full-grown Iraqi male, he could've passed as a stunt double for a younger Saddam Hussein – especially when he'd cant his beret just right. If you think about it, that's some Delta Force shit. Regular units don't typically do stuff like that. But we did. I'm sure we were in violation of one stupid Army regulation or another, but we didn't care. It was tactically clever and we believed it gave us a huge leg up on our enemies. Especially before heading out on raids. Anything to save a life, right?[††]

Still, nothing changed. The violence continued. Our enemies had an immense advantage to fighting us on their turf. Everybody we spoke to who lived in the villages we patrolled claimed to have zero knowledge as to who was behind the attacks, as if there wasn't a concerted effort by some of the locals to drive us from "the land of the two rivers," or as this place was more commonly referred to by some of my buddies: the biggest shithole on Planet Earth.

When I'd be out on patrol, all I could think of was how in the opening scenes of *It's a Wonderful Life*, James Stewart's character, "George Bailey," all chipper and wearing a smile, boasts of his wanderlust ambitions to travel the far ends of the Earth – of his

---

[††] Allow me to clarify this passage, as it requires further explaining: Fox Troop never baited the insurgency with Hispanic soldiers. On the one or two occasions we utilized this strategy, only NCOs of the rank staff sergeant or higher participated, and by their own freewill. In fact, they may have even proposed the idea. Moreover, they were trailed from a safe distance by friendly forces that backed them up the whole time. It was an unconventional strategy for an unconventional war, and it yielded useful intel ahead of raids. Also, this was earlier in the war, before the insurgency began using IEDs.

desire to escape the pleasant town of Bedford Falls and someday visit Baghdad. Now here we were, smack dab in the Cradle of Civilization, Abraham's birthplace, a land that's home to one of the Seven Wonders of the World, the Hanging Gardens of Babylon. And all we could think about was how much we hated the place.

Chapter Ten
RISK

BUSH'S COWBOY RHETORIC had finally reached its crescendo when he delivered his infamous "bring 'em on" speech, which came off as though he were challenging the insurgency to a duel on national television. Though yet another gaffe he'd later regret, it came at a time when attacks on Coalition forces were on the rise and our enemies were availing themselves to increasingly sophisticated means of targeting us.

In the midst of Iraq's crumbling stability, a certain member of our platoon received a package in the mail one day. In it was *Risk – the Game for Global Domination*. Oh, how we loved that game! We played it daily for hours on end. The objective in Risk is to subjugate every region on the board by defeating your opponents wherever they're at and maintaining a troop presence in every country. Then, and only then, is victory achieved.

One of our guys cleverly refined his strategy for global dominion to that of a fine art. First, he'd gain complete control of the South Pacific, prioritizing the capture of East and West Australia. These territories would be taken at any cost. Then, from his newly established base of operations in the Outback, he'd gradually push north, conquering Indonesia, Papua New Guinea, and several additional territories with little resistance until he controlled all of Southeast Asia. This method of attack always bought him just enough time to build up his small and fledgling army of plastic game pieces, which he'd use for an aggressive expansion into the Middle East and up the eastern shoreline of Asia. At this point, he was virtually unstoppable. Occasionally, when several of us would play and I stood zero chance of winning, I'd deliberately pit my weaker army against his, choosing to martyr my own troops in a suicidal campaign to prevent Asian supremacy of the globe. This always pissed him off and would usually cost him the game.

As for me, I usually took a far more nationalistic approach, making a point of first capturing the good ol' U.S. of A. After centralizing most of my troops there, I'd expand the American empire at any cost. I'd place a huge contingent of forces in Alaska to obviate the possibility of a Russian invasion via Siberia. However, I was keen enough not to place all my eggs in one basket, since I also required a large and mobile ground army to conquer foreign lands. Unfortunately, my strategy for American domination of the world rarely panned out. I found it nearly impossible to defend our southern border because I was always getting bogged down in quagmires all over the globe, particularly in the Middle East. At which point I'd usually be stretched too thin to take on foreign aggressors at home. Before I knew it, China was creating problems for me in Asia, Russia was creeping into Western Europe, and all Latin America was flooding my southern border.

By then, my army was in complete disarray, morale was low, and my troops would usually die off somewhere in Southwest Asia, in those badlands known as the Hindu Kush. Some twenty-three hundred years ago, it was there that Alexander the Great's conquest for world domination finally ran out of steam. Today we know it as Afghanistan. With American troops in over 130 countries (despite the end of the Cold War and our victory over Soviet

Russia), it seemed our foreign policy was beginning to resemble the underlying objective in the board game Risk. Our unwarranted invasion of Mesopotamia seemed like a real-life push for regional domination – one that unwisely diverted resources away from the effort to decimate al Qaeda and hunt down Osama bin Laden. And just like those plastic cavalry pieces used as cannon fodder in Risk, our individual chances of surviving Iraq hinged in part on dumb luck. It didn't matter if we were on a patrol in triple-digit temperatures or thrashing our way into the homes of Ba'thists at 0400. There was always a very real chance of getting shot or blown up. For each man, living in this matrix of constant fear and uncertainty was a living hell. I know it was for me.

But not every waking moment of our lives was spent fretting dangers that lay just around the corner. The majority of our missions went pretty smooth. On base, we passed the hours at FOB Mallard just as we had done at Dreamland. While some played Texas hold 'em and reminisced endlessly about past rendez-vous with women, I preferred to keep to myself, usually tucked away somewhere reading a book. When there wasn't jack shit going on, some would even put back a drink or two. One of our guys had been cleverly smuggling alcohol into Iraq via the US Postal Service; it was sent to him in glass bottles labeled "Dad's Bug Juice." There was actually vodka in all of those bottles of "homemade mosquito repellant." Nobody ever got wasted on the job, but they'd drink to take the edge off after a mission or long patrol.

One evening, just a few days after our arrival to FOB Mallard, we got an unexpected surprise. All of us peons were waiting around for the platoon sergeants' meeting to adjourn so we could get *notes* (a nightly ritual in the Army in which everyone stands around on pins and needles to find out what's on the agenda the following day).

After the meeting, Dupéré marched back upstairs and sat on his cot. As we gathered around, he looked down at his notepad and asked a simple question:

"Who wants to see Kid Rock tomorrow?"

"Funny," I said, puzzled by the offer. "For real though, what's up?"

"Damn it, I asked: 'Who wants to see Kid Rock?!'" he replied, looking at me and another soldier. "'Cuz if I don't get an answer *real quick*, us NCOs are gonna go."

I looked back at him, dumbfounded by the words coming out of his mouth, though wise enough to answer his question with "I do!"

"Alright then, that's more like it! Turns out Kid Rock is putting on a little show for the troops tomorrow afternoon at BIAP [Baghdad International Airport]. So, first thing tomorrow morning, ya'll meet up at Headquarters. From there, you're gonna pile into some trucks and Humvees and move out. Got it?"

"Roger, Sergeant!"

The next morning, we did just as we were told. Dozens of us piled nonchalantly into the backs of un-armored vehicles, without a care in the world. It was like we were all back in high school and heading to a party or something. Just a few minutes before our departure, one of the mechanics whipped out his balls. Mimicking something you'd only expect to see on MTV's *Jackass*, he fastened a plastic zip-strip around his nutsack, only to realize that he couldn't get it off. One of our medics had to remove it with the use of a bladed surgical tool, carefully sawing through the plastic to avoid lacerating one of his testicles. We all laughed our asses off, momentarily forgetting that we were in Iraq.

In fifteen minutes, we were on our way, traveling back down the same strip of highway on which we had just come a few days prior. We continued eastbound, passing Fallujah at a safe distance as the City of Mosques petered out of sight. Provided we made it back before sundown, we didn't feel there was too much to worry about. Especially since our adversaries only struck at night, like vampires.

Shortly after arriving at BIAP, I found myself drifting through a fetid crowd of sweaty soldiers and Marines. Thousands had amassed for one purpose: to rock 'n' roll! That afternoon we weren't soldiers. We were just a bunch of dudes having fun. It was the first time in three months that I felt like a normal human being. Not even war could rob me of the good time I was having.

Then came the man of the hour. I'll admit, I had doubts as to whether he'd actually show up, but he did. Kid Rock always comes through for the troops. That's why they love him. With style and ease, he meandered through the crowd, signing autographs and high-fiving soldiers before making his way onstage. He was chaperoned by a handful of clean-cut officers and several women of astonishing beauty, a sight that only drove us all the more wild. We all muscled one another out of the way, everyone vying to catch a glimpse of them as our frenzied herd parted in two. I squeezed my way into the mass and snapped a crooked picture of Kid Rock, who was sporting a sweaty wife-beater and had a big grin plastered across his stubbly, goateed face.

For a moment, I felt as if I were back in high school. Years earlier, my buddies and I used to go to rock concerts all the time. The last show I went to before signing up was Ozzfest 2000. It was the best concert I ever saw, and not simply for the music. While I was there, I managed to sneak backstage and hang out with a few rock stars, including Dirk Lance and DJ Kilmore of Incubus. Prior to getting chased out by security, the three of us played a couple rounds of putt-putt golf. Afterwards, I linked back up with my friends, who all looked upon me with great envy for the rest of the evening. And not only did I have the autographs to validate my story, a couple of them had seen me standing off on the side of the stage between sets, carefully blended in with roadies.

But my point is this: I wasn't born a soldier. If, as a high school senior, I had accidentally stumbled into a time portal and been whisked several years into the future, I wouldn't have recognized myself in that crowd at BIAP. At seventeen, I was a straggly-haired teenager with baggy pants and a chain wallet. I didn't care about my grades and had few aspirations in life outside of ditching class. The guys I used to chum around with were no different; even worse I'd say. It was like we were perpetually raging against the machine. We all scoffed at the idea of military service and saw college as a useless endeavor for academic chumps. About the only thing I had going for myself was that I had a job, working as a farmhand on my brother-in-law's dairy. And that job saved me from permanently falling in with the wrong crowd.

Now here I was three years later, decked out in Army fatigues and carrying a machinegun. I used to hate "the man." Now I worked for him. If someone had told me this is where I'd be in the not so distant future, I would have said they were out of their mind. But I matured a lot in that year after I dropped out of high school. I had done the unthinkable – I cut my hair, ditched my stoner friends, started spending time at the library, earned my GED (Good Enough Diploma), and somewhere in the mix, became a registered Republican. It was like I had grown up overnight. Somehow, I doubt the younger me would approve of my new conformist lifestyle. I was nothing more than a smalltown loser going nowhere fast, so I decided to get my act together. Now I was in Iraq on a pitstop in my journey to manhood.

—

Around the same timeframe as Kid Rock's visit to Baghdad, we also caught word of some very disturbing news. Famed actress and musician Jennifer Lopez and her darling hubby, Ben Affleck, had died in a car accident. It was our platoon quidnunc, Private Calvin, who first told me the heart-wrenching story of their demise. He seemed thunderstruck, as though someone had just knocked the wind out of him. He had beads of sweat running down his forehead and was out of breath.

"Calvin, what is it?" I asked.

"J.Lo and Ben Affleck are dead!"

"Oh, well that sucks. Where'd you hear this?"

"From some guy in Squadron. I can't believe it…"

This must have come as a terrible loss to Calvin, who, along with his extensive collection of chick flicks, had recently purchased *Maid in Manhattan*, in which "J.Lo" played the lead role.

The better part of a month elapsed before the story was permanently unmasked as nothing more than baseless gossip. Nothing even remotely similar to this had happened to either of them. But that didn't keep the story from spreading like wildfire through all of Southwest Asia and reaching us in late June.

Funny thing – to cite author and OIF veteran Paul Rieckhoff, founder of IAVA (Iraq and Afghanistan Veterans of America), in his memoir *Chasing Ghosts*, he also recalls hearing this same rumor. Only he and his guys heard it when it was first birthed in Kuwait at the gates of Camp Victory earlier that April. "Everyone was flabbergasted," he writes:

The story must have been passed to thousands of soldiers before noon. I couldn't believe it. This was without a doubt the most devastating news gotten – the biggest loss of the war so far…

That really sucked. I liked watching J.Lo shake her ass on TV. Third Platoon was seriously depressed. I thought I might have to order a bereavement period for these guys. The idea of J.Lo's ass being gone was killing them…

—

If there was any indication that we were fighting a politician's war, it would have been when our new squadron commander issued an official decree that forbade the soldiers under his command from carrying non-NATO weapons (i.e., the ever-popular AK-47). But it wasn't his decision. This was coming down the pipes from higher.

Many of us had begun using weapons confiscated from insurgents out of necessity to defend ourselves. On a *conventional battlefield*, each member of each crew in an armored scout platoon has a specific set of tasks that limit him to either the driver's hull, one of two places in the turret, or the crew compartment. Therefore, there isn't much need for anyone but the dismounts to get issued a long-barreled rifle, such as an M16 or its slightly shorter cousin, the M4. Not when you can unleash hell on your enemy from behind the sights of a 25mm.

But that's under strictly ideal circumstances. In this post-Saddam "cluster fuck" of a war, we found ourselves on the ground a lot, with each man taking on various new roles within our platoon, being forced to operate in an increasingly hostile environment under atypical conditions. Some extra M4s were divvied out to each company before the deployment, but there still weren't enough for everyone. This shortage in personal weaponry left half our guys packing nothing more than a 9mm Beretta, a standard sidearm that only holds fifteen rounds and has a maximum effective range of 50 meters. Now, compare that to our enemy's first line of defense, the AK-47, which has twice the stopping power of an M16 and is semi-accurate at up to several hundred meters. So we did exactly what anyone else in our situation would have done – we took every unauthorized Kalashnikov for ourselves until each member of our platoon had his own rifle. Problem solved!

Instead, that's when the top-down "regimental ass-pounding" began. We soon enough were informed that even though killing Iraqis is permitted under justifiable circumstances, such as offensive and defensive actions, because the United States is a signatory to the North Atlantic Treaty Organization, doing isn't permitted when it's done with a non-NATO weapon.

So, in layman's terms, if I shoot an Iraqi in the guts with an M16, I'm a *war hero*. But if I do so with a Kalashnikov, I'm acting in violation of NATO policy. Anyhow, that's the way it was explained to me by Dupéré (I'm sure there were other reasons for the ban that I wasn't privy to). From what I understood, only in the rare circumstance that one runs out of his or her own ammunition are they permitted to use the enemy's weapons – at which point they're pretty much screwed anyway. So you're damned if you do and damned if you don't.

I remember thinking, *This has got to be the stupidest thing I've ever heard!*

Had this been another day and age, it wouldn't have been an issue at all. We'd be given a wink and nod as tacit approval. Nobody in their right mind would have expected us to abide by such absurd regulatory claptrap.

Unfortunately, some of the officers in Regiment and their enlisted yes-men seemed to have a knack for enforcing mindless Army regulations. Nonetheless, even though we complied with Regiment, surrendering our beloved Kalashnikovs, there were still a couple guys who kept theirs on hand. God willing, there wouldn't be any need for us to brandish them. But if so, they were tucked away under boxes and duffel bags, where no fobbit could see them.

—

Before we knew it, we were told that we'd be returning to Fallujah toward the end of July. And not to Dreamland, but to some compound known as the "M-E-K."

But first, we were given a mission that would span several days and send us trekking halfway across the al Anbar province, searching for weapons and reconnoitering large swaths of unfamiliar desert terrain. I welcomed the operation as a timely divergence from our drab routine of patrolling from dusk till dawn. As a dismount, there wasn't a whole lot for me to do. So I just took in the scenery from the rear of our Brad. Iraq had a certain charm that I seemed to appreciate. Even with the desert sun beating down on my face, I loved the serendipity of each new adventure, and the sheer pleasure that came with taking in all these new sights. I couldn't get enough of it, to be honest.

We logged hundreds of kilometers that mission, touching ground in barren lands that only armies and Bedouins dare set foot. We searched random pockets of mud huts and stone hovels that looked about a thousand years old. I remember finding one packed to the brim with crates of munitions and anti-aircraft shells left over from the first Gulf War. We'd find this stuff, then wait around for EOD teams to come out and blow it all to pieces. We also probed a couple abandoned military outposts, but all we found were old, dirty uniforms and a few gas masks scattered about. No underground laboratories with stockpiles of biological weapons. No nuclear-tipped missiles. No hidden bunkers with neatly-rowed canisters of sarin gas. Essentially, none of the stuff that the Bush Administration had assured us would most certainly be there. Just a lot of old, rusty munitions. That's all we ever found.

Between missions we had a good bit of downtime, too. One afternoon, our spunky new platoon leader came up with a fantastic idea.

"Bryan, go grab your gear! We're gonna blow something up. Consider it a demo course."

Perched at the top of a nearby hill was a small, lonesome building, standing perfectly intact, though appearing to serve no real function. As I tagged along behind Lieutenant Keegan, he grabbed a claymore mine that had been stowed away somewhere in the back of his vehicle.

"Are we going to blow that building up, Sir?"

"You're goddamn right we are!"

Until then, I had never met somebody so infatuated with things that go *Boom!* As he removed the claymore and detonator from the canvas bandolier, uncoiling its wiry spool of det cord, he had this half-crazed look in his eye, like a meth addict feening for his next hit.

I was forced to inquire, "Sir, were you the kid who used to cut apart bottle rockets and firecrackers to make small, homemade explosives?"

"Yeah," he replied. "But I was smart enough not to blow my fingers off in the process."

The mine was neatly laid in the building's hindmost room, in a way that was sure to maximize the blast effect. Keegan gave me the honors. We hunkered down from a safe distance, and with a small squeeze of the detonator, I blew the back half of the building out – not flattening the property outright, as I would have liked, but cracking the foundation and splitting the structure in two.

"Wow! That was awesome!!!" I shouted, nearly deaf from the blast.

Keegan had made my day. If nothing else, this is why I joined the Army – to blow shit up!

But the real highpoint of that mission was the time we got to cool off by taking a dip in a huge lake we stumbled upon. As we approached the beachfront, we scanned everything in the vicinity, including the bluffs overlooking our position. All we could see were a couple fishermen, but no one else. The place was all ours. Upon reaching the shoreline, we faced our Brads outward, giving second thoughts to anyone hoping to attack us.

Once given the okay, our ramps lowered and we poured out of our vehicles. As we stripped down to our boxers and lunged into the cool waters, a couple of our gunners remained in their turrets, on high alert. Words can't describe how good it felt, the waves smacking against our faces as we swam and dunked one another. Sure, this wasn't exactly Cancun, and the air reeked of smoke from our diesel engines, but the lake was crystal clear and the water felt unbelievably good. From the shoreline, this place could have passed for a getaway resort along the Gulf of Aqaba, in the Sinai, had the beachfront not been littered with bomb craters and the rusting armaments of a war long past.

Our splendid little excursion ended with our return to FOB Mallard a couple days later, though not before netting some very bad people in a raid – mid-tier Saddam loyalists responsible for organizing attacks on American troops.

By now, we had just a week left in Ramadi. Most of us dreaded the thought of returning to Fallujah –

that is, until we learned that our new base was equipped with various amenities left behind by the 3rd Infantry Division: TVs, satellite dishes, air conditioners, refrigerators, etc. Rumor had it there was even an on-base restaurant, phones, and incredibly enough, a souvenir shop that sold beautifully detailed glass hookahs, or what the Arabs call *sheesha* pipes. Suddenly, the pros of relocating to Fallujah seemed to outweigh the cons of staying in Ramadi. Besides, Ramadi wasn't much safer. Enemy attacks were on the rise and our living conditions sucked. We had been there a month and were just now getting electricity.

We were told that we'd be moving out first thing Thursday morning, July 24. Until then, it was business as usual. That Tuesday evening, all of Fox Troop squeezed into a small room on the first floor of our living quarters to watch *Old School*. I'm a huge fan of Will Ferrell, so you can only imagine what a treat that was. We roared with laughter at every scene, especially halfway into the film when Ferrell's character, "Frank the Tank," wails in anguish over the loss of his dear friend and fellow pledge, "Blue." He breaks down at the old man's funeral and begins yelling his name after singing a dramatic rendition of *Dust in the Wind*.

Captain Byers howled at the top of his lungs, echoing the words of Frank the Tank, causing us to laugh that much harder: "You're my boy, Blue!"

A couple hours after everyone bedded down, our crew geared up for a late-night patrol. We hit the streets just before daybreak and got back sometime around breakfast. I grounded my gear in the vehicle, grabbed a little something to snack on, and then raced upstairs to catch some shuteye. The past forty-eight hours had been unusually calm. No car bombs. No snipers. No RPG assaults. No late-night mortar strikes on our base. With fighting season in full swing, the tranquility of the last two days seemed odd, if not too good to be true. One thing I love about Iraq is that life lacks routine. It would seem even the *Muj* prefer their mornings off, which was fine by me.

Along the way I passed Captain Byers, who greeted me with "What's up, Stud?" as I ascended the stairwell.

"Not much, Sir!"

I wanted to stop and chat, but he was getting ready for his leader's reconnaissance to Fallujah – a necessary prelude to our unit's relocation there the following day. Once upstairs, I scarfed down a small plate of food and immediately passed out on my cot. The moment I lost all consciousness, I felt someone tugging at my arm. It was my driver.

"Bryan, wake up! Captain Byers just got killed, and Sergeant Murphy's in pretty bad shape."

That got my attention real quick. I sprang to my feet in disbelief.

"No…that's impossible," I said. "I just talked to him like fifteen minutes ago. What the hell happened?"

"They got hit by an IED."

"What the hell's an IED?!"

"Improvised Explosive Device."

Chapter Eleven
THE MEK

NOBODY SAW IT coming. Their convoy was barely out of the gates of FOB Mallard when Captain Byers' Humvee got rocked by one of the first IEDs to be employed against American forces in all of Iraq.

Riding with him that day had been his driver Specialist Terry Brewer, Lieutenant Keegan, a civilian interpreter, and our platoon sergeant, SFC Daniel Murphy. The blast shredded everything and everyone on the passenger's side, killing Byers almost instantly and severely wounding Sergeant Murphy and the interpreter. Keegan and Brewer were shielded by the men to their right, whose bodies sustained the bulk of the shrapnel. Byers never stood a chance, and whether Murphy would pull through was now a matter of fate. Word had it he was in terrible shape, dangling somewhere between life and death, with a slim chance of surviving.

Out of courtesy to our unit, following the attack Byers' Humvee was supposed to get parked in a dusty field adjacent to our billets – far removed from those in Fox Troop. Instead, some numbskull from Squadron dropped it off right in front of our company headquarters. There it sat like a bloody horror show, with fresh crimson stains splattered about. The entire right side was pockmarked with small holes from where the shrapnel had torn apart everybody seated on the passenger's side.

By our own volition, a few of us headed out with wet rags in hand and proceeded to scrub it clean and remove any of the bloodied gear that had been left inside. I wasn't sure if Brewer had realized it yet, but just inches above where his head had been, there was a gaping hole in the framework of the Humvee. A huge chunk of whatever had just barely missed his cranium. An inch or two lower and he would have gotten half his face removed. As horrible as it all sounds, it could have been much worse. Despite the intensity of the blast and having never been trained on how to react to this sort of attack, Brewer managed to keep the vehicle from veering off the side of the road and crashing. Keegan attributed their survival to his good driving skills.

We spent that evening coping with the loss of Byers and wondering whether Murphy would make it. Regardless of what had just happened, the show had to go on, just as Byers would have wanted. His last words were: "Keep moving forward!" And so we did, metaphorically speaking. In his stead, our old commander, Captain Reinhardt, was sent back to Fox, and not long after, we received a replacement for Sergeant Murphy from Eagle Troop.

In those first couple days after reassuming control of Fallujah, a beautiful memorial service was held for Byers – one suited for a hero. We said our final goodbyes and recognized a life well-lived. Byers was arguably the finest officer any of us had ever had the pleasure of serving under. More than that, he was a son, a brother, a friend, a husband, a patriot, and above all, a man of unwavering faith in God. Many of us took comfort in knowing that he was now in a better place, looking down on us from a higher altitude. In the Cav, we call it Fiddler's Green. It's where our dead spend eternity. According to legend:

Halfway down the trail to Hell

In a shady meadow green
Are the souls of all dead troopers camped
Near a good old-time canteen
And this eternal resting place
Is known as Fiddler's Green

Marching past, straight through to Hell
The Infantry are seen
Accompanied by the Engineers,
Artillery and Marines
For none but the shades of Cavalrymen
Dismount at Fiddler's Green

On this most somber of occasions, I expected myself to be all tears, just as I had been at Quinn and Broomhead's memorial service. But in all honesty, no more than a few teardrops trickled down my sun-beaten cheeks. Though all of us were clearly hurting inside, as I looked around, those surrounding me didn't appear to be all too grief-stricken either. Beckett wore a hard-boiled straight face, as did Kublai Khan. Even Brewer seemed incredibly well-composed, and not only had he survived the attack, he was Captain Byers' right-hand man. Yet there he stood, showing little emotion, his buddies patting him on the back.

It was a chilling sign of how desensitized to war we'd grown.

Byers was the fifth man in our squadron to have given his life in Iraq; the third to die in an actual enemy attack. That first cut is always the worst, but after a while your heart calluses over and you become less receptive to human misery. Every day, I'd flip through the *Stars and Stripes* and read about other young soldiers who'd just made the ultimate sacrifice. American troops were being killed in Iraq at a rate of about one or two per day. With each month it was only getting worse, and there seemed to be no end in sight. I could only hope and pray that my name wouldn't be the next to grace the pages of some newspaper back home.

—

We've just gotten our replacement for Murphy, who remains in critical yet stable condition. Meet Sergeant First Class Anthony Brentford. Together, he and Lieutenant Keegan are Blue Platoon's dynamic duo. At just a shade over forty, Brentford is only twelve months or so shy of retiring. With nearly twenty years in, he looks a full ten or fifteen years older than his actual age. That's what the unwholesome combination of chain-smoking and years in the field do to a man.

He's a grizzled fellow who reminds me of a cross between John Wayne and an aging Clint Eastwood, like he could have played the town sheriff in an old spaghetti western. His rough-and-tumble appearance is matched by a no-bullshit persona, quickly earning him the title *ODB* – short for "Old Dirty Brentford." Already I've seen him tear Kublai Khan a new asshole, a sight that brought me great satisfaction as I laughed hysterically from an unseen location. He may be as ornery as they come, but so far I like our new platoon daddy. He's not exactly easy to warm up to, but overall he's pretty laid back and seems to know his stuff.

Our first run-in was one for the books. Upon settling in at the MEK, he decreed that no longer would he tolerate the sight of people walking back from the showers without a towel.

"If I see that shit…people walkin' around buck naked, well so help you God. Is that understood?"

As I'm showering later that evening, Beckett creeps up to the plywood stall I'm in and snatches my towel as a joke, without me even noticing. He knows full well I have to pass Brentford's enclave of our new living quarters in order to get back to mine. After cleaning up, I feel around for my towel and notice it isn't there, draped over the door, where I had left it. Nor has it fallen to the ground. Almost instantly, I realize that I've been set up for an all-nude confrontation with Brentford – and who set me up for this potentially awkward exchange.

"Beckett," I murmur, clenching my right fist.

I'm not sure why, but he seems to take endless pleasure in embarrassing me in front of our platoon. The roughhousing I'm used to by now, but this isn't cool. My options are few, and I have a 50/50 chance of getting caught. So I chance it and go dashing past ODB's room as quickly as possible. But I'm not fast enough. The old seasoned vet spots me.

"That's it! Who's that?! Who the fuck's runnin' around here naked?!"

Busted, I freeze. I begin to panic. Not wanting to leave the man waiting, I do an about face and march back out into the hallway to meet him halfway…in the nude. I feel about three inches tall as he towers over me at nearly six and half feet, glaring at me in total disgust, with furrowed eyebrows.

"Who the fuck are you, Soldier?" he snarls. "And why the hell are you running around without a towel?! Did I not make myself clear? What part of 'Don't walk around here naked' don't you understand?"

Like a total jackass, I snap to the position of parade-rest.

"Sergeant, I'm Private Bryan."
Bad mistake! Now Brentford thinks I'm mocking his authority. He loses it and goes berserk. I step back a foot or two, girding myself for the major ass-reaming that's about to ensue. All the while, Beckett stands off to the side, snickering while ODB tears into me.

Fortunately, a non-com from Alpha quickly intervenes, coming to my rescue: "Well shit, Bryan, don't just stand there with your pecker hangin' out. Go throw some clothes on, ya fuckin' idiot!"

After nervously explaining what happened, I was absolved of the crime. Not wanting to snitch on Beck, I swore up and down that somebody must have taken my towel by mistake. First impressions always last, and this wasn't exactly the kind of start I had hoped to get off to with our grumpy new platoon sergeant. But in no time all was forgiven.

Looking back, life at the MEK wasn't half bad. The fact we were back in the saddle for another round of Fallujah was entirely overshadowed by the considerable improvement in our new living conditions. On base, there was a fully operational PX and chow hall, and if you couldn't stand feasting on canned Army food, you were free to spend a couple dollars at a Middle Eastern restaurant. The menu featured a variety of savory entrées, including shish kabob and chicken shawarma sandwiches. There were even two or three DSN (Defense Switched Networks) phones up and running. They looked more like Vietnam-era handmics used for calling in artillery strikes than actual telephones, but they worked. Of course, whether or not you'd actually get through to your family was another story altogether. On a good day, you could usually get through on the first several tries. On a bad day, however, you'd waste a half-hour dialing your family and not even reach an operator, or get cut off after that first *hello*.

Our company had its own section of the base, too, with just enough room to squeeze everyone in. It was a gated facility with high concrete walls, affording us lots of privacy. We even had an air-conditioned game room with a refrigerator and satellite television, and beside that, a makeshift workout center complete with dumbbells and a weight bench. When not tied up at the front gate or patrolling vast stretches of highway, however one chose to spend their free time was entirely up to them. Some liked pumping iron, while others just napped or sat around watching porno for hours on end. Calvin's philosophy to surviving Iraq was, "the more one sleeps, the shorter their deployment," because unconsciousness meant temporarily losing all awareness that you were deployed in the first place.

And how can I forget the porta-potties? The inside walls of our shitters were like pages torn from a soldier's journal, with random thoughts jotted down in permanent black marker that gave voice to the gripes of every man who had ever marched in there to pinch a loaf. Mostly, it was "FUCK IRAQ," written over and over in varying fonts and on every wall of every porta-potty. Of course, there were also racial slurs, Bible verses, drawings of large-breasted women being impaled by men with jumbo-sized penises, and I learnt that somebody had just lost their girl to Jody.

But life at the MEK wasn't all catnaps and grab-assing, just as Byers' Humvee getting blown-up wasn't a one-time thing. In just a matter of weeks, IEDs began cropping up all over the "Sunni Triangle." Now it was our job to keep our sector's supply routes clear. The threat posed by roadside explosives quickly surpassed the dangers of getting bush-whacked by gunmen or RPG teams. They were neatly camouflaged along the right margins of every heavily traveled route, where they'd lie in waylay much like a rattlesnake waiting to strike its prey. Sometimes there'd even be multiple ordinances daisy-chained together, concealed behind brush or mounds of dirt.

One day, one of our tanks in Green Platoon veered too far to the right while on patrol, rolling over one and setting it off. *KABOOM!* It shattered one of the road wheels and blew their track clear off the suspension system.

Logistics are the lifeblood of every army. When access to various supplies dries up, wars are lost. Therefore, we couldn't afford to lose control of the supply routes in our area of operations. Every day, we'd patrol long strips of highway that snaked in and out of our sector and past key areas of interest, to include a US-run prison facility named "Abu Ghraib or something like that."

If you were safely buttoned up in a tank or Bradley Fighting Vehicle, the chance of getting hit by an IED was pretty slim. Earlier in the war, the blast effect of a roadside bomb couldn't pierce the thick metal girding of a well-armored vehicle (in just a year's time, they'd figure it out through lots of trial and error). On the other hand, if you were consigned to a unit that cruised around in light-skinned Humvees, then you were in for a wild ride. Our troops extemporized as best they could by adopting better defensive driving techniques. Some even welded old chunks of rusty scrap metal to the sides of their vehicles to shield themselves in the event of an attack.

To avert such attacks, I even saw one platoon of National Guardsmen go so far as to paint their Humvees with mud. See, their Humvees were the older models, lined with thin metal sheeting, though shaped identically to the newer tan armored Humvees that had just rolled off the assembly line in time for the invasion. By painting their vehicles with mud, they hoped to fool their enemies into believing that they were equipped with the tan "up-armored" models that could sustain an IED blast. Though a crafty idea, it was equally pathetic. But in Iraq this is what the greatest military on the face of the Earth had been reduced to.

Throughout summer, the IED threat grew worse. Not only did the number of attacks increase exponentially, so did their lethality. In time, we began to see "new-and-improved" IEDs. They were often fitted with EFPs (explosively formed penetrators), or what the average grunt might call a "shaped charge." Imagine a shallow copper dish that's been horizontally sealed to a vertically positioned cylindrical device. Now imagine that same device packed to the brim with high explosives. When the triggerman sets it off, the explosion is funneled in a single direction and the malleable copper plate instantaneously takes on the form of a deathly molten rod. Traveling at speeds of up to 1.2 miles per second, it can easily destroy an up-armored Humvee from the side or pierce the underbelly of an Abrams tank. While this technology has been in use since World War II, it was new to the battlefields of Iraq.

Get hit by one of those and you're history! It's like you're rolling along and all is fine one second, and the next your entire vehicle is engulfed in flames and half of your crew is dead. There's usually nobody to shoot back at, and your platoon is left cleaning up the wreckage on a crowded city block, bagging its dead while the locals just stare at you. Where's the glory in that?

—

In our first days at the MEK, there were two questions that weighed heavily on my mind: *Why is our new base called the MEK?* It seemed nobody could provide me an answer. I assumed *MEK* to be a common acronym drawn from the military's vast alphabet soup, some shorthanded phrase I had yet to memorize. After all, there are so many it's hard to keep them all straight. Secondly, I wanted to know: *Who are all these swarthy-looking foreign nationals I see hanging around on base, totally unguarded?* There were a lot. I just assumed they were local workers we hired to perform menial labor and do other unsavory jobs – like pumping the raw shit from our porta-potties and spreading it in the nearby fields.

Well, I was wrong. They were Persians.

Persians? I thought. *Now I'm totally confused…Why are there Iranians on our base?*

My curiosity ran wild until I was able to get the answers I was looking for. That August, we clocked a lot of man-hours standing guard at the front gates of the MEK. It was a mindless assignment that kept us off the streets of downtown Fallujah, so I had little reason to complain. More often than not, we were accompanied by a tall, doughy, grey-haired gentleman named Mr. Ahmed. I'm not sure if that was even his real name, but it seemed to stick and was much easier to pronounce than some of the more throaty-sounding Arabic last names one hears over there. He'd assist us in clearing local civilian personnel seeking entry to our compound.

An Iranian political dissident who'd spent half his life in exile, he was intellectually astute and fluent in several languages. He had even lived in France at one point. Mr. Ahmed was a soft-spoken Marxist with a studious persona. From an ideological standpoint, the two of us couldn't have been more opposed to one another's views on economics. But as a political junkie and fellow bookworm, I got along with him just fine. Besides, I liked the man and found him to be a genuinely interesting fellow. I remember thinking that if he weren't stuck in Iraq, he could be lecturing in the ivory towers of UC Berkeley.

"So what's a guy with your smarts doing here, in Fallujah of all places?" I asked.

His life story was not a short one. I spent the better part of that August getting to know my new friend on a personal level while biting my lip every time he'd go off on some crazy political tangent. I didn't want to come off as overly intrusive, but I was genuinely curious about this man's background and had to know more. I wanted to know why he'd fled Iran, what the nature of his business was in Europe, and how he had wound up in Iraq. So I'd carefully pry for personal details, listening attentively as he spoke while sipping my chai and nibbling on dates and pita bread.

As it turned out, he and his colleagues belonged to the "People's Mujahadeen of Iran," better known as the MEK (Mujahadeen-e-Khalq), which our State Department and several foreign governments had long ago branded a terrorist organization. Hence, the name of our squadron's new base.

Now it makes sense! I thought.

Still, figuring out what exactly the MEK stood for on a philosophical level took a good many conversations with Mr. Ahmed. I also spent a considerable amount of time thumbing through pro-Mujahadeen pamphlets and magazines, which sat in piles in a little rest hooch at the front gate of our compound. Though most of this material was in French and Farsi, some of it was in English.

To pass time, I'd read their literature while on break. On the front cover of some magazines, I noticed the image of a red hammer and sickle – an iconic trademark of the international communist movement. In one of these publications, there were photographs of an MEK field training exercise, with one of the images seeming to stand out among the rest. It was a static tank column whose lead vehicle was being commanded by a female. A female tank commander – now that's something you don't see every day, I thought. It was intended to highlight their advocacy of women's rights (a radical concept by Middle Eastern standards).

After a couple weeks of poking around, I learned that our Iranian friends were basically hard-line socialists. Their political ideology was defined by a bizarre hodgepodge of ideas melding elements of their Shia Islamic faith with a revolutionary Marxist doctrine. In short, their whole aim was to overthrow the Islamic Republic of Iran and establish a secular socialist regime in its place.

Founded in the political unrest of the Sixties, the group's original intent was to confront Western interference in the internal affairs of their country. Over the course of the following decade, they assassinated a handful of American military attachés stationed in Tehran. They also teamed up with radical Islamists in 1979 to overthrow the Shah of Iran, who our CIA installed in 1953 after leading a coup against the democratically-elected Mohammad Mosaddeq (who had sought to end foreign control over Iran's oil supply by nationalizing it). The MEK also gave its stamp of approval to our embassy workers being taken hostage, and subsequentially opposed their release in 1981 – 444 days after the fact.

However, after helping to successfully depose the Shah, they soon found themselves at even greater odds with Ayatollah Khomeini and his rabid legion of followers. What ensued was a homicidal government-led crackdown on the MEK and their leftist sympathizers. The Mujahadeen came to detest the Islamic fundamentalists even more than the Shah, who had acted as America's puppet for two and a half decades.

Now backed into a corner, the MEK declared war on the newly forged Islamic Republic of Iran, launching a guerrilla campaign against Khomeini's regime. Scores of public figures and government officials were killed in a series of attacks initiated by their organization. Having been driven underground, they reestablished their party headquarters in France, but were subsequently expelled in 1986. Apparently the French wanted nothing to do with them, and refused to play host to an endless death match between the Mujahadeen and the belligerent new government of Iran.

With nowhere to go, they pleaded with Saddam Hussein for aid and comfort. Their timing was perfect. Iraq and Iran were already embroiled in a war of attrition, with upwards of a million combatants having perished on both sides. Saddam was more than delighted to bring the MEK into the fold, and they seemed equally thrilled to participate in his murderous crusade against Khomeini's regime. Soon enough, their ragtag army was outfitted with tanks and firearms, all courtesy of Saddam.

During guard one afternoon, I struck up a conversation with my new acquaintance, posing questions of a more personal nature.

"Mr. Ahmed, what of your family?" I asked. "Do they live here on base or somewhere in Europe?"

He paused and then sighed, and with a stiff look on his face replied, "My family is dead."

I wasn't sure what to say. I offered my deepest condolences. I didn't mean to sound nosey, but pressed him for more information. With bleary eyes, he told me of a government-led crackdown in Iran in 1988, in which thousands of civilians were killed — mostly political dissidents and the relatives thereof. Some mysteriously disappeared, never to be seen again. Others were openly hanged in the streets to dissuade the masses from stepping out of line.

This fellow's life wasn't short of tragedy, that's for sure.

In a separate conversation, I learned that some of his comrades were killed when their compound was bombed by American fighter jets during the invasion several months earlier. Apparently they were mistaken for Iraqi ground forces. Yet he seemed to have no axe to grind against the United States. It was the Iranian government he detested. He held a genuinely contemptuous view of the mullahs and the theocratic police state they had established.

One day, one of our guys joked with him, "Ya know, if Iran keeps pissing us off, we might have to invade them, too!"

His eyes lit up and a smile came to his face. "Oh, I pray this day comes! I pray Bush brings their government down!"

Still, for all the tragedy Mr. Ahmed has endured, I can't say that I feel entirely sorry for the MEK. Despite having recently renounced their past use of violence, they are by every definition a terrorist organization and maintain a cultish hold over their followers. What's more, after being granted asylum by the Iraqi government in the 1980s, they allegedly collaborated with Saddam's regime to stomp out the Kurdish rebellion in northern Iraq – better known as the *al-Anfal* campaign. That ultimately amounted to genocide. They're believed to have also been complicit in helping to put down the Shia uprising during the first Gulf War, in the spring of 1991. For that reason, many Iraqis want the MEK permanently expelled from their country. Last I knew, their status is in limbo, and I don't know what ever happened to Mr. Ahmed. I like to hope he made it out of that dusty old camp, but I don't know for sure and likely never will.

—

The second anniversary of 9/11 was fast upon us. Two years had passed in the blink of an eye, just like that. While in Iraq, I had been having recurring nightmares of that second plane – Flight 175 – slamming into the South Tower of the World Trade Center. I'd wake up every time in a cold sweat, relieved that it was just a dream, only to realize that it hadn't been. Suddenly, my eyes would shudder open. I'd find myself lying on a cot in a very strange room, with an M16 tipped against the wall and a pair of dog tags around my neck. A second or two would pass before I'd realize where I was at. It was a rattling experience every time.

I spent one of my last guard shifts at the MEK squabbling with Beckett over the wisdom of invading Iraq.

"So, Bryan, what do ya think of Bush now?"

"What the hell's that supposed mean?"

"You know exactly what I mean."

I'd been hoodwinked into supporting this war; Beckett had not. Though no conspiracy theorist, he believed the White House had ulterior motives, and that a lot of it had to do with oil. I tried dancing around the question, using a few Republican talking points to defend Bush's indefensible logic for plowing into Iraq without an exit strategy or any kind of plan for keeping the peace.

"So, you don't think Bush was just a little too eager to point the finger at Iraq for 9/11?" he asked. "Tell me, where are the weapons of mass destruction? Where're the al Qaeda?"

"No!" I exclaimed. "Because he couldn't risk letting us get hit again! He did it to keep us safe. Those days after September 11 were a very frightening period…what with all those anthrax-tainted letters floating around in the mail. And just knowing that Saddam was sitting on an arsenal of chemical and biological weapons…which, by the way, no one has proven they *don't* exist. It's a big desert, my friend. They're here somewhere. We'll find them. For all we know, they're probably sitting in a warehouse in Syria."

"Oh, so now they're in Syria? How convenient…" he said, shaking his head in disbelief at how gullible I was.

I knew what Beck was getting at. He was right. Operation Iraqi Freedom was a war without merit – a horrific machination dreamt up by starry-eyed military fanatics like Dick Cheney, Deputy Secretary of Defense Paul Wolfowitz, and Richard Perle, chairman of the Bush Administration's Defense Policy Board Advisory Committee. For years, these men had argued for the ousting of Saddam Hussein. Finally they'd gotten their way; September 11 was just the pretext they needed to embark on this ill-conceived conquest of theirs. Sure, their intentions were good (in wanting to democratize Iraq). But the path to hell is paved with good intentions.

Of course, I wasn't yet willing to accept that notion. So I continued about like a brainwashed automaton, equating patriotism with blind loyalty to the state – all while snubbing those who didn't support the war.

In reality, the decision to invade Iraq didn't materialize in light of new intelligence concerning Saddam Hussein's alleged stockpile of WMDs, or for that matter any effort on his part to reconstitute the programs which produced those weapons. Team Bush began piecing together their war plans shortly after 9/11, the narrative for regime change matching carefully selected intel designed to make a strong case for doing so. It's as if they acted on pure intuition, assuming their most unreliable sources to be rock solid, while not giving due consideration to any contradictory information that didn't fit their preconceived storyline.

Months earlier, on Feb 5, 2003, Secretary of State Colin Powell appeared before the UN Security Council, revealing to the world what America knew – or at least thought itself to know at the time – about Iraq's WMDs. In his possession, a thick dossier, complete with the transcripts of intercepted phone calls and a slideshow featuring high-tech satellite imagery and sketches of mobile laboratory facilities used to produce biological weapons. The mood was tense, this being the final inning for diplomacy. The talks had failed, and now war seemed imminent:

> My colleagues, every statement I make today is backed up by sources, solid sources. These are not assertions. What we're giving you are facts and conclusions based on solid intelligence. I will cite some examples, and these are from human sources…

> Numerous human sources tell us that the Iraqis are moving, not just documents and hard drives, but weapons of mass destruction to keep them from being found by inspectors…

> One of the most worrisome things that emerges from the thick intelligence file we have on Iraq's biological weapons is the existence of mobile production facilities used to make biological agents…

Powell knocked it out of the ballpark, at one point displaying a small glass phial, stating, "Less than a teaspoon full of dried anthrax in an envelope shut down the United States Senate in the fall of 2001…UNSCOM estimates that Saddam Hussein could have produced twenty-five thousand liters. If concentrated into this dry form, this amount would be enough to fill tens upon tens upon tens of thousands of teaspoons. And Saddam Hussein has not verifiably accounted for even one teaspoon full of this deadly material."

It was American political theatre at its finest. And that's just a sample of his speech, which he's now ashamed and embarrassed of, calling it a "blot" on his record as America's chief diplomat. Apparently he feels taken advantage of, his legacy forever tarnished by the sinister ambitions of lesser men. I remember watching bits of this presentation on TV a couple months before getting shipped off to the Middle East. I was totally sold, and so was the American public (yes, it was that compelling). But there's no point in shooting the messenger. Powell's a decent man, I believe. In fact, he's since called for a complete investigation into this whole debacle – an investigation that's unlikely to happen anytime soon, as it hasn't yet, and most likely never will.

As for President Bush's role in all this, I believe a very good man got *very* bad advice. Bush had campaigned on rebuilding the military and maintaining peace through strength, much as Reagan had done in the Eighties. But 9/11 changed his worldview, and he was persuaded to opt for regime change in Iraq at the bidding of Cheney, arguably the most powerful vice president in American history. Some called Iraq a war for oil; others claimed it was all about lining the pockets of defense contractors. Me personally, I think it mostly came down to a lot of half-baked ideas on how to bring democracy to the Middle East. I like George W. Bush, and believe he had the best of intentions. I just wish he hadn't gone down the path of toppling Saddam Hussein. In doing so, he unleashed something on the world we've yet to fully contain.

—

In Fallujah, our battle for hearts and minds amounted to an ineffectual strategy of one step forward, two steps back. For every enemy we greased, we must have killed two or three civilians by accident. That didn't sit well with the locals, nor was it a point of pride for any of us. Believe me, no soldier in his right mind wakes up thinking, *Ya know, I really feel like killing innocent people today.* But in war, shit happens. And if killing a few locals put a dent in our image, what happened August 17 really made us look bad.

Green Platoon was patrolling the Abu Ghraib district when a man aimed what appeared to be an RPG at one of their tanks, carefully steadying the device on his shoulder while facing them head-on at just under a hundred meters. In the spur of the moment – in what must have felt like a kill-or-be-killed situation – one of the tank commanders fixed the sights of his rifle on the man and fired six shots, killing him instantly. As it turned out, they hadn't killed an insurgent, but instead a *Reuters* cameraman. They had mistaken his bulky, shoulder-hoisted camera for an RPG.

The gentleman killed by Fox Troop wasn't just any reporter, but none other than *Mazen Dana* – an award-winning Palestinian journalist famed for his daring coverage of the Israeli-Palestinian conflict. In a follow-up article written by the *Washington Report on Middle East Affairs*, the following was said of Dana:

> Mazen Dana was a very brave man. As a cameraman for Reuters and a Palestinian living in the occupied West Bank city of Hebron, Dana had been shot, beaten, his bones broken, and chased and jailed by armed Israeli troops so many times that the sheer numbers blur into a surreal image of the cruelties of military occupation. Yet Dana carried on.
>
> There is no small irony that the final gunshot that took his life was not by an Israeli but an American, and not in Palestine but Iraq.

Ironic, indeed. The article goes on to note that international media rights groups such as the Committee to Protect Journalists have "called for a full inquiry" into what *really* happened. I know through other readings that similar organizations have even brought their grievances to the United Nations, demanding the world body pay greater attention to the substantially high number of journalists who've lost their lives covering the war in Iraq.

Dana's boss, Tom Glocer, then chief executive of *Reuters*, snootily pointed out that, "All of us have seen what a shoulder-held television camera looks like, it is a different-looking beast certainly during the afternoon sunlight. One should be able to tell from 50 yards away." But he acknowledges that "in conditions of war, young soldiers fearing for their own lives don't have a lot of time to make fine distinctions." Regarding this latter point, he's absolutely right.

The internet is rife with conspiratorial guesswork as to why Dana was killed, written by people who weren't even there when it happened. They inculpate us with trying to "kill the truth." Some have even speculated that he was deliberately wiped off the face of this earth for reporting on Abu Ghraib, as though he were on the verge of uncovering something big when the powers that be martyred him on camera.

But that simply isn't the case.

In reality, the platoon that gunned him down had been ambushed in an RPG attack just days earlier. One of their squads had been guarding a relatively secure site well outside of Fallujah when an RPG came screeching in, hitting their position dead-on as several of them were standing around outside of their tank, getting ready to bed-down for the evening. Fortunately, the round ended up being a dud, and nobody was killed or seriously wounded. Still, the warhead managed to brush the fingertips of one soldier and halfway removed one or two of them, leaving him with severed nubs for fingers.

If our guys seemed a little quick on the draw, their near brush with death is the only reason why. It's unfortunate that such a remarkable person was killed in an otherwise avoidable tragedy, but these things happen in war. Dana knew that. He knew what he was getting himself into when he came to Iraq. In fact, he can be referenced as having said all the way back in 2001 that, "I will continue with my work regardless of the hardships and even if it costs me my life."

Of course, the mother of all blunders came just one day after the second anniversary of 9/11. Our time at the MEK had drawn to a close, and we had just handed over control of Fallujah to a newly-arrived battalion of troops from the 82nd Airborne. While patrolling the eastern outskirts of the city, they intercepted two or three paramilitary-style FPF (Fallujah Protection Force) pickup trucks that were chasing a group of men involved in a highway robbery. They must have gotten spooked and assumed they were enemy targets because they shot up the trucks, killing no less than eight members of the FPF and wounding several others.

Then, believing themselves to be acting in self-defense, they trained their weapons on several armed guards standing outside a nearby Jordanian-run hospital, killing at least one or two Jordanian nationals. This time they had really screwed the pooch. Because that hospital had also served as a centre for various diplomatic exchanges, what the 82nd Airborne had done was practically tantamount to launching a unilateral strike on the sovereign nation of Jordan. Or at least that's how it was explained to me by Lieutenant Keegan. It was a public relations nightmare for the United States government. The State Department must have had a wonderful time explaining this "mishap" to the Jordanians. Colin Powell had to personally apologize for the incident.

Chapter Twelve

BURNT WAFFLES

OUR MARCH OUT of Fallujah was significant in that it marked the halfway point of what would end up being an almost year-long deployment. I tried to look at the situation through rose-colored lenses, as though I had just scaled an enormous mountain, and that it'd be "all downhill" from there on. I kept telling myself: *I can do this! If I made it this far, the rest will be a cakewalk.* Of course, I hadn't the slightest clue what to expect in the months ahead. All I knew was that we were relocating to al Asad. It's an enormous airbase located several hours west of Fallujah, somewhere in the heart of the Iraqi desert.

We took everything from the MEK that wasn't bolted down. We did so not out of necessity, but in hopes of ensuring a higher standard of living for ourselves in the months ahead. If it could fit somewhere in or on our Bradleys, it was coming with us. The air conditioners and all. Someone had even strapped a refrigerator to the front of their vehicle.

But we had other motives, too. There was simply no way we were leaving anything behind for the 82nd Airborne. Like a pair of rival football teams, we didn't like them, and they didn't like us. Since the birth of modern warfare, the Infantry and Cavalry have been locked in an endless squabble over who's more badass. Whereas they do most of the fighting, we're the tip of the spear. About the only thing we agree on in matters of war is that we both hate Marines (and I say that as the son of one). On more than one occasion, our guys nearly came to blows with theirs. Usually while standing around in crowded spaces, like the phone room and chow hall. It'd start with somebody cutting in line or talking shit about the other person's unit, and it would end with all the usual displays of machismo, with one guy threatening to beat the other guy's ass, though not following through on it.

So we made a point of leaving the 82nd with little to nothing, even taking the metal shit-burning barrels with us. Play silly games, win silly prizes! That's how we saw it. As our convoy passed through the front gates of the MEK, bidding farewell, we must have looked like a band of traveling Gypsies. That's how loaded down our vehicles were.

Later that afternoon, we reached al Asad. On our way in to base, I noticed an awkward sight – the fins of dug-up fighter jets protruding from the desert floor. During the invasion, the Iraqi Air Force had been missing in action. Now we knew why. They had literally gone underground, so to speak. Saddam's military never recovered from the beating it sustained during the first Gulf War, especially with sanctions in place. In lieu of fighting an air battle they couldn't win, they opted to just bury their planes rather than watch them get shot down. In the far-reaching search for Saddam's WMDs, no stone was left unturned. And since those weapons didn't exist, the most our hunt ever turned up were a bunch of Soviet-era fighter jets – mostly leftover relics from the Cold War that were in no shape to fly.

I wasn't in al Asad a week before getting sent out of country for some much-needed R&R. A bunch of us were flown by helicopter to BIAP, and from there we caught a C-130 to Qatar for several days of rest and relaxation on an Air Force base in Doha. There, a soldier's idea of vacation means lolling about like an airman, copping z's in an air-conditioned building. It was something we hadn't done in a while. Like any military base, it was a heavily controlled environment. There was even a three-beers-per-day drinking limit that was enforced through a computerized tracking system. Still, it was an opportunity for us grunts to blow off steam and get caught up on sleep. So I didn't take my time there for granted.

With our eyes alone, we ravaged the body of every decent-looking Air Force girl stationed at Camp Doha, carefully sneaking glances as we crossed paths. I'm sure we must have come off like a bunch of sexually deprived brutes, but these were the first sleeveless women we'd seen in five months. Even in uniform they looked cute, especially in those sexy little blue and grey running shorts.

If all that eye candy wasn't enough, the real treat was whetting our appetites on actual food. Apart from the usual string of fast food restaurants, there was even a Chili's on base. For the past three months, Fox Troop had been kept on a steady diet of canned "Country Captain Chicken." It was fed to us nightly at chowtime. Rumor had it a supply sergeant at Squadron didn't like our first sergeant, so he kept sending our unit the same field rations. A favorite in the coastal South, the Army's version of this meal was the most reviled dish on our menu, tasting something like stewed roadkill. Lieutenant Keegan described it as "the most vile concoction known to man." So Chili's legendary Baby Back Ribs were like manna from Heaven.

After taking our seats and placing our orders, several of us broke out into song, using our eating utensils as musical instruments: "I want my baby back, baby back, baby back, I want my baby back, baby back, baby back. I want my Chili's baby back ribs! Chili's baby back ribs! Barbeque sauce!!!"

Many of the airmen at Camp Doha looked at us as if we were a bunch of Neanderthals, obnoxiously crowding them out with our undesired presence. It wasn't out of disrespect; there was just no frame of reference by which these Air Force guys could relate to what we'd been through the last few months. Though we're all cogs in the same machine, each one serving his or her intended purpose, we're the ones who get worked harder than most everyone else – and it really shows. You could see it in the bags under our eyes.

In the short run, none of us wanted to go back to Fox Troop. Especially after seeing how well the Air Force treats its people. Nearly everything about the Air Force seemed better than Army life, from their shorter deployments to their drastically higher stand-ard of living. Along with rarely being placed in harm's way, they don't treat their lower-ranking en-listed personnel like chattel. Plus their chow halls are nicer, and their barracks rooms are like studio apart-ments compared to what we live in.

That got a few of us thinking: *Man, screw the Army! When I get out, I'm joining the Chair Force. Those guys have it made!*

—

Something cool happened shortly before I went on R&R: I was promoted to the rank of "specialist." During the ceremony, which took place at the MEK, the "private" insignia on both of my collars was yanked off and replaced with specialist rank – an honor eighteen months in the making. Once known as "Private Fuck Face," I had ascended the ranks, earn-ing the title "Specialist Bryan." I couldn't have been prouder...

Then the "blood ranking" commenced.

Blood ranking is an archaic rite of passage, now gone with the Army's decision to modernize its wardrobe. Before the Army switched over to its new, fashionably chic, digitally camouflaged combat uniforms (with their spiffy shoulder pockets and Velco rank, nametags, and unit patches), in the rear soldiers wore green and black BDUs, or "Battle Dress Uniforms," and while deployed to the Sandbox, DCUs, or "Desert Camouflage Uniforms." As was custom back then – before the days of Velco insignia – each soldier above me in rank or time in grade lined up to congratulate me by pounding down on my rank with both hands and all his might, as if each of them was trying to break me in two. One by one, all the NCOs in Blue Platoon filed through to get their shot in, including Kublai Khan, a onetime user of anabolic steroids.

To each side of my neck the flesh just below my collar bones was lacerated, as the "dammits" (the little bronze caps shielding the pointy metal tips on the backside of the rank) are always removed prior to a blood-ranking ceremony, maximizing the pain with each blow. I looked as though I'd just been mauled by a gang of vampires; the collar of my Army-brown t-shirt stained with little patches of blood. But I didn't care. I was too busy reveling in the glory of my promotion.

Well now it was time to get new rank sewn onto my uniforms. So while I was in Qatar, I drifted into a Korean-run alterations shop on base, no different from the ones on and around Fort Carson.

I remember waiting to get new rank sewn onto my raggedy, desert-colored uniforms. As I stood there, I noticed a few unit patches for sale. They were pinned on the wall behind the cash register in neatly lined rows. Each one had been sewn from scratch – the 101st Airborne, Special Forces, 1st Armored Division, and yes, my unit, the 3rd Armored Cavalry

Regiment. Or as we're known back home, the "Regiment of Mounted Riflemen." I never liked our unit patch. The design is outdated, and it looks too much like a Boy Scouts merit badge. It's small and round, depicting a lone bugle with two words stitched above in bold lettering: *BRAVE RIFLES*. That's our regimental slogan.

But this patch was different. Something about it was off. As I squinted some, I exploded in a fit of uncontrollable laughter, noticing that it actually read "BURNT WAFFLES." But there was some truth to this. Five months into our deployment, I felt more like a burnt waffle than a brave rifle.

Chapter Thirteen
MARCHING ONWARD

ON NOVEMBER 2, about three dozen soldiers slotted for R&R filed in through the back of a Chinook helicopter destined for BIAP. Most of them were from the 3rd ACR, to include some from our squadron. Less than an hour later, they were unexpectedly shot down by a shoulder-fired anti-aircraft rocket, forcing their bird out of the sky somewhere near Fallujah. In all, fifteen soldiers were killed and many more wounded. It served as a devastating reminder that our enemies were growing stronger by the day. In just six months, they had gone from pelting us with stones in April, to blowing up our Humvees in July, and now downing our helicopters in November.

Months earlier, we clashed with Ba'th Party apparatchiks who simply wanted us out of Iraq. But these guys were far more extreme. For they fought with a machinegun in one hand, and a Koran in the other. In essence, we were battling al Qaeda in Iraq (AQI). And their goal wasn't limited to driving the "American infidels" off their soil. They had a grander vision of someday establishing an Islamic Caliphate.

In the counterterrorism community, they're commonly referred to as *Takfiris*. As any observer of Middle Eastern affairs can tell you, *Salafism* is a fundamentalist strain of Sunni Islam that's native to the Arabian Peninsula. Whereas many Salafists are sympathetic to al Qaeda and its affiliates – if not outright supportive – most are not. Takfiris, however, are Salafist crazies who claim the right carte blanche to carry out Allah's will through armed force – to include suicide bombings, decapitations and kidnapping. You're familiar with the 9/11 hijackers? Yeah, those types. Call it the bin Laden school of thought. As few as their adherents may be, they'll stop at nothing to prove their point – even if it comes down to steering a truck bomb into a crowded marketplace and razing an entire city block, killing hundreds.

At the time, our company had been occupying FOB Byers, named after our late commander. It was situated somewhere between the small city of Ar Rutbah and the H3 Airfield, which are both located near the Jordanian border and well within the hem of the al Anbar province. Encircled by a long and windy stretch of barren acreage, we'd been there for the last few weeks, reconnoitering the western frontiers of Iraq.

While there, Fox got tasked out on a special assignment to gather information on the possible whereabouts of Captain Michael Scott Speicher, a missing Navy pilot whose fighter jet was shot down over western Iraq twelve years earlier, during the first Gulf War.[‡‡] It was believed he may have been taken alive and held prisoner, having probably been executed sometime before the initiation of Operation Iraqi Freedom. Saddam's regime had long denied those charges. But given its lack of respect for human rights and international law, it wouldn't have been unlike them to execute a prisoner of war – especially an American fighter pilot. Unfortunately, the crash site

---

[‡‡] It wasn't until August 2, 2009 that the mystery of Captain Speicher's disappearance was finally solved. An Iraqi national living in the area lead a group of U.S. Marines to his burial site. Turns out he didn't survive the crash, and according to the locals, was buried by a group of Bedouin tribesmen. May he rest in peace.

of his F/A 18 Hornet only seemed to verify the unknown, providing no clues as to whether he even survived the attack.

A separate afternoon, we drove out to the H3 Airfield. For as far as the eye could see, at varying intervals of the base there were a great many concrete bunkers, all containing vast amounts of unguarded munitions – the kinds used to blow apart our Humvees and supply trucks – there for the taking. It was like a terrorist free-for-all. There were also stockpiles of mortar rounds and RPG warheads just lying out in plain sight, rusting under the low blue skies of the Mesopotamian desert. We're talking tens of millions of dollars in weapons. An arms dealer would have gotten a serious hard-on just being there, imagining how to offload it on the highest bidder.

I noticed fresh tire tracks leading away from many of these sites. It was evidence that scores of people had already helped themselves to truckloads of assorted weaponry. Probably jihadists and common criminals hoping to sell the stuff on the black market. In the Eighties, most of Iraq's arms purchases came from Russia and China, some from France. Of course, during the Iraq-Iran war, we also supplied Saddam with a good bit of weaponry to defeat the Ayatollah. It was ironic and perhaps a little unnerving to occasionally find *MADE IN THE USA* stamped on the sides of certain armaments. Just like those overpriced fighter jets buried beneath the desert floor of al Asad, the money spent on this stuff could have gone towards building schools, roads, libraries, and hospitals. Instead, it went towards feeding the despotism of Saddam Hussein, our onetime ally.

The H3 Airfield was just one of many unguarded weapons sites throughout Iraq.

Prior to the invasion, then Army Chief of Staff General Eric Shinseki publicly stated that if we were to invade Iraq, we'd need "something in the order of several hundred thousand soldiers" to not just hold the country, but to effectively secure locations like the H3 Airfield. Instead, his concerns were brushed aside by the likes of Donald Rumsfeld and Paul Wolfowitz (the latter of whom I've always thought to resemble an oversized ventriloquist dummy).

Wolfowitz, a Republican whiz kid with no military background, said that Shinseki's troop estimates were "widely off the mark." Consequently, their gross miscalculation in the number of soldiers needed to secure Iraq cost our military dearly. Because there were not enough boots on the ground to secure these unguarded weapon depots, the insurgency now had free access to an arsenal of weaponry that could be used to impede the Bush Administration's lofty postwar reconstruction plans. And whereas Shinseki was believed to have been quietly forced into an early retirement for voicing such concerns, his civilian bosses were given a pat on the back for their *brilliant* execution of the war. Adding insult to injury, Bush even awarded Paul Bremer the Presidential Medal of Freedom for his "meritorious contribution" to the security of the United States. How's that for irony?

—

With the holidays approaching, a few of the guys in my unit latch onto a new rumor that we'll be home by Christmas. Word has it that Lieutenant Anderson's father, a brigadier general, had spoken with Donald Rumsfeld, inquiring into the date our unit is scheduled to return to Fort Carson. It's said that Secretary Rumsfeld had personally assured him that we'd all be having "a very Merry Christmas," those being his exact words.

Aside from the fact that no such exchange had even taken place, and that any rumor to the contrary is complete horseshit, many take comfort in the thought that *Just maybe it's true! Maybe we'll all be home by Christmas!* Well, I'm not buying it! But either way, I sense that Fox won't be so lucky as to ride this war out sitting on the edge of nowhere. Since coming to FOB Byers, we've done little more than sit around all day watching *Bang Bus* and *Girls Gone Wild.* All whilst guzzling down can after can of non-alcoholic Budweiser. That cushy lifestyle we've readapted to is about to come screeching to a halt, as we're being sent back into the meatgrinder of Iraq.

As of late, we've been receiving daily reports that our counterparts in Tiger Squadron are catching hell in al Qa'im, a small though volatile city on the Syrian border. That doesn't augur well for any hopes of some grand yuletide homecoming. As I see it, unless I intentionally shoot myself in the foot, there's simply no way I'll be home in the loving embrace of my family before the year's end. A huge operation is in the making, and Fox Troop has just been designated a "regimental asset," assuring that we'll get "hey youed!" the moment higher-up feels the need to shuffle us around on the geopolitical chessboard of western Iraq.

Sure enough, about two weeks later we're out there in al Qa'im, just a stone's throw from the Syrian border. Dubbed "Operation Rifles Blitz," we've been sent to aid Tiger in their big push to cleanse the city of insurgent activity.

It's November 22, and my spirits are as downcast as the weather. In Iraq, "winter" is typically met with brisk temperatures and torrential downpours. It's the weekend, and today marks my twenty-second birthday. In war, nobody gets Saturdays off, much less their birthday. Instead of a night on the town in Colorado Springs, I'll be spending this evening in the damp and chilly confines of my lonely driver's hull —

with just me and my thoughts. I've long been cursed with having a birthday that falls on the yearly anniversary of John F. Kennedy's assassination. Ever since kindergarten, I was reminded on every birthday by my elders that "on this day in history, President Kennedy was assassinated" x-number of years prior. This time around my birthday coincides with the fortieth anniversary of his untimely death; or just five days shy of Thanksgiving.

I'm cold and wet. My clothes are muddy, and the temperature is just a few degrees above freezing. Steady beads of water are trickling in through my driver's hatch, soaking the entire lower half of my body. As I sit there taking orders from Keegan, who's perched in the turret, I try to warm myself up. I detach the main hose connected to the gas particulate air filtration unit to my left, cleverly running the device in through the crotch of my pants. I turn it on, cranking the heat all the way up. In the event of a chemical attack, the machine's sole function is to provide the driver with a clean and filtrated air supply. Well, I've just found another use for it: heat.

We're just two days into this mission, and already Lieutenant Keegan wants to put a boot in my ass. Mostly on account of my erratic driving. Back in August, his usual driver received orders for Fort Polk, Louisiana. As a result of his departure from our platoon, I was "promoted" and reassigned to Blue 1, taking over where he left off. I've handled a Bradley before, but have had little experience operating one in urban terrain. On relatively short notice, I've been thrust into the driver's seat for the largest operation of the entire deployment. I'm desperately trying to "be all I can be" from behind that steering column, but at every turn all I can seem to do is piss off Blue 1.

"Bryan, can you explain why you just rolled over that shiny, metallic disk lying in our path?"

"Because it was just hubcap, Sir."

"And you know this because you're an ordinance specialist?"

"No, Sir."

"Then don't drive over things that look like fucking landmines!"

"Yes, Sir!"

I won't lie. Overall, I'm a pretty lousy driver. Right now, Keegan has every right to be pissed off. Tiger has already lost one Bradley to an anti-tank landmine. So it's important that I not drive over suspicious-looking objects or cut corners too sharply, where hidden explosives lay. Otherwise, I can get our whole crew blown to kingdom come.

Still, I'm having one hell of a time trying to read his mind. This mission kicked off at 0500 on November 20, and already we've reached loggerheads. When our column is at a standstill and I see the vehicle in front of us slowly creep forward, I try to show some initiative by moving ahead without being told. That usually gets me hollered at: "Hey, dipshit, did I say go?!" But when I don't move on instinct and choose to wait for his command, I also get yelled at for not stepping on the gas: "Bryan, move out!!! You need to wake up and get with the program! When Blue 5 moves, you follow! Is that so hard to understand?"

"No, Sir!"

"You go when I tell you to go," he says, "and you don't stop until I say so. Is that understood?"

"Yes, Sir!"

"OK, that's what I like to hear."

He tells me to pivot right, and that's when I decide to play stupid. We're not in enemy contact, so I decide to push his buttons right then and there. I know full well what he meant. He wants me to spin us around, doing a full 180, and then follow Blue 5. Instead, at his command to pivot right I do just that, pivoting clockwise until given the order to stop. See, when told to "pivot right" just seconds earlier, Keegan never specified when to stop. So I continue pivoting in circles as if I'm a deranged circus carnie refusing to let terrified children off my carousel wheel.

By the second or third around-we-go, I'm quickly beseeched with the following question: "Bryan, why the fuck are you pivoting us in circles?!"

"Sir, you said 'pivot right.' So I'm pivoting right," I reply, awaiting his response.

"You know what I meant, dipshit!!! Now spin us around and follow Blue 5. Don't make me come down there and skull-fuck you with the turret wrench!"

Keegan is livid. In the Army, a proverbial "skull-fucking" is an expression of serious disapproval with one's subordinates. I've pissed him off, and this is just the beginning.

Sometime before noon, we're parked and I happen to glance at our vehicle from the engine deck. I suddenly notice that my rucksack (which I had strapped to the right side of the track's exterior, along with everyone else's duffel bags) is missing. This isn't good, and not because I dread the thought of wearing the same pair of water-logged socks and underwear for the next two weeks. Of greater concern, I don't want any of my uniforms falling into enemy hands.

Earlier that morning, I was ordered to pull up next to some brick wall so that a sniper team from the 101st Airborne could easily disembark from the rear crew hatch of our Bradley and set up an observation point on a nearby rooftop. At every command to nudge closer and closer to that old brick wall, my rucksack was mangled and ripped until it finally broke free, only to be left behind in the streets like a gift bag for whoever was lucky enough to find the thing.

After alerting Lieutenant Keegan of the situation, we drive back to where it all happened. With the patience of a saint, he starts bartering with the locals to get it back. Yet nobody claims to have seen it. So he makes them an offer they can't refuse (no, he didn't threaten to kill them). The deal is that if they return my rucksack and all its contents, they'll be generously rewarded with a full box of MREs and a case or two of bottled water. It's a pretty sweet offer, especially given the fact it's Ramadan. Within minutes of Keegan's proposal, it magically reappears. Whoever had found my rucksack at daybreak must have rifled through it and taken some of the contents, but I don't care. I still have my uniforms, socks, t-shirts, and underwear. I can live without the missing beanie and AA batteries, and since there are no weapons of mass destruction in Iraq, I don't have much need for the anti-chemical weapon protective outerwear (some of which is gone).

We were told this mission would last ten days. Well, twelve hours in, I've already had enough. As evening approaches, it's obvious we'll be doing a lot of around-the-clock patrols meant to keep our enemies off the streets. Normally, I'd install my "night sight" device by fastening it to the center periscope of my driver's hatch, allowing me to see in the dark while out on patrol. But I'd been having mechanical issues with mine, and found it much easier to roll about with my hatch popped open and a pair of night-vision goggles in my right hand.

Later that evening, we're patrolling a certain district in the nearby city of al Karblah, driving through a skein of labyrinthine streets delineated by tall concrete walls on each side. As I approach a narrow T-shaped intersection, I pan my head to the right to see if I'm clear to make the turn. Suddenly, there's a massive explosion at the nose of my vehicle. From the corner of my left eye, I see a bright fireball. I instinctively coil back in my seat, slam on the brakes, and jerk my head to the left, realizing that in failing to make the turn, I've just plowed into an electrical transformer. I breathe a sigh of relief and am thankful to discover that I haven't rolled over a landmine. But this isn't entirely good – for the entire district of eastern al Karblah goes black, porch lights and all.

And it's my fault…

I've just knocked out the electricity to an entire city grid, like I'm some kind of one-man demolition crew.

At daybreak, we pass by to inspect the damage. It's even worse than we thought. As we approach the site, all that can be seen is a muddy set of vehicle tracks leading up to the scene of the crime. The transformer is all mashed up, and clearly inoperable. Even worse, I learn there'll be no repairing it until our Civil Affairs team can allocate the many thousands of dollars needed to get the power back up and running. I feel like a colossal moron. The locals are irate and probably think that my actions were a deliberate measure intended to punish them for passively supporting the insurgency.

For the next day or so, everyone in the platoon was busting my chops.

"Bryan! Watch out -- a transformer!!! Hahaha…"

I thought I'd never hear the end of it. Some charged that I had fallen asleep at the wheel, while most others accepted my earnest admission to being the worst driver in all of Fox Troop.

—

By the time all was said and done, we had spent over a month in the western deserts of Iraq supporting

Operation Rifles Blitz. It was a far cry from the ten days we were originally told it would last.

We came crawling back to al Asad on December 23, just two days before Christmas. I remember that day all too well. It was cold out, and I was shivering from inside my driver's hull. The Army had just issued us these really nice black winter fleeces – the kind you might see advertised in a North Face catalog, minus the logo. Everyone loved them. Not only were they comfortable, they were stylish, too. The only problem was that even though they were issued to us by the US Army, they weren't considered "Army-issued" military apparel – meaning that, cold weather or not, it was a violation of Army Regulation "670-1" to wear them outside the wire. Therefore, they rarely got worn at all. So as I sat there dreaming how much cozier I'd be if only I could wear what the Army itself had issued me, my new winter fleece remained balled-up somewhere in the bottom of my duffel bag, completely unutilized.

As we pulled in through the front gates of our base, there was a nasty rainstorm underway, and the internal comms on Blue 1 temporarily shorted out. Keegan's voice was reduced to a dull murmur, barely audible through my CVC (Combat Vehicle Crewman's Communication Helmet). So I just trailed Blue 5. There wasn't much else I could do. Nor was there any use in getting pissed off about it. We'd made it back – all of us! Together, as one, we survived that final mission, having lost no men nor taken any casualties. Our vehicle could have seized-up right on the spot, overheating and dying of engine failure, and I wouldn't have given two shits. I was through with this place. From the moment I hung that final left turn into al Asad, I knew I'd be making it home alive. With a major sense of relief washing over me, I felt as though I had just finished a marathon.

Back at our hangar on al Asad, there was a small mountain of care packages awaiting us, as well as a Christmas feast in the making. Sure, this wouldn't be the same as spending Christmas at home, but our camaraderie helped ease the strain of being away for the holidays, six thousand miles from our loved ones. So either way, I had to count my blessings.

As I sat in the chow hall two days later, gorging on my Christmas dinner, I paused for a moment to give thanks and remind myself how fortunate I was to have grown up in the United States of America. That strong sense of thanksgiving was spurred on by a story I'd recently heard.

Weeks earlier, in al Qa'im, a saga unfolded that was unique to anything we'd encountered since setting foot in Iraq. In one of those small villages near the Syrian border, an Iraqi boy – age thirteen – approached Dragon Troop one afternoon, claiming to have insider's knowledge of the insurgency. He said that his father was a local insurgent ring leader, as well as an abusive tyrant who was demanding that he take up arms against the Americans. He also claimed to know the who's who of those creating problems in Tiger's AO (area of operations), plus the whereabouts of various weapon caches.

As a clever ploy, he requested to be taken into custody, to give his family and friends the impression that he had just been forcibly detained by American troops. Naturally, this roused the suspicions of every soldier in Dragon Troop, since there was no telling who this kid was, or whether he was in cahoots with the enemy. But his story proved solid. In the following weeks, the intel he provided helped Tiger Squadron dismantle an entire network of enemy fighters in the western al Anbar province, resulting in the capture of several dozen high value targets, including his own father, a former officer in Saddam's Republican

Guard. In the short run, enemy attacks in the area withered to a near standstill, sparing the lives of numerous servicemen. News of his good deeds spread like wildfire, as even the White House took notice.

He continued to work closely with Dragon Troop, identifying terrorist suspects and revealing the exact locations of their weapon caches. Given all he'd done to support us, it wasn't long before the guys developed a great fondness for this kid. They became like older brothers, nicknaming him "Steve-O." Their first sergeant, Daniel Hendrix, all but took on the role of surrogate father, treating the boy as if he were his own son. He didn't have to, but it was the right thing to do, and so he did.

As their bond grew and young Steve-O cozied up to his new American pals, becoming their chief informant, local fighters grew wise to who'd been leaking all their secrets. By then, his father was already in custody, and his family began receiving death threats. Before Dragon Troop could swoop in to save them, insurgents ruthlessly executed his mother in retaliation for conspiring with us. If it was of any consolation, First Sergeant Hendrix was the first to tell Steve-O that his mother had been killed. From that moment on, he selflessly vowed to fight tooth-and-nail to get this kid into the United States, no matter how long it'd take. He promised the boy he'd make it happen.

As the 3rd ACR returned to Fort Carson, Steve-O remained in country, continuing to live on base with a group of Marines who relieved us that February. Meanwhile, on the home front, Hendrix dealt with miles of red tape in trying to get Steve-O entry into the United States. Fortunately, he wasn't alone. There were many people in high places who were eager to help, realizing the sacrifices this boy had made on our behalf. After six months of behind-the-scenes paperwork, Steve-O finally got his visa. He was bumped to the front of the line and permitted entrance into the US later that September.

Not only had First Sergeant Hendrix kept his word, he took the boy under his wing, moving the teen into his home until better living arrangements could be made. In a symbolic gesture intended to give Steve-O a feeling of what it meant to be on top of the world, on his first day in the US, Hendrix drove the boy to the top of Pikes Peak in Colorado Springs, fourteen thousand feet above sea level, overlooking Fort Carson. The story's as heartwarming as it is tragic. I remember thinking that if this hadn't happened in real life, it would have made a great plot for a novel. In fact, many would later read about it in the pages of *A Soldier's Promise: The Heroic True Story of an American Soldier and an Iraqi Boy*. The two even made a guest appearance together on Oprah, where Steve-O got to meet his favorite actor, John Travolta.[§§]

So as I sat in the chow hall that evening, banqueting on a generous helping of mashed potatoes with gravy, I tried to remind myself that in spite of everything I had endured in the past year, I was blessed to have grown up in Ashtabula, Ohio, and to have been raised in a society that values freedom, tolerance, reason, and individual liberty. As they say, God bless America!

[§§] In researching this story, it was with utter shock that I received the news of what's since become of Steve-O, or "Jasim Mohammad Hassin Ramadon." Eight years after being granted entrance to the US, he was charged in connection to the July 21, 2012 sexual assault of a 53-year-old woman in Colorado Springs, along with several other Iraqi males. The responding officers described it as one of the most gruesome crime scenes they had ever witnessed – the poor woman still alive, though beaten to a pulp and bleeding heavily from the attack. For his crime, he's currently serving twenty-eight years to life.

—

We spend that January servicing our vehicles in preparation for redeployment. I've never worked harder in my life, but we get the job done on time, and that's about all that matters. After turning in our Bradleys, I assume there'll be little more for us to do than idle away on perimeter guard. As usual, my assumptions are wrong.

Blue Platoon is informed that we'll be drawing a platoon's worth of light-skinned Humvees and heading back out to secure vast stretches of highway for the "safe passage" of Iraqi Muslims making the "Hajj," – i.e., the annual pilgrimage to Mecca, Saudi Arabia, their holiest of holy cities. In accordance with the Five Pillars of Islam, every God-fearing Muslim is required to make the Hajj at least once in his or her lifetime. Each year, millions of loyal adherents to the Koran descend upon Mecca for an event that leaves many in a state of spiritual ecstasy. It's considered a rite of passage for every able-bodied Muslim who's in tune with their faith and capable of making the journey. And due to the ever-revolving nature of the Islamic calendar, all this religious hoopla just happens to fall on those last couple weeks we're in town.

Well, la-di-frickin'-da! With just two weeks left, here we go again…

We load our Hummers up and exit through a break in the fence just beyond the guard towers, driving off en route to FOB Quinn, several hours away. The outpost is named after Staff Sergeant Michael Quinn of Eagle Troop, who was killed in Fallujah back in May of the previous year (the same night my vehicle took an RPG).

At FOB Quinn we do route clearance patrols all day long, and for the sole purpose of preventing attacks on Shia pilgrims by al Qaeda. In recent months, there's been an influx of foreign troublemakers hoping to upset the applecart in Iraq. Their goal is to foment a holy war between the Sunnis and Shia. Part of me feels this mission borders on complete insanity, especially this late in the game. No doubt, the last thing I want to read about in the news is a busload of Shia pilgrims going up in flames. But I don't want their safety to come at the cost of American lives. Iraqis, I'm convinced, should be doing this – not Americans.

Twice a day, we drive in a straight path for hours on end, chasing the horizon, just waiting to get hit by an IED – only to turn around and head back to base. Then we wake up the following morning and do the same thing again. I'm nervous as hell each time we head outside the wire. At the beginning of each patrol, I say a *Hail Mary!* and hope to God we'll make it back without incident. The mission lasts about two weeks. Though we take no casualties, I don't like the idea of jeopardizing American lives to quell Iraq's domestic troubles.

I begin to think, *Why should we get blown to pieces defending a bunch of people who probably don't even want us in their country?*

Part of me feels this mission is well outside the purview of American jurisdiction and exceeds what was asked of me upon taking my oath of enlistment. I had sworn to "support and defend the Constitution of the United States against all enemies, foreign and domestic." Nowhere in that oath did I pledge to give my life doing for Iraqis what they ought to be doing for themselves, no matter how well-intentioned the endgame. If I wanted to die in somebody else's civil war, I would have signed up as a U.N. peacekeeper. But at the same time, I don't want all we've fought for to go to waste. If Iraq gets overrun by jihadists, then we're all screwed. So what's the solution? I'm not sure there is one, to be honest.

Chapter Fourteen
HOMECOMING

A COUPLE WEEKS later, we ceased operations at FOB Quinn and returned to al Asad. By then, the Marines had moved in to relieve our unit. Sometime near the end of February, we boarded a large military aircraft that swept us off the face of Iraq and deposited us at a small airbase somewhere in neighboring Turkey. From there, it was on to Germany, and then Banjor, Maine, where everyone in our company was greeted by a group of old flag-waving vets who'd fought in Korea and Vietnam. I'm not sure how they even knew we were coming, but a whole squad of them had shown up in the hours past midnight to welcome us home. As our plane was being refueled, we stood around exchanging war stories and munching on some homemade cookies their wives had baked us.

Like Iraq, neither of those wars was very popular when they were our age. Especially Vietnam; everyone else forgot about Korea, as if it never happened. The men who fought and spilt their blood there came home to a nation that didn't appreciate their sacrifices or honor its commitment to its veterans. I guess this was their way of righting history, to make sure we didn't show up at that airport feeling unwanted or somehow out of place.

On this otherwise joyous occasion, not everybody was smiling. Somewhere between Point A and Point B, one of our guys got dumped by his fiancée via telephone (apparently Jody got his girl), and another was busted in Germany trying to score some pot between flights. He tried talking one of the mechanics into arranging a drug deal with his boys in Colorado Springs, and it all went south from there. In battle and play, our unit's reputation always preceded us. Seeing how nearly ten percent of Fox Troop had "pissed hot" just weeks before the deployment, testing positive for the use of marijuana and cocaine, the latter came as no surprise. But that's how we roll in Fox Troop. Sure, a few of our guys may have been unfit for garrison life, but when the going got tough, our reliability in combat was unmatched by the other units of the 3rd ACR. That's why we were regarded as a "regimental asset," even if we probably seemed more like a liability to our chain of command.

Just before dawn, our plane touched ground in Colorado Springs. From there, we were shuttled to Fort Carson in commercial buses. As we were ferried home, many of us scanned vigilantly from the vehicles' side windows. Some eyeballing suspicious objects like trashcans and curbside shrubbery, others scanning rooftops and dimly lit alleyways. If we seemed a little on edge, as though something could blow up at any given moment, it's only because our collective sense of survival was stuck in overdrive.

In ebullient anticipation of our welcome home ceremony, we filed out of the buses and quickly assembled into formation, just outside the Special Events Center. Then Captain Reinhardt marched us inside. There were thousands of camera flashes, and an enormous *WELCOME HOME!* banner dangled overhead. The crowd was ecstatic, many gushing with emotion. Like us, they had waited with great patience and uncertainty for this very moment. A handful of smiling reporters paced the sidelines of this gathering, snapping photos of us as if they were paparazzi stalking a group of celebrities. It felt wonderful standing before them, knowing that after all these months we hadn't been forgotten.

Everything was handled very procedurally. The ceremony concluded with Reinhardt rendering a salute to his higher-up, pivoting around on the ball of his right foot, facing us, and then bellowing out as loudly as he could: "FOX TROOP…DISMISSED!" Those with family in attendance dashed off to be with their loved ones, while those of us who didn't have anybody waiting around for them hung out just long enough to shake a few hands and exchange smiles with reporters before getting driven back to the barracks.

How I spent the next couple days is sort of a blur, but later that week, I came back to work clean-shaven and well rested – though not at all eager to dive back into the usual grind of our unit's six-to-five work routine. Something about those eleven-hour workdays just didn't appeal to me.

A few of us were involuntarily selected to participate in an upcoming welcome home parade for the 3rd ACR, myself included. It was being held downtown on Saturday morning. The City of Colorado Springs couldn't fit all five thousand of us on Tejon Street. Instead, each squadron contributed x-number of personnel to stand in for our regiment.

I could think of a hundred good ways to spend that day, and marching around in some dog and pony show wasn't exactly what I had in mind. After five days behind the wheel of his big rig, my dad had just gotten off the road. We hadn't even seen each other since I got back. I had originally intended to drive up to his cabin that morning, but now my plans would have to be postponed until after the parade.

I called him up, fuming over how I wouldn't be making it up to the cabin until later that evening.

"Dad, they're always pulling this shit at the last minute! It never ends…It's like the Army thrives on constantly dicking us Joes over…"

Then I was calmed by his words.

He reminded me, "Son, I know you're not looking forward to this and all, but a lot of really good people went to the effort of throwin' this thing for you guys because in their eyes, you're all heroes. Keep in mind that when we came home from Vietnam there was no one standing around waving flags and 'welcome home' signs, showering us with praise. In fact, we were spit on by college students and called 'baby killers.'

"Some of my friends didn't make it back, and neither did some of yours. So when you're out there today, enjoy it, and be grateful that you made it home alive and in one piece. Keep your head up and march with pride, and don't let anyone take this day from you, because you boys earned it."

Chapter Fifteen
STOP-LOSS

JUST ONE MONTH after returning, we learn that we have orders for a deployment to Iraq in Spring 2005. That means I'll be getting "stop-lossed," or held past my contractual obligation of three years and sent back to the Sandbox...along with a bunch of guys who had pegged their hopes on either getting out in the coming year, or altogether retiring. According to Title 10, United States Code, Section 12305(a): "...the President may suspend any provision of law relating to promotion, retirement, or separation applicable to any member of the armed forces who the President determines is essential to the national security of the United States."

It's a major kick in the balls! We all knew it was coming. It was only a matter of time...But Not. This. Soon. We've literally just made it home, and now we're chomping at the bit to make deadlines for a second go at this splendid little foray into nation building. A year may sound like ample time to prime any unit for combat, but when you consider the sheer amount of training and preparation that goes into readying an entire armored cavalry regiment for battle (to include the overseas transportation of military equipment), it's all barely enough time for things to play out according to schedule.

With everyone taking leave and our war toys stuck in transit, life is pretty calm the first three months we're home. But after this brief respite, our days regain their old and toilsome pace. Sixty-hour work weeks become the norm – and that's not including field time. During the previous deployment, our regiment's scout platoons were outfitted with state-of-the-art ODS (Operation Desert Storm) Brads, as our actual vehicles had been stripped of all their mechanical innards and left rotting in the motor pools of Fort Carson for the past year and a half. This time around, it's the older models we'll be taking to war. We now have the insanely arduous task of resuscitating them from the dead – bolt by bolt – for an uphill race back to the Sandbox. If that's not bad enough, orders have just come down and some of the most seasoned members of our company have been transferred to other duty stations, leaving our unit short of personnel amid a deepening workload.

But this is what I signed up for, and I wouldn't want to be getting out so long as everyone else is going back. Call that blind devotion or just plain mad, but I know these guys and we've stood through the fire. Even the ones I don't especially like have my back, and I've got theirs. Not to mention, all the new openings in Fox Troop mean I'm sure to make sergeant in the coming year. So there's plenty of room for growth, and I feel I'm up to the challenge of leading men – even if it's just a few guys. Apparently so does my leadership. Shortly after getting back, I'm made a gunner and told if "you don't fuck up, then just *maybe* we'll send you to the promotion board." Eventually, that promise comes to pass and I make rank ahead of our deployment.

As an up-and-coming leader, the greatest conundrum I face is what to make of our fresh crop of rookie soldiers arriving from Fort Knox. Most are squared away; others need some improvement. That's to be expected and can be easily corrected through remedial training. However, all through 2004 and into the following year, we keep getting these shitbags who have absolutely no business whatsoever being in the Army, much less combat.

One kid showed up with our unit patch stapled to his BDUs; Kublah Khan smoked him till he threw up. Another was severely depressed and tried twice, without success, to commit suicide within the first month of coming to Fox Troop. The first time he threw himself down a flight of stairs in the barracks, though failed to seriously injure himself. That got him placed on LOS (line of sight), where he was closely monitored following the incident. Then, while under the close supervision of an NCO, he tried slitting his own wrist with a piece of splintered wood from the chair he was sitting in. Him I felt sorry for, as he was clearly not well; the other guy I didn't pity for a second. Both men were quickly routed out of the Army, though not before causing us a lot of headaches and wasting our time – precious time that could have been spent readying the other guys for Iraq.

Though the worst of the bunch was this pimply-faced virgin who had the personality traits of a mass shooter. Not only was he an incompetent, he was a mentally unstable loner with no friends – not exactly the sort of guy you want to be equipping for battle. I remember he was an avid gamer so addicted to the internet that he'd lose track of time and miss unit formations; nor could he manage his own finances. I'm not sure if he was off his meds, or was never on them to begin with, but he was definitely in need of professional help. We knew we had a real freak on our hands when he began writing each of the *seven deadly sins* on the magazines of his M4. He didn't last a month in Fox Troop. Somebody caught him rubbing one off in the driver's hull of their Brad, so that became the pretext for immediately getting him out of our platoon and chaptering him out of the Army.

Normally, those types get weeded out in the first couple weeks of Basic Training. Though I suspect that due to the stop-loss and dwindling recruitment numbers, the Army was under intense pressure to retain as many soldiers as possible for the war in Iraq. When I went through Basic in early 2002, 5/15 Cav broke off half the guys in our unit. Two years later, however, standards were being lowered across the board in a clear push for quantity over quality. On paper, it may have helped shore up the number of troops in Iraq, but it also had an adverse effect on frontline units, as we kept receiving incorrigible soldiers. I'm just glad we got those three out of our platoon as soon as humanly possible. In Iraq, they would have been a greater threat to our platoon than the enemy.

—

When prompted, the man in the video calmly uttered his final words: "My name is Nick Berg. My father's name is Michael, my mother's name is Susan. I have a brother and sister, David and Sarah. I live in West Chester, Pennsylvania, near Philadelphia."

Under the ward of five armed men to his rear, Berg sat before a rolling camera in an orange jumpsuit, oblivious to what his captors were saying: "We tell you that the dignity of the Muslim men and women in Abu Ghraib and others is not redeemed except through blood and souls. You will not receive anything from us but coffins after coffins...slaughtered in this way." I doubt Berg knew what was coming next.

A young and well-traveled businessman, he had come to Iraq hoping to land a contract rebuilding communication antennas. Instead, he was kidnapped sometime in April 2004, and was now at the mercy of Abu Musab al-Zarqawi, head of al Qaeda in Iraq. At the close of his venomous edict, Zarqawi unsheathed a long butcher's knife and personally decapitated

Berg, chanting "God is great!" while slicing through his neck.

The video was every bit as painful to watch as I imagined it'd be. Yet out of some morbid sense of curiosity, I had to see it. As did most everyone in Fox Troop and millions around the globe. By the week ending on May 15, "Nick Berg" was the number one internet search term, narrowly besting Britney Spears and *American Idol*'s Clay Aiken for first place. In an ominous turn of events that would damn the American occupation of Iraq, his beheading paralleled an equally gruesome event – the murder of four security contractors in Fallujah just a month and a half earlier. They were in the employ of Blackwater USA, a private army of guns-for-hire headquartered in the backwoods of Moyock, North Carolina. After their convoy was targeted by insurgents and two of their vehicles set ablaze, a mob descended on the charred remains of those inside, dragging their corpses through the streets of Fallujah in a gory procession and hanging the bodies of two from a bridge on the western rim of the city.

As I read of this crimsoned trail of events unfolding overseas, it was crazy to think we had just come from there, and even crazier that we'd soon be going back. But at least this time we knew who we were fighting, and that's the first rule of war – know thy enemy. In just a few months we'd know them well.

—

On New Year's Eve, I was on leave and didn't feel much like celebrating. So I stayed in to watch the ball drop on TV. As I sat in my mother's living room, fixated on the images of all those people squashed together in Times Square, I began to ponder my own mortality. I was struck by the sudden realization that the next time I come home, it might be in a flag-draped casket. *This could be the last time I ever see my family*, I thought. Things in Iraq were getting ugly, and there was no silver lining in the dawn of another calendar year. Not with deployment just around the bend.

Sometime around midnight, I made a New Year's resolution. A single promise worth keeping: *I'm bringing myself home alive. Screw Fiddler's Green. I'm not dying in that fucking desert…*

A week earlier, I was channel surfing when I happened upon breaking news of an attack in Mosul. A suicide bomber had waltzed into a chow hall undetected and blown himself up. 22 died, including 14 servicemen. Dozens more were wounded. News of the attack in Mosul drove a wedge through every notion of mine that we should simply "stay the course" in Iraq. That doesn't mean I thought we should just up and leave, but we definitely needed a new strategy, because what we were doing simply wasn't working. What's the definition of insanity? According to Einstein, it's doing the same thing over and over again and expecting different results. Well I'm no Einstein, but as I saw it, we could either get this thing right and win, or we could come home in defeat. But staying the course was not an option.

Chapter Sixteen
TAL'AFAR

Tel Afer was once a town of some importance; it is mentioned by the early Arab geographers. It has been three times besieged within a few years. On each occasion the inhabitants offered a vigerous resistance.

- Austen Henry Layard
Nineveh and its Remains
1867

**Tal'Afar, Iraq
April 17, 2005**

I KNEW THIS deployment would suck; I just didn't realize how badly. In the spring of 2003, I genuinely believed in our cause. But I had since rethought the wisdom of America going to war against Saddam; didn't seem like such a great idea in hindsight. This time around there's no rousing sensation of stepping into the unknown. Nor any grand illusions of bringing democracy to Iraq. We know exactly what to expect. In the preceding year, 2004, some 849 American troops had given their lives there. Mostly in the Sunni Triangle. Since then the whole paradigm of who we were fighting and why had completely shifted, and in more ways than one, it feels like we're playing Russian roulette. Statistically speaking, we all know that at least two or three of us won't be returning home. Among those of us who will be fortunate enough to survive, chances are several more will be seriously wounded in battle. Though I keep thinking, *just maybe* we'll all make it home alive.

Sadly, any hope that might happen was quickly smothered out by word of a devastating attack that rocked the 3rd ACR at its core. On April 17, Regiment's Command Sergeant Major John Caldwell had been rolling along in his Humvee somewhere in the district of Mahmudiyah, south of Baghdad, when it was struck by a powerful roadside bomb, killing his twenty-one-year-old gunner, Private Joseph Knott, and leaving him in almost as bad of shape. It was terrible. We had yet to even commence operations in Tal'Afar and already we were losing men – and of all people, Regiment's top enlisted man.

Revered by thousands, Caldwell, a former Alabama State linebacker, had a larger than life personality that suited him well. He was a barrel-chested African American whose imposing stature was smoothly offset by his easygoing personality. In the rear, he could often be spotted moving between squadron motor pools, offhandedly dropping in on his soldiers as they worked on their vehicles. Caldwell had remarkable executive skills. Without second guessing names or faces, he'd wade into a crowd of soldiers and lighten the mood with a few jokes, then move on to weightier conversations pertaining to training, deployment, and troop morale. And now he was lying on an operating table in some distant aid station, swollen beyond recognition whilst braving life-threatening injuries. It did little to ease our wary minds. I start thinking, if not even the highest-ranking enlisted man in Regiment is safe, then how screwed are we?

—

A couple days after our arrival to Tal'Afar, I'm standing around in a gaggle of Joes, bullshitting. One of our guys waltzes up with some grim intel, having just gotten back from his own little fact-finding mission.

"Man, I just got through talkin' with some of the fellas in 2-14," he says, a bit frazzled. "Turns out half of 'em got Purple Hearts. They said this place is horrible…some of the worst combat they've ever seen!"

Days earlier, we showed up hoping that maybe the situation in Tal'Afar might be different. But after mingling with some of the guys we've come to relieve, we realize that isn't the case. It comes as a real gut punch: First Caldwell and his gunner, now this…

We don't know it yet, but we've just been handed the keys to a city that our command has dubbed the "Fallujah of northern Iraq." Because Tal'Afar is so geographically far removed from the more densely populated cities haloing Baghdad, and not part of the Sunni Triangle, the situation there has all but evaded any serious coverage by the press. Instead, news outlets have focused their attention almost exclusively on the war-ravaged al Anbar province. That explains why until now nobody's heard of this place.

Tal'Afar is in northern Iraq, which people associate almost exclusively with the Kurds (who are relatively pro-American), as well as other ethnic minorities who pose no security threat whatsoever, including Yazidis and Assyrian Christians. Well, it turns out there are a lot of bad dudes up here, too.

Our mission is to relieve 2-14 Cavalry, a Stryker battalion that's been working alongside the Iraqi Security Forces in a hopeless struggle to regain some semblance of security in Tal'Afar. In the past few months the city had been overrun by insurgents. It now serves as the northern base of operations for AQI; predecessors of the Islamic State. If that's not bad enough, all the makings of a civil war are brewing among the city's various tribal factions.

Tal'Afar wasn't plunged into a state of anarchy overnight. Its violent unraveling was nearly two years in the making, and if anything, a foreseeable consequence of American policymakers' mishandling of the war. This ancient city, which had once been under the heel of Alexander the Great, is not at all comprised of American-friendly Kurds, as I had initially hoped. By and large, its inhabitants are predominately Turkoman. There are over eighty tribes in Tal'Afar. In terms of religious demographics, three-quarters identify as Sunni; the remainder are Shia.

As the insurgency spread into northern Iraq and reared its head in Tal'Afar, that previous fall, 2-14 countered the threat by launching "Operation Black Typhoon." Unfortunately, little if any thought was put into how the operation might shape the city's perception of American forces, much less the extent to which it would galvanize the Sunni majority.

In an official account of our squadron's mission in Tal'Afar, then Lieutenant Colonel Christopher Hickey observed:

> ...the operation utilized both Coalition and Iraqi forces. By utilizing a predominately Shia Commando Brigade from the Baghdad area, BLACK TYPHOON further alienated the Sunni population. While tactically successful, the operation had cascading effects that were still being felt upon the arrival of Sabre Squadron in April of 2005.
>
> The first effect created by the operation was distrust. The use of predominately Shia forces caused severe distrust among the Sunni population. Allegations of abuse, feelings of persecution, and a series of Shia Turkoman-driven leadership changes among the local government further flamed the animosity of the Sunni Turkoman. Secondly, the subsequent establishment of a Shia Chief of Police and

> his unilateral decision to fire the predomi-
> nant Sunni Turkoman Police Officers left
> the remaining Shiite security forces within
> Tal Afar nothing more than a hollow shell,
> relegated to the security of their own areas
> – mainly along tribal lines. Finally, the
> failure to maintain an adequate security
> presence or address reconstruction griev-
> ances within the city upon completion of
> OPERATION BLACK TYPHOON
> served to validate the anti-coalition views
> held by many local Sunni Turkoman.

Hastening the city's inevitable slide towards civil war was not 2-14's intent. Operation Black Typhoon, though poorly thought out, was an earnest attempt to prevent insurgent activity from spreading in Tal'Afar. Just as the architects of this war never imagined that their grandiose plans for Iraq's future would enflame long-suppressed cultural divisions as they had, stifling any hopes of national reconciliation between Sunni and Shia.

Now we had a huge job ahead of us. Not only would we be wrestling the city back from al Qaeda, we'd be doing so while trying to stand up local security forces, rebuild the city, and broker a cessation of hostilities between the various tribes. It seemed we had our work cut out for us, alright. In political terms, it's known as the "oil-spot strategy." The idea being to combat the enemy while re-enforcing security and creating opportunities for the local populace. Otherwise known as "clear, hold, and build," we're on the cutting edge of developing a new counter-insurgency strategy for Iraq. Maybe it's not the job we imagined ourselves doing two years earlier when this thing first kicked off, but it's now the task at hand – and we've only got one chance to get it right. So we're going to give it our all. Besides, we can't afford to fail!

—

Within days of our arrival, we venture outside the wire on our first mounted patrol, trailing 2-14's Strykers as they set upon Tal'Afar and pierce the outer-rim of the city, leading us in from the west. We nervously dart from one area to the next, cross-referencing each stop with the coordinates on our black and white aerial maps.

2-14 has just a week or so remaining on this leg of their deployment, as their official relief date is set for April 30. For this bedraggled troop of cavalrymen, Tal'Afar will soon be nothing more than a bad memory – a sort of living nightmare that'll contract in sight the moment they drive off out of town. We don't spend more than five minutes at any one location, as their non-comms seem wary of doing so. I can't say I blame them. Nothing would complement a year in Iraq quite as badly as getting greased on one of your final patrols.

It's dreary out and the murky skies have cast a long, darkened shadow over the city. After six months of tribal warfare and pitched street battles, Tal'Afar is a mess. Entire neighborhoods are under enemy control, and its people, hopeless and milling around like zombies, appear as if the life has been sucked right out of them. Most storefronts are black, having long ago been chained shut by their fearful owners, and the local government has all but ceased to function, leaving most residents without electricity or access to running water. Out of fear, children have stopped going to school, and their parents only leave home when necessary.

This is NOT the Iraq we left behind in February 2004.

At varying intervals of our patrol, there are small Iraqi-run military outposts, all loosely connected by heavily cratered supply routes. Within the walls of each compound, we find a platoon of skittish Iraqi soldiers who rarely set foot beyond the sprawls of razor-sharp concertina wire safeguarding their base. It's obvious these guys don't want to be here anymore than we do and are as eager to leave Tal'Afar as the men of 2-14. But they're trapped. Like us, they're now prisoners of this city.

We continue about our business, exploring every nook and cranny of our newly assigned AO. Fox Troop will be responsible for the westernmost areas of the city, patrolling an invisible fault line bisecting Sunni and Shia territories. Tensions there are especially high. The guys in 2-14 give us the skinny on key points of interest, telling us who we can and can't trust, and explaining in which neighborhoods we'll likely encounter the most resistance.

Tal'Afar was built upon the raw umber moonscape of the ancient Assyrian empire, cobbled together stone-by-stone over the course of many centuries. At its heart stands a high-walled citadel perched above a grassy hilltop, overlooking the city's narrow streets and alleyways. Built from carefully layered stone, this ancient mega-fortress resembles something right out of a History Channel documentary on the Crusades. Constructed centuries ago by the Ottoman Turks, it's now used to garrison Iraqi and American troops, and will serve as the main operational hub for the local government – once we're able to get it back up and running.

The city's timeworn feel plays right into the whole aura of battling Muslims in a strange and foreign land, and is strategically advantageous to the cause of our adversaries. For starters, there's just something about the sight of American tanks patrolling the age-old streets of Tal'Afar that's sure to draw the ire of Muslims, attracting long-bearded fanatics from all over the place. The extremists we're at war with seek to capitalize on this reality, as well as the now strained relationship between Sunni and Shia tribal factions. If American forces are to maintain any level of credibility among the locals, we can't afford to be seen as catering too closely to the interests of the local Shia minority.

2-14's as ballsy a unit as any I've seen. But they're short on manpower, and their nimbly armored Strykers lack the muscle needed to get the job done. What's more, under their watch Tal'Afar has become a magnet for hardcore jihadists. As one of the least manageable cities in all of Iraq, terrorists operate in broad daylight. They murder at will, doing little to cover their tracks, as virtually no one has the power to challenge their stranglehold over the citizenry of Tal'Afar.

2-14 couldn't pierce the city without being pushed back by an impregnable wave of enemy resistance. Their long-bodied Strykers made for easy targets, and outside of their punishing repertoire of nightly raids and daytime patrols, it was beyond their capacity to establish an American stronghold in any quarter of the city. In the end, they had lost the objective. Even worse, the Iraqi Army is too cowardly to stand its ground and fight. And whenever the Shia are attacked, the local police force responds in kind, exacting revenge on unarmed Sunnis by rampaging through their neighborhoods in paramilitary-style vehicles, indiscriminately shooting at men, women, and children.

So, not only do we have Shia militia to contend with (backed in all probability by a meddling Iran), there's the head chopping savages in al Qaeda who are trying to establish an Islamic Caliphate. Those guys are the worst of the bunch. In their eyes, even children are fair game. For instance, in the months prior to our relief of 2-14, Takfiri guerillas had kidnapped and murdered a small boy in retaliation for his family having allegedly provided American troops with intel on local insurgents. What I found more unsettling than the murder itself was the nature of the crime. They had purportedly ripped the child's upper body open and stuffed his rib cage full of explosives. Next, they tossed his remains out into the streets, their goal being to take out his relatives if they attempted to retrieve the corpse.

While slaughtering innocent civilians fit perfectly into al Qaeda's diabolical plot to disrupt Iraq, for our adversaries, no target was prized more than that of an American serviceman. It was as though each of us had a bounty on our heads.

The new Iraqi government was little more than a house of cards still under construction; one propped up by the courageous young men patrolling her streets. It was clear from the outset of our deployment that the bane of our existence would be IED attacks – a threat that had evolved considerably over the course of two years. In 2003, homemade IEDs were strung out along our most heavily trafficked supply routes, hidden beneath mounds of trash in reptilian fashion. This crafty innovation in modern-day guerrilla warfare spelt bad news for Coalition troops tasked with patrolling Iraq on foot or in light-skinned Humvees. Though a threat to be taken seriously, when detonated on well-armored military vehicles, like ours, these cheaply constructed explosive devices proved little more than menacing at best.

Unfortunately, a lot had changed since then. The IEDs were now so powerful they could flip a tank – or blow a hole clear through it, killing everyone inside.

There were other threats, also. Most of the suicide bombers in Iraq came not from local towns and villages, but from neighboring Saudi Arabia – an overwhelmingly Sunni country. Of course, there were also a lot of fanatics from Jordan and Syria, too. Nowhere was this more evident than in Tal'Afar, which is seated between Mosul and the Syrian border. We were even told that prior to our arrival, a Chechnian sniper had been stalking her streets, picking off American troops one-by-one over the course of several months. Eventually, a Navy SEAL sniper team was brought in to "neutralize" that particular threat.

In addition to a fierce overrun of locally born "backyard insurgents," a sizeable number of Tal'Afar's most hardcore fighters had just relocated there from Fallujah, where they'd recently been disgorged from their rat holes following the Marines' initiation of Operation Phantom Fury that previous November, in 2004. Many of those who were not killed off or captured in the Battle of Fallujah avoided death only to resurface in Tal'Afar. For all we knew, we had probably already battled some of these guys two years earlier, back in Fallujah. It was like playing a game of whack-a-mole, and now it was our turn at bat.

—

Most combat units filtering into Iraq would typically endure their heaviest losses during the earliest phases of their deployment. The 3rd ACR was no exception. There was a whole learning curve to familiarizing oneself with the people, culture, and terrain of Iraq's cities. Our enemies were quick to seize on this reality, striking us hard before we could get wise to our surroundings. We had learned this the hard way in 2003.

It was only a matter of how and when?

On April 28, a few others and I had just stepped out of the chow hall. As we passed a small group of soldiers, we caught word of an attack on Grim Troop. "A huge IED or something!" we were told. Within the next hour or so, more information trickled in: Four

KIA. Two guys from Grim, and two from 2-14 Cavalry.

Just as planned, Grim Troop had set out to reconnoiter the Sarai district with various elements from 2-14, the Stryker battalion we had come to relieve. They were now just two days shy of the finish line. Whereas Tal'Afar is shaping up to be far worse than we had ever imagined, its Sarai district is a netherworld of Sunni militancy, hands down the most violent square kilometer in all of Iraq – and that's no exaggeration!

As I heard, before rolling out of Camp Sykes, several guys in Grim Troop had innocently volunteered to ride along in one of 2-14's Strykers. On any deployment, intense fascination with the war toys of other military units always abounds in fighting men. I can understand why those guys in Grim Troop would temporarily abandon the safety of their Bradleys for a onetime joyride in the back of a Stryker. Hell, I would have done the same. The Stryker is a thinly armored eight-wheeled vehicle with a .50 caliber machinegun mounted on top. It's an excellent piece of equipment, though far better suited for the stony foothills of Afghanistan than the concrete jungles of Iraq.

At the tail end of their mission, just as they were exiting the city, an enormous explosion ripped through the belly of that same vehicle, killing four soldiers in all. Grim Troop's dead included Specialist Ricky Rockholt and Private First Class Robert Murray. From 2-14: Sergeant Eric Morris and First Lieutenant William Edens.

I wasn't sure what stung more: The timing of the ambush or the fact these young men never stood a chance of fighting back.

If that wasn't Morris and Edens' last patrol, then it would have probably been their second to last, because our unit transition was nearly complete. On the other hand, Murray and Rockholt of Grim Troop had barely gotten a taste of Iraq before getting killed on some miserable stretch of road in the most dangerous corner of the world. What a tragedy!

May they rest in peace.

Like that attack that had nearly claimed the life of Command Sergeant Major John Caldwell, this one seemed just as ominous – a forewarning to what lay ahead. Exactly two years earlier, Sabre had rolled into Fallujah unopposed, earning the full wrath of its people after the 82nd Airborne killed a dozen and a half civilians – a mess we inherited. But this April 28 was different. It was American troops who were dying, and for us that made all the difference in the world.

Chapter Seventeen

THE BELLY OF THE BEAST

Most people rarely venture from their homes. Streets are deserted. Vehicle traffic is almost nonexistent. Storefronts are shut. For those who knew Tal'Afar before, it is a painful memory.

- Arwa Damon, CNN

IT'S MAY 1 and today is an important milestone, one of many to come: Sabre Squadron has just assumed control of Tal'Afar. Already we're off to a bloody start. Not three moons have passed since that IED attack on 2-14's Stryker, and a suicide bomber has just plowed an explosives-laden vehicle into a Shia funeral procession, tearing asunder a crowd in mourning. Nearly three dozen are dead; dozens more are wounded. It's not how we intended to start the day, but it is what it is.

After the initial shock wears off, total chaos ensues. The victimized Sada tribe takes to the streets with Kalashnikovs, vowing to avenge their dead. They descend upon Tal'Afar General Hospital, taking it by storm so their loved ones can get treated there without fear of being dragged off by insurgents. One might think a public hospital would be neutral territory, but that isn't so. Not here. Following large-scale attacks on the residents of Tal'Afar, Zarqawi's forces are known to prey on those seeking medical treatment. Whenever they feel the urge to kill, they simply show up and do a quick walkthrough of the hospital.

If they spot someone of interest, they snatch them up. It's that easy, and nobody dares to stop them. Maybe they get held for ransom, if they're lucky. Though usually they end up bound and gagged, only to be decapitated or shot in the back of the head, then dumped somewhere in plain sight. When captured, one can only hope and pray for a quick death.

The hospital's staff are a sketchy bunch, some with questionable ties to AQI. Circumstance dictates they walk a very fine line, neither sucking up to their foreign occupiers, nor giving the fanatics a reason to kill them. While the idea of "hear no evil, see no evil" comes as second nature for the locals, this rule holds especially true for city workers. Their survival is based in part on an inherently selfish ability to stay off al Qaeda's kill list – at any cost. Even if that means turning a blind eye to the horrors unfolding in their own neighborhoods.

With the situation in Tal'Afar having come to this – what the city's mayor Najim al-Jibouri has fittingly described as a "human slaughter house," Fox Troop is called on to restore law and order at the hospital. Upon doing so, dozens of Iraqi soldiers are trucked in for reinforcement, assuming control of the facility's internal security. Sandbagged observation posts are established on its rooftops, and concrete blast walls mark every entranceway to the property. In the coming weeks, Tal'Afar General Hospital will become our home away from home, serving as a springboard for future military operations throughout the city. It's part of our long-term strategy of chasing off the insurgents and transforming Tal'Afar into an island of stability. We've got to start somewhere, and this place is it.

—

On July 9, I arise at the crack of dawn, pulling myself up from the back ramp of my Brad. It's been a long night. I'm feeling a bit off-center – sort of nauseous – like I have a hangover. Completely out of it, I nearly tip over the moment I stand up. It seems I've come down with something. Probably a head cold. Plus I'm beat – in part from having not eaten anything the night before, though mostly on account of having not gotten a wink of shuteye in the last twenty-four hours. I curse the fact that all I had done was toss and turn all evening, peevishly scratching my neck and forearms as though I were a human flea-bag. Like two summers earlier, I'm finding that *Off* bug spray is no match for the unstoppable army of tiny insects gnawing at my skin.

For the past couple days, we've been camped out of a small cluster of one-story government buildings on the southwest corner of Tal'Afar. There's an ongoing rotation between Red Platoon and ours, in which either or spends a minimum of two days in the city conducting around-the-clock missions – all while the guys in the other unit get caught up on sleep in the rear, at Camp Sykes. So there we are, minus Bravo Section.

I feel a bit queasy, but right now there's not a whole lot to gripe about. The past forty-eight hours have been unusually calm, or at least on our end.

I take a long swig of water, step down from our ramp, then stumble off to the side of our track to take a piss. As I unbutton my fly, I mosey around the front of our vehicle and glance east, towards Tal'Afar. My head is starting to throb. I take comfort in knowing that we'll be out of here in two short hours, just as soon as Red Platoon shows up.

The countdown begins…

I train my thoughts on what I plan to eat for breakfast just as soon as we get back: A huge stack of buttermilk pancakes topped with five packets of maple syrup, and a tall glass of orange juice on the side. That'll hit the spot, alright. Afterwards, I plan on taking a cool shower, toweling off, cranking up the AC in our hooch, then slipping into bed and falling fast asleep. Oh, what bliss. I can barely wait!

Then my thoughts are cut short by the static hum of our troop radio. I brace myself, knowing it can be none other than Fox HQ. They're summoning us for one reason or another. But why this early? I hope it's regarding some negligible piece of information that needs passed on to Sergeant Brentford. Or perhaps it's an update from Red Platoon, informing us they're getting an early start on the morning (which is highly unlikely because they're usually running late).

It's Sergeant Hernandez. He comes over the net, ordering our platoon to get on standby, or what's known in the Army as *REDCON 1*. Something big has just happened. As we crank on our engines and suit up in full battle rattle, we learn that one of Grim Troop's dismounts has just been shot while on a raid in Sarai.

The details aren't totally clear. But from what I understand, earlier that morning, Grim, along with the Iraqi Army and Special Forces, had stormed several buildings in Sarai, to include an elementary school that had reportedly been overtaken by jihadists. They were said to have transformed it into an enemy safe house. Grim's objective was to "confirm or deny" this intel-ligence – and confirm it they did. As they funneled into the school, a hailstorm of bullets rained down on them from the second floor. At some point they took a casualty, later identified as Specialist Hoby Bradfield. He'd been shot multiple times, at least once in the neck.

We haven't a second to waste; Grim Troop is counting on us. We know these guys. If the shoe were on the other foot, they'd have our backs in a heartbeat.

Soon we're en route to Sarai – the belly of the beast – with Kublai Khan spearheading our four-vehicle column of Bradleys. We race past the citadel, heading southeast toward Sarai, via a frightful stretch of road that I had long hoped we'd never venture down since that big raid a month earlier – where we lost Colonel Crowe.

Within seconds of looping into Sarai, an RPG sizzles past our lead vehicle, barely missing it. Un-hindered, we race into the action, positioning ourselves just a few blocks from Grim Troop, impeding other hostiles from descending on the school. Still licking their wounds from the pounding they received on June 7, it seems our adversaries have learned a few lessons from that battle – more specifically, how to dig in and fortify themselves against a much stronger army.

I'm hoping the situation will calm down with our arrival. I figure once Bradfield is stabilized, we'll pull off the objective and leave Sarai behind in a trail of dust – along with a few bad guys in flex cuffs and a cache of weaponry. As a bonus, I hope our Apaches flatten that school, killing the terrorists inside.

Damn, I wish that's what happened!

Instead, we hold tight and sit there like ducks in a row, getting shot at for hours as the situation deterio-rates and then spirals wildly out of control. As Brad-field is getting patched up, our platoon holds a small stretch of road cleaving through Sarai. Right now, we're more of a distraction than anything, a sort of mechanized defense barrier intended to draw the at-tention of insurgents. It's pure chaos. Shit's blowing up all around us – with RPGs whistling overhead and bullets flying everywhere, pecking away at our vehicles. We're basically trapped in a cyclone of enemy fire. We're pretty well buttoned up, but they've got us right where they want us.

Part of me wishes I could claim to have greased a dozen terrorists that morning, but that wouldn't be true. This is no turkey shoot; the enemy's so sneaky you almost never see him. At least not from my vantage point. I place a few rounds through a nearby window, but otherwise don't do a whole lot of shooting.

Meanwhile, with the CASEVAC underway, enemy contact picks up. One of our birds is knocked out of the fight after a burst of machinegun fire tears through its mechanical innards, damaging a fuel cell. But we're undeterred in our mission. We're not leaving here until we finish what we've started. Under heavy fire, American and Iraqi ground forces press onward in their search of adjacent properties. At one location they find a shitload of weapons and jihadist propaganda, including RPGs and a suicide vest. It's a major score.

By now the CASEVAC is almost through.

Bradfield is still alive and has just been loaded into the squadron med track. As it speeds off, an utterly horrifying explosion rings out, sending shockwaves through every single one of us. On our end, it feels as though a lightning bolt has just struck within feet of our crew. I recoil in my seat, gnashing my teeth as the city floor trembles and a hot plume of smoke and fire rise from the point of origin.

It turns out the med track has just rolled over an enormous IED. It detonated under the crew compartment, flipping the vehicle from nose to rear, killing Bradfield and another soldier.

Squadron medic Private First Class Eric Woods was killed instantly, crushed under the tonnage. Another medic on board, Sergeant Lenard Schultz, lost his right leg and suffered countless injuries. And Bradfield, who'd just survived one attack, was violently flung around in the latter, the blast having ravaged his frail body with shrapnel. He survived, though only for a short while. After being flown to a combat surgical hospital in Mosul, he was pronounced dead.

It made my blood curdle. In conventional warfare, medics and wounded military personnel are usually spared from the onslaught of opposing armies. But in the urban jungles of modern Iraq, none of our adversaries adhere to the laws of war. The fact they don't play nice comes as no surprise. After all, these are the same monsters who recently bombed a funeral procession. Here, it's kill or be killed.

As reinforcements pour in from Camp Sykes, they too are attacked. One of Eagle's tanks gets hit by an IED, and Fox Green is ambushed with RPGs. Fortunately, neither platoon suffers any casualties; though Blue 3 almost loses his head as a rocket darts over the turret of his Brad.

Then, two hours into the fight, Sergeant Brentford gets shot in the chest by a sniper. He collapses into his commander's seat and lets out a frightening howl over the radio. The airwaves fall silent. For the time being, I think he's a goner. But then he gets back on the mic and lets us know that he's okay. The round nearly penetrated his breastplate, knocking the wind right out of him and severely bruising his chest. I can't remember what he said as he came back on the mic, but our spirits were renewed by the first word that came out of his mouth.

By the time we finally exfiltrate the area, it's almost noon. As we gradually pull out, Sarai erupts in a seismic display of violence – with scores of jihadists pouring into the streets to fire on those units trickling out of southeast Tal'Afar. Along with a few ground elements observing Sarai, our choppers stay around to patrol the skies from way high up, closely monitoring the scene below. Enraged swarms of Mujahadeen are spotted dragging their dead and wounded from out of their shithole dwellings. We must have waxed enough bad guys to fill the back end of a dump truck, and right now their grief is our joy.

I wish I could offer a clearer account of what transpired that morning, but I can't. Even with up-to-the-second information spilling over the troop net, there were so many moving pieces in that fight that it's too hard to recall everything that went down. All I know is that I was scared to death. We all were; anyone who claims otherwise is a liar. This mission should have taken an hour, tops. Instead it dragged on for six.

I remember sitting there in the turret, utterly petrified, my heart pounding more intensely than a set of war drums. All while sweat drizzled down my forehead, stinging my eyes. This was the scenario I had long dreaded. It felt like an eternity, as though the hands on my watch were stuck in place. Every passing minute seemed like five. I can only image how those guys in Grim Troop felt, pinned down in that school, exchanging fire with an enemy who'd rather go out in a glorious hailstorm of bullets than throw up a white flag and surrender. God, it was awful!

Tit for tat, the "Muj" lost that morning. No question about it; we kicked their asses. But this victory of sorts mattered little, as there seemed to be an endless pipeline of Muslim youths eager to replenish their ranks. We gave 'em hell, but it came at a steep price. And with no end in sight, I had to wonder if we'd ever win this thing.

—

Sometime after that big raid in Sarai, I'm sitting in a small wooden shack at Camp Sykes, pulling radio guard. It's late at night and I'm struggling to stay awake. So I pour myself a cup of coffee.

I'm a little on edge. The past few days have been pretty wild. But we're used to this by now. Here, daily life is punctuated by well-coordinated acts of mass murder. The key is to not let it get to you, so I'm trying not to.

Just then, Beckett comes barreling in through the side door with a magazine in hand.

He throws it at me.

"Sergeant Bryan, you gotta read this…That's the motherfucker who attacked us in Fallujah!"

"What?" I reply, unsure what he's even talking about.

"The guy who lobbed the grenades over the wall of our base. Remember? Two years ago? That's him…in the magazine!"

It's the June 26 edition of *Time*. I pick it up and flip to an article entitled, *Inside the Mind of an Iraqi Suicide Bomber*, by Bobby Ghosh. There's a headshot of an Iraqi youth from Fallujah. He's going under the alias Marwan Abu Ubeida. His face is wrapped in a black *keffiyeh*, and bears a cold, murderous stare.

As I glide my right index finger over the text, I can't believe what I'm reading. Beckett's right. This is the guy. I'm seized by an eerie sense of *déjà vu*, as though I've just been yanked back to that night of the attack. The article describes in precise detail the events of our encounter:

> Marwan joined the insurgency in April 2003 when U.S. soldiers fired on a crowd of demonstrators at a school, killing 12 and wounding many more. Marwan, who took part in the protest, escaped unharmed, but the event proved decisive. He says that a few days later, he and a few friends collected grenades and small arms

from a military site abandoned by the Iraqi army and mounted an attack on a building occupied by U.S. soldiers. "They shot back but couldn't hit any of us," he recalls. "It was my first taste of victory against the Americans."

It goes on to detail how in two short years, young Marwan was lured into the ranks of Zarqawi's feared al Qaeda in Iraq network, and how his warped desire to be martyred in combat was recently fulfilled by his commander's decision to select him for a suicide mission, after months of pleading.

"He doesn't know when or where he will be ordered to climb into a bomb-laden vehicle or strap on an explosives-filled vest," writes Ghosh, "but says he is eager for the moment to come."

"Man, this whole war is a big damn mistake," I said, sipping my coffee as I handed the magazine back. "Al Qaeda wasn't even in Iraq till we showed up. Now there's five thousand little Marwans running around here wanting to blow themselves up. And to think, I signed up for this!"

Chapter Eighteen

TOUR DE FORCE

The offensive in Tal'Afar, which wound down last week, was this year's Fallujah -- a mass assault involving 7,000 U.S. and Iraqi soldiers and hundreds of Bradleys, battle tanks, artillery pieces, all combined with AC-130 Spectre gunships, F-16 fighter jets and attack helicopters.

- Michael Ware, TIME
September 18, 2005

IN THE LAST week of August, the 3rd ACR endured a rash of killings in Tal'Afar that left three dead and one wounded. It started on the 27th, when Eagle Troop's Specialist Joseph Martinez was shot and killed by an enemy sniper while on a foot patrol. Then, only two days later, First Squadron's Second Lieutenant Charles Rubado of Crazyhorse got picked off while sitting in the turret of his Abrams tank. As one of our Kiowas swooped in to provide air cover for the MEDIVAC, it too was fired on, killing Chief Warrant Officer Dennis Hay, and leaving his co-pilot CWO Gerald Torres with gunshot wounds in both legs. Torres, who must have been in a world of pain, somehow managed to land without crashing, sparing both himself and his bird.

I was on mid-tour leave when it happened, and first heard about it on the news, the evening before I returned to Iraq. By the time I make it back to Camp Sykes, the place is all but deserted. There are a few souls on post, though not many. Mostly support personnel. I'm forced to wait around for another day or so until I can hitch a ride into the city with another platoon. As expected, I missed the September 2 kick-off of "Operation Restoring Rights." We'd been planning this *tour de force* for the last several months. It's the surprise attack that'll enable us to take back the city. In the two weeks I've been gone, thousands of additional troops have converged onto Camp Sykes for a long-anticipated showdown with the enemy. There are reinforcements from Tiger Squadron, hordes of Iraqi foot soldiers, Paratroopers, Rangers, Green Berets, Kurdish Peshmerga. You name it, we have it – and they're all here to crush the enemy. With this kind of manpower at our disposal, AQI doesn't stand a chance.

When I get thrown into the fight a day later, I expect to find my platoon dug in somewhere in Sarai, exchanging lead with the enemy as they inch forward ever so slowly, block by block, taking casualties every step of the way.

That isn't the case.

Having learned from the slaughter of their brethren in Fallujah a year earlier, only a few of Tal'Afar's most committed jihadists stood their ground. The rest scattered like rats on the deck of a sinking ship. With each passing hour, they lost more and more ground. Then, not three days into the mission, they just sort of threw down their arms and melted into the general populace. They couldn't mount a good defense, not with their lines of communication crippled. The ones who did stay and fight were quickly killed off, their bodies left to rot in the streets.

Over the next few nights, the ground trembles every couple hours or so, waking soldier and civilian alike as our Apaches and Spectre gunships soar overhead, pounding targets and blowing up booby-trapped homes. And by day, we press on the enemy from all sides, cornering them in Sarai. From there, all innocents are allowed safe passage out of the city, while those suspected of being in cahoots with the enemy are held for questioning. Some fighters even try to blend in with ordinary families fleeing the city, only to get dimed out by their fellow Iraqis. Others go as far as disguising themselves as veiled women, hiding beneath black *niqabs*. But we're on to them and their little ruse doesn't work. By the time we cease all major combat operations, Tal'Afar is still standing, more than 150 insurgents are dead, and six hundred military-aged males have been detained for questioning.

Chapter Nineteen

REBUILDING A CITY

NO SOONER DOES the fighting cease than does Sabre launch Operation Unalienable Rights. Months of intense urban warfare have left Tal'Afar in a state of disrepair. In many corners of the city the electricity hasn't been on in months and there's no running water. Raw sewage is backed up into the streets. Entire families are malnourished. Most shops remain closed for business, and at least three-quarters of adult males are without a job. The schools haven't opened their doors to children in nearly a year, and civil servants are forced to conduct their affairs at the castle, under the guardianship of their American protectors. With just five months ahead of us, we're now faced with the daunting task of trying to breathe life back into this place while checkmating what remains of the insurgency.

Our enemies are down but not out, and remain but a pulse or two away from recommencing their murder spree. After suffering major losses in September, al Qaeda officially declared war on the nation's Shia population. Zarqawi released an audiotape denouncing the "Crusader-Shi'ite" alliance, falsely accusing the Americans of wanting to exterminate the Sunnis, and warning all Shia they're now fair game.

I suspect they'll fly beneath the radar for a while and then strike when we least expect it. But for now, things remain calm. At last we finally control the city and will now be permanently operating forward of Camp Sykes, living in makeshift bases. The idea is to deny our adversaries the ability to regain a foothold in the communities they ravaged. In areas deemed to be of strategic significance to our overall mission, abandoned properties are taken over and turned into patrol bases. Within a four or five block radius of these outposts, we patrol the areas on foot and establish rapport with the local community, allowing the people to voice their grievances while cleverly gathering intel on the enemy.

Additionally, we also have the elections to deal with. The October 15 constitutional referendum is less than a month out, and the people of Tal'Afar seem about as eager to vote as they are wary of leaving their homes to do so. Back in January, as Iraqis poured out by the millions to elect representatives to oversee the drafting of their new constitution, Tal'Afar was so racked by gunfire and explosions that most chose to just stay home, forgoing their right to vote. In all, only one thousand people made it to the polls that day. But this time around there's reason to be optimistic. Even with Tal'Afar's Sunni majority threatening to boycott the referendum, it's a major step forward. Not so much the referendum itself, but the fact that voters can go to the polls with minimal interference from the insurgents.

Working closely with the locals, we also launch a multi-pronged effort to address both the general lapse in security and the fact that many thousands of people are living without access to electricity and running water. One of our chief priorities is establishing a fifteen hundred-man police force that more closely matches the demographics of the city, and thus can't be used as a retaliatory force by one sect against another.

Back in May, the local police operated as a Shia death squad. They'd carry out attacks on Sunni residents in reprisal for attacks that had been carried out on their fellow tribesmen in southwest Tal'Afar. We put an end to that real quick. With so many young men desperate for work and tired of having their communities under constant siege, for the time being, differences in tribal affiliation are laid aside, loosely uniting previously warring factions. Tal'Afar is now on its way to having a fully integrated police force that's neither Sunni nor Shia, but instead Iraqi. It's not a perfect solution, but it's a start.

Our efforts to quell the violence are coupled by a major push to get the electricity back on and the water running. Our Civil Affairs team pledges over four million dollars for various reconstruction projects; a million just to get the power back on. As a result, broken water mains are repaired and new wells are dug. In neigh- borhoods that don't have running water, we have it trucked out to them until these projects are completed. There's also a well-staffed civilian workforce that be- gins repairing the streets. And at the local granary, large flatbeds arrive and load up with enormous amounts of rice and flour, and then, on our dime, dis- tribute the goods to those in need.

All of this is done in coordination with the Iraqi national government, which is finally stepping up to the plate to do something for its own people. That fall, it shelled out a little of the oil money it'd been sitting on to hasten Tal'Afar's recovery. A total of 4.5 billion dinar was dispersed among the people, appor- tioning each family with the equivalent of $100.

Our efforts pay off. Soon enough, parents begin allowing their children out of the house to play, and the schools re-open their doors. Traffic picks up, too, along with local commerce. People start visiting the market again, and adults can be seen hanging out around storefronts, playing dominos and sipping chai. It's as though the people of Tal'Afar have just come out of hibernation. After all that human suffering we had witnessed through the summer, I must say the change in scenery is rather heartening. It appears there's some merit to winning hearts and minds after all. If only we had gotten it right the first time we were here, maybe we wouldn't have had to come back two years later. I mean, the country would have still been a wreck politically, but maybe it wouldn't have been as violent.

Chapter Twenty

THE FINAL STRETCH

NOT ONLY WAS the constitutional referendum just three weeks out, the Iraqi parliamentary elections were set for December 15. Suffice to say, we had our hands full. Come October, our enemies embarked on an all-or-nothing campaign of terror that spanned clear through the final three months of the year. Though Sarai was now one of the safest neighborhoods in town, Fox AO became a last-ditch battleground for the enemy. It was here they'd commit their most horrific atrocities yet. All in hopes of fomenting a "holy war" between Sunni and Shia, and preventing Iraq from becoming an electoral democracy.

Upon regrouping, AQI and its affiliates arose from their state of dormancy. Now it was game on. I had made the mistake of assuming the worst of the fighting was through. I couldn't have been more wrong. Our enemies may have just gotten their asses handed to them, but it only strengthened their resolve. Sure, the number of insurgent attacks had dwindled to around only several per week, but when our adversaries did strike, it was usually with precision and sheer brutality.

They had regained the element of surprise. I called it al Qaeda's Fourth Quarter Rampage; it cost us lives, plus our patience and sanity. In fact, it nearly derailed our plans ahead of the elections, but we stood firm.

Red Platoon, which had already lost one man, suffered a dangerously close call. They were in this neighborhood, camped out of some abandoned home when a car came peeling around the corner of a nearby intersection. The driver slammed on the gas and aimed for their patrol base. As he steered in their direction, I'm sure his face bore the same depraved expression as Mohamed Atta's as he was piloting Flight 11 into the North Tower. Both men hellbound in their pursuit of Paradise; their minds like one and their prayers the same: *Allahu Akbar! Allahu Akbar!*

But that's when you might say his plans went up in smoke, no pun intended. At homestretch, the man set off his explosives just one second too early, blowing down the front wall of the property, though causing no bodily harm to our men inside. It was a flawed impact, or what you might call "premature detonation."

However, as fortunate as Red Platoon may have been, if I recall, one of the neighbor kids was killed in the blast. So it was still a tragedy in every sense of the word. It always is whenever innocents are lost in war, especially children.

In the coming weeks, we got hit on multiple occasions. Our enemies knew they couldn't beat us in a firefight, nor outmaneuver us during a raid. So it was IEDs every time.

Red lost two Bradleys. In the first attack, a gaping hole was blown clear through the rear end of Red 2. The blast left their vehicle mangled and unserviceable, with sharp spikes of twisted metal pointing upwards around the area of impact. It happened on "IED Alley," the scariest stretch of unpaved road in all of Tal'Afar. Quite miraculously, none of their dismounts had been riding along in the crew compartment that afternoon. But if they had been…well, let's just say none of them would have survived.

In the second such attack, an IED detonated under the front-right corner of Red 1's suspension system, nearly flipping the vehicle. Fortunately, nobody was killed or severely wounded. Footage of that attack would later wind up on the internet in some al Qaeda propaganda video. It's eerie; I get shivers every time I watch it.

On a separate occasion, Blue 4's crew almost got rubbed out while traveling down one of the main routes in our AO. They drove up on an IED that detonated right under the front lip of their vehicle, scarring it some, though causing no major damage. The blast packed such a wham that it knocked the gunner right off his seat, sending him to the floor of the turret. Minus one sore ass and some rattled nerves, nobody was injured in that attack either. But had it detonated just a microsecond later, it would have ripped clear through their Bradley, swallowing half the crew in a fiery wave of shrapnel.

It continued like this for three months, with no signs of letting up. Short periods of tranquility were frequently interrupted by loud explosions. At times, it was utterly demoralizing. And not just for us, but for the thousands of helpless souls we'd sworn to protect. The locals continued to take it on the chin well through the October 15 referendum. As we'd pull out of one abandoned home and relocate to the next, terrorists would level the place we just vacated. It was their way of sending a message, and that message was crystal clear: *Conspire with the Americans, and we'll kill your whole family!*

On the southeast rim of FOX AO, there's a bustling marketplace in the heart of Tal'Afar's commercial district. Lined with shops and kiosks, it rests on a long stretch of paved road just a couple hundred meters from the citadel. This market has long been a major hub for local trade and commerce, drawing Sunni and Shia patrons from all corners of the city. Given Tal'Afar's current state of affairs, it was also regarded as a place of major strategic significance. After all, crowd sizes at the local market were but one variable through which our leadership could determine whether security conditions were improving throughout the city.

Those normally large crowds that were nowhere to be seen earlier in our deployment had begun to re-appear. For us, it was a good sign. It meant we were doing something right. For our enemies, however, it was an indication that they were slowly losing control. For their cause was much better served when the people of Tal'Afar were penned in at home, too frightened to leave.

Determined to use whatever horrifying means necessary to scare people away from the polls, on October 11, some al Qaeda-inspired maniac drove a car bomb into that very same marketplace. He set it off in the midst of a large crowd, killing several dozen and wounding more than eighty. Limbs were strewn about. Bodies everywhere. Storefronts burning. Some people dazed, others screaming. It was a portrait of chaos if ever there was one. I wasn't present for the CASEVAC. But quite a few of our guys were there, and they all described it as the most awful thing they had ever seen, the victims painted in a kaleidoscope of blood and guts.

The sheer number of casualties was overwhelming. Within minutes, a wounded mass of Iraqis appeared at the gates of our base, pleading for medical attention. I had never seen anything like it, such desperation in their eyes. All of this as others were being transported to the hospital or bandaged up amid the carnage. We didn't have enough medical supplies to sufficiently treat all of them, but we treated those we could as best we could. We did so at risk of depleting the supplies in our med bags. But we didn't care. It was the right thing to do.

Then, just a day later, some woman donned a suicide belt, waltzed into a group of police recruits and blew herself up, taking out nearly three dozen young men. Only once before in Iraq had a female done such a thing, and it was during the invasion.

Following the attacks, Sabre pumped thousands of dollars into the local economy to keep the city from veering off course and returning to its previous state. With the help of a Civil Affairs team, a compensation program was established to get the market back up and running. The attacks were "a whole new level of fucked up," to quote a friend. But instead of allowing themselves to be deterred from moving ahead with the referendum, Tal'Afar's Shia population decried the bombings and made it clear that no amount of violence or intimidation would stop them from casting their ballots come October 15.

Four days later, the referendum passed with nearly eighty percent of Iraq voting in favor of adopting the new constitution. As expected, the Sunnis stayed home in protest. But in Tal'Afar, 17,000 poured out to vote. Just two months earlier, that would have been impossible. But thanks to us it did.

—

Beyond the wire, there were occasional moments of relief. And believe me, I relished every one of them – be it a good laugh or some pleasant distraction, like watching the morning sunrise.

I remember standing in the courtyard of this one family's home, just ahead of the December 15 parliamentary election, complementing the owner in Arabic on his flower garden. He smiled and thanked me, offering us some chai as his little girl dashed over to the garden and picked me a small bouquet of yellow flowers. I pinched off several and slid them under the elastic name band on the left side of my helmet, causing her to break out in a spate of giggles.

She then ran back and plucked me a few more, each one different from the next. With a huge smile on my face, I took them from her little hands and began adorning myself with them. Soon a flourish of rain-bow-colored blossoms sprung from the buckles and straps lining my tactical gear. I looked like a human flowerpot.

More giggles.

As we continued along on our foot patrol, marching house-to-house, all those flowers drew the unwanted attention of my new section sergeant. He warned me I shouldn't forget where I'm at. "No shit!" I told him, as if the M4 in my hands wasn't a dead giveaway. I'm not afraid to show my warface, but I also know when to smile. My thinking was, if you can't get down to the level of the people, you can't win the war. Sometimes you have to put yourself out there and shake a few hands, let them know we're not the bad guys, because if you don't, somebody else will convince them that America's the Great Satan.

—

The parliamentary elections were an absolute success. By the end of the day, 40,000 people showed up to the polls – more than twice the number who voted in the referendum, two months earlier. That's a considerably impressive figure, given that Tal'Afar comprises only around two hundred thousand residents, and that the election was carried out in a friggin' war zone.

Though more important, the number of Sunnis who participated was commensurate to the amount seen trickling in from the neighboring Shia precincts. While the Sunnis had stubbornly boycotted the constitutional referendum just two months earlier, they were quick to realize that if they forewent voting in the parliamentary elections, they'd wind up even more underrepresented in government than they already were.

As expected, al Qaeda tried to scare off those hoping to vote in their first free election. They attempted to mortar the largest poll site in Fox AO. Their calculations were way off the mark. Instead, they hit two nearby homes, wounding a young mother standing in the courtyard of her house, and later that day, killing a small child who'd been playing in his backyard. But none of their vile tactics were enough to scare people away.

Our year in Iraq had all come down to this day. Never could I have imagined that our greatest strategic victory would come not in battle, but in our ability to secure a few election booths from a terrorist attack. From my turret, I observed many thousands of people exiting the polls. They strolled home in small packs, their right index fingers stained purple from having just dipped them in small jars of ink. It was history in the making. Across the globe, those watching cable news saw live-streamed images of Iraqis marching to the polls, braving possible death to have their voices heard at the ballot box.

It was an inspirational sight, but I was still a man divided. Though every shred of my being hated this war and I wished it had never happened, there was a certain righteousness to our cause in Tal'Afar. We were the good guys, and at the core of my soul I knew we'd be leaving this place in much better condition than we found it. That much I could take solace in.

By year's end, the men of Fox Troop would grace the pages of *Rolling Stone*, and later appear on the front cover of *Soldier of Fortune*. Even Bush was now touting our success in Tal'Afar. In a sense, we had just laid the groundwork by which future counterinsurgency operations in Iraq would be fought. Without demolishing the city, we had come about as close to defeating our enemies in Tal'Afar as any military unit in Iraq could have ever dreamt of doing. It was not an absolute victory, per se, but a victory nonetheless. As Lieutenant Colonel Hickey observed, "In a counterinsurgency there is no decisive victory, but the constant pressure maintained throughout the area during this time began to result in a large decrease in attacks."

He's right. Our enemies built up a lot of steam in their assiduous effort to derail the elections, but most of that activity tapered off by the end of December. Sure, they'd burn off some rage every now and again – usually by shooting someone or blowing something up. But their weakened capacity to strike us where it hurt was becoming more and more evident. We may not have been home free just yet, but as New Year's Day set upon us, it was obvious our mission there was done. We won. They lost. And very soon we'd all be flying out of Iraq with our heads held high.

Ai-ee-yah! We'd made it!

Chapter Twenty-One

THE MAYOR'S LETTER

IN LIGHT OF our accomplishments in Tal'Afar, the city's mayor, Najim al-Jibouri, penned the following letter, praising those in the 3rd ACR. A translated version was circulated throughout Regiment, and then read aloud on the floors of Congress. Hereunder is that letter:

In the name of God, the compassionate and merciful, to the courageous men and women of the Third Armored Cavalry Regiment, who have changed the city of Tall 'Afar from a ghost town in which terrorists spread death and destruction, to a secure city flourishing with life. To the lion hearts who liberated our city from the grasp of terrorists who were beheading men, women, and children in the streets for many months. To those who spread smiles on the faces of our children and gave us restored hope through their personal sacrifice and brave fighting and gave new life to the city after hopelessness darkened our days and stole our confidence in our ability to re-establish our city. Our city was the main base of operations for Abu Mousab Al Zarqawi.

The city was completely held hostage in the hands of his henchmen. Our schools, governmental services, businesses, and offices were closed. Our streets were silent, and no one dared to walk them. Our people were barricaded in their homes out of fear; death awaited them around every corner.

Terrorists occupied and controlled the only hospital in the city. Their savagery reached such a level that they stuffed the corpses of children with explosives and tossed them into the streets in order to kill grieving parents attempting to retrieve the bodies of their young.

This was the situation of our city until God prepared and delivered unto them the courageous soldiers of the Third Armored Cavalry Regiment, who liberated this city, ridding it of Zarqawi's followers after harsh fighting, killing many terrorists, and forcing the remaining butchers to flee the city like rats to the surrounding areas, where the bravery of other Third Armored Cavalry Regiment soldiers in Sinjar, Rabiah, Zumar, and Avgani finally destroyed them.

I have met many soldiers of the Third Armored Cavalry Regiment; they are not only courageous men and women, but avenging angels sent by The God Himself to fight the evil of terrorism.

The leaders of this Regiment, Colonel McMaster, Colonel Armstrong, Lieutenant Colonel Hickey, Lieutenant Colonel Gibson, and Lieutenant Colonel Reilly embody courage, strength, vision, and wisdom. Officers and soldiers alike bristle with the confidence and character of knights in a bygone era.

The mission they have accomplished, by means of a unique military operation, stands among the finest military feats to date in Operation Iraqi Freedom and truly deserves to be studied in military science. This military operation was clean, with little collateral damage, despite the ferocity of the enemy. With the skill and precision of surgeons they dealt with the terrorist cancers in the city without causing unnecessary damage.

God bless this brave Regiment; God bless the families who dedicated these brave men and women. From the bottom of our hearts, we thank the families. They have given us something we will never forget.

To the families of those who have given their holy blood for our land, we all bow to you in reverence and to the souls of your loved ones. Their sacrifice was not in vain. They are not dead, but alive, and their souls are hovering around us every second of every minute. They will never be forgotten for giving their precious lives. They have sacrificed that which is most valuable.

We see them in the smile of every child and in every flower growing in this land. Let America, their families, and the world be proud of their sacrifice for humanity and life. Finally, no matter how much I write or speak about this brave Regiment, I haven't the words to describe the courage of its officers and soldiers. I pray to God to grant happiness and health to these legendary heroes and their brave families.

Epilogue
THE HOMEFRONT

Colorado Springs, Colorado
February 21, 2006

THE FEELING WAS much different coming off our unit's *second* deployment to Iraq. There were fewer camera flashes, less balloons, and not as many party streamers. If there were any reporters at all, the only ones covering the event would have been with the Fort Carson *Mountaineer* and maybe the Colorado Springs *Gazette*. Perhaps it's just my imagination, but as we exited the shuttle busses that carried us there, those awaiting our arrival seemed less riveted by our presence than before. This time around, they looked at us not so much as heroes, but as a distinct class of men to be pitied for what we had just lived through. I don't know; maybe they no longer believed in our cause and were just glad to have us back.

But that sure wasn't the case in 2004. When we came home from Iraq two years earlier, virtually all of Colorado Springs was festooned in yellow ribbons, affirming local support for the troops, and "welcome home" banners hung from every overpass on S. Academy Boulevard, near base.

I even remember every man in our regiment being presented a special "thank you" coin from Anheuser-Busch, the largest brewery in the US. At 1.6 ounces, it was twice the weight of an Eisenhower cupronickel dollar, and slightly larger in diameter. Engraved on the front was a bald eagle with a bright

American flag in the backdrop, along with shiny gold lettering on both sides and a commixture of other patriotic slogans and imagery. On the back it read: "SALUTING THOSE WHO PROUDLY SERVED." There are 300K of those coins in circulation. I still have mine; number: 111,235.

However, a lot had changed since then. Apparently we were no longer America's cause célèbre. As public support for the war began to wane, so did people's interest in keeping up with the events related to it. Because so few were personally affected by the ongoing conflict in Iraq, the masses just sort of buried their heads in the sand, tuning out the ugly realties of this war. Instead, people refocused their attention on the random spatter of day-to-day bullshit that clutters the human mind: mostly sports and reality TV. Slowly, the public grew more interested in actress Lindsay Lohan's coke addiction than the immense sacrifices of those shedding their blood in the far-off sands of Iraq. It wasn't that the American public had forgotten about us; it just seemed we were no longer foremost in their thoughts and prayers. But whatever – just spare me the crocodile tears.

—

Following our 2006 homecoming ceremony, I woke up the next morning in the hallway of some roadside hotel. I was hungover and wishing I hadn't gone out the night before. I was the only person awake. Everyone else in our little circle of friends was still fast asleep, with some passed out on the floor in the room behind me. I can't even say for sure what led me to bed down out in the hallway of all places, but for one reason or another I did, using my jacket as a pillow.

Though I had some recollection of how I got there, I had no idea when I'd be leaving. It seemed that Beckett had "lost" his truck. He lent it to one of our buddies the night before, and now that person had no idea what bar he left it at.

On that early a morning, I'd normally be fast asleep. But to ring in the celebration of our long-awaited return, every unwed soldier in Fox Troop set upon Colorado Springs in search of a good time. What I really needed was sleep, and lots of it. I had been awake for going on two days, and was still jet-lagged from the long flight home. I would have gone to bed earlier that night, but I got coerced into going out with the guys for "a couple drinks." Well, as is too often the case, one drink turned into three or four, then quite a few more.

So there I was, lying in a hallway…

I could see a kitchen off in the distance. I figured a little caffeine might help me shake my hangover, so I pulled myself up off the floor, my nose following the bold scent of freshly percolating coffee. The TV was on and I noticed that the hotel staff had set out a box of donuts and a small basket of fruit. So I grabbed a plate, loaded up on food, poured myself a hot cup of coffee, and then took a seat, leaning back in my chair. With the room spinning and my liver still processing the alcohol that was coursing through my veins, the aftereffects of the previous night were really bearing down on me. I had a throbbing headache and felt a little off-balance. And though I was starving for something to eat, I wasn't so sure I'd be able to keep my food down.

As I sat there, I started to fiddle with the aluminum memorial bracelet on my left wrist. In remembrance of our dead, Fox Troop had ordered a whole bunch of them online. It was our way of assuring we'd carry their names with us the rest of our days. With a heavy heart, I dragged my right thumb over the inscription:

SGT JACOB SIMPSOM
F TRP 2/3 ACR KIA 16 MAY 05

SIMPSOM. All I could do was shake my head. The company we purchased them from had botched the spelling of his last name. Though an honest mistake, I took offense. As far as I'm concerned, if you work in the engraving-the-names-of-dead-servicemen-on-small-metal-bracelets industry and it's beyond your ability to not screw up the spelling of a dead American soldier's last name, then maybe you should consider a new career. The guy had a last name, and it was Simpson: S-I-M-P-S-O-N.

On May 16, 2005, Simpson had been guarding the front gates of Tal'Afar General Hospital. As his shift wound to an end, he returned to the building his platoon was camped out of. He ascended the stairwell, waltzed into Red's sleeping quarters and immediately grounded his gear. As the rest of his platoon joked and played cards, he raced off down the hallway to the latrine. Minutes later, as he finished his business and stepped out of the restroom, an RPG came rocketing in through the hallway window, ricocheting off the wall and striking him in the head. It was a one-in-a-million shot. Here today, gone tomorrow. I'm just glad he didn't suffer any. Today he occupies a plot in Section X of the Willamette National Cemetery in Portland, Oregon.

May he rest in peace.

Nor would Simpson be the only member of Fox Troop to take his last breath in Iraq. There was also Sergeant Tyrone Chisholm of Savannah, Georgia, a twenty-seven year old father of two. He died on November 11, swallowed up in the nearly impenetrable hull of his Abrams tank by an IED.

Though I didn't know "Chiz" as well as I would have liked to, I had always gotten along with the man.

He was a tall, lanky black guy who spoke in a thick Southern drawl. Laidback and always full of cheer, that's how I remember him. A damn hard worker, too, and a great NCO. He'll be missed.

May he also rest in peace.

Bizarrely enough, in the rear Chiz had roomed with Simpson, who was killed six months earlier in that RPG attack on the hospital. Together they maintained an apartment just outside the north gates of Fort Carson. By sheer coincidence, Chiz died on Veterans' Day – which, believe it or not, would have been Simpson's twenty-fifth birthday. It's stranger than fiction, but I swear it's true.

While Chiz and Simpson were the only two in Fox Troop to die on our second deployment to Iraq, there were a lot of close calls.

Like this one time, our platoon got word that some guy was rigging an abandoned home with explosives. Since one of our squads was already out prowling the streets, they were the first to come peeling onto the scene. As the rest of us piled into our Brads, they stayed put outside the objective, choosing to wait on reinforcements before entering the property.

In the past two years I had been on my fair share of wild goose chases, and had long ago stopped taking these "intelligence" reports at face value. I just assumed this was another bullshit mission based on bullshit intel.

Well not this time…

At just a minute out from our arrival, the entire building exploded. *Kabooooom!* It was a perfect lateral blast, flattening the property and showering those on site with raw chunks of brick and mortar. The structure had been wired to blow, and when it did, it damn near came down right on top of our platoon. Whoever did it, they had patiently waited for us, hoping to bury our dismounts under the rubble by triggering the explosives with a remote-controlled device. In fact, the people who called it in were probably the ones who set it off.

From their vantage point, they must have assumed we had already charged inside. Maybe the triggerman thought we were in there hanging around, admiring his handiwork. Had we arrived just a couple minutes earlier, half our platoon would have been eaten alive in the blast. I doubt our bodies would have even been recognizable. We'd be little more than ground meat, crushed between rebar and thousand-pound blocks of concrete – and perhaps the most casualty-ridden platoon of American soldiers to have ever stepped foot in Iraq. Like those few lucky New Yorkers you read of who were employed at the World Trade Center and called off from work on 9/11, a mere two minutes spared us from no uglier a fate.

But now I just wanted to put all that behind me. After all, I had made it home. I was set to process out of the Army in four months, and didn't want to think about what I saw over there.

So I redirected my attention to the morning news. Then something grabbed my attention, causing my ears to perk up. There had just been a major bombing in Iraq – no surprise. Lately, that's all people seemed to hear about – daily bombings in Iraq and the ever-rising toll of dead American servicemen. But this was different. It wasn't the number of casualties that stood out, but the target itself: the al Askari mosque in Samarra, better known as "the Mosque of the Golden Dome." Built in 944 AD, it's one of the holiest sites in all of Shia Islam. One of the oldest, too. But it's more than just a house of worship – this mosque is a symbol of Iraq itself. There it stood for eleven centuries, its iconic golden dome and minarets penetrating the skies of Samarra. And now there it was on TV, in a miserable heap of rubble.

It was pretty obvious who was behind the attack: al Qaeda. It had to be. That kind of viciousness is in close keeping with their pathological bloodlust. And if it wasn't them, then it was some twisted band of individuals affiliated with their organization – perhaps an even more radical splinter group. On and off, Iraq's Sunni and Shia have clashed for over a thousand years. And for the last three, the tensions between them had been steadily rising. Now things had just boiled over, begetting a new cycle of sectarian violence that was sure to reach every province in Iraq.

To those Americans catching this broadcast as they headed out the door on their way to work, it wasn't worth a second of their time to stay and watch. After all, it was just a mosque, and nothing less is to be expected of Muslims. Right? But I knew exactly what it meant. Iraq was about to come unspooled, and it'd be our troops who'd bear the fallout from this attack, as another two thousand Americans would have their lives cut short over there.

I left Iraq cautiously optimistic about its future. I had hoped that 2006 would be some kind of turning point in the war, and that after the turmoil of the last three years, the situation there would gradually cool down, ushering in a period of relative calm. But I was now realizing that wouldn't be the case. Things were about to get much worse.

By year's end, the country would be fully embroiled in civil war. Over one hundred thousand civilians would perish, and four-and-a-half million would be displaced. In Tal'Afar, where Simpson and Chiz and so many other fine young men had given their lives, the city would once again be plunged into a state of anarchy. And in neighboring Sinjar, where most of our unit's ethnically Yazidi interpreters were from, 796 civilians would be vaporized in a single coordinated bombing – the largest terrorist attack since 9/11. But the American public wouldn't hear too much about it. Instead, they'd be focused on the news surrounding Lindsay Lohan's recent DUI.

It was simply heart-wrenching, just thinking about it. So I shut off the television and finished my coffee in silence. I was relieved to be washing my hands of that tortured land. As I sat there, I told myself it was time to put what I saw behind me, and to start looking ahead to the future. Though at the core of my soul, I knew I'd never be the same person I used to be, as Iraq would forever be a part of me, and I a part of it.

In remembrance of

Captain Joshua T. Byers
KIA July 23, 2003
Ramadi, Iraq

Sergeant Jacob M. Simpson
KIA May 16, 2005
Tal'Afar, Iraq

Lieutenant Colonel Terrence K. Crowe
KIA June 7, 2005
Tal'Afar, Iraq

Sergeant Tyrone L. Chisholm
KIA November 11, 2005
Tal'Afar, Iraq

NOTES AND ACKNOWLEDGEMENTS

First and foremost, I'd like to thank Marianne Page for agreeing to proofread my initial manuscript. I also value her various editorial contributions to this project. I'd also like to thank Zachary Sestak for writing the product description of this book. His words were a wonderful addition to my own. If I was half the writer he is, this book would have turned out much better.

Additionally, I'd like to note that all material cited herein has been referenced below. With that material I have also provided a wealth of historical references that serve to validate my story, providing the reader with web links for easy access. Finally, the photo on the front cover of this book is one of me in the turret of Blue 2 during a raid in Tal'Afar. It was taken in the summer or fall of 2005. The rear cover features an overhead view of Tal'Afar.

Prologue:

Hickey, Christopher M., Lieutenant Colonel. MEMORANDUM FOR THE RECORD. "SUBJECT: 2/3 ACR Actions in During Operation Iraqi Freedom." 30 Jan 2006. *Department of the Army, Headquarters, 2nd Squadron, 3rd Armored Cavalry Regiment, Forward Operating Base Sykes, Tal'Afar, Iraq, APO AE 09379*

Combat Zone Season 1, Ep. 1. "Battle of Tal Afar," The Military Channel.

"Fallen Heroes of Operation Iraqi Freedom," Army Lt. Col. Terrence K. Crowe.
http://www.fallenheroesmemorial.com/oif/profiles/croweterrenc
ek.html

Chap. 1
Armon, Rick. "Summit County Has Third Most Methamphetamines Sites In the U.S," *Ohio.com.* 5 Sep. 2008

http://www.ohio.com/news/summit-county-has-third-most-
\methamphetamine-sites-in-u-s-1.111446

The Urban Dictionary. "Ashtabula"
http://www.urbandictionary.com/define.php?term=Ashtabul a

ARMY STRONG. "Cavalry Scout (19D)"
http://m.goarmy.com/careers-and-jobs/browse-career-a nd-job-
categories/combat/cavalry-scout.m.html

Chap 2.
Leo III, Shane. "Website Again Ranks Military Among Worst
Jobs," *Stars and Stripes.* 23 Apr 2013.
http://www.stripes.com/blogs/stripes-central/stripes-central-
1.8040/website-again-ranks-military-among-worst-jobs-
1.217803

Chap. 3
Published by 3rd Cavalry Public Affairs in collaboration with
the Third Cavalry Museum (Fort Hood Texas), "The History,
Customs, and Traditions of the 3rd Cavalry Regiment."
http://www.hood.army.mil/3rd_cr/files/pdfs/BloodAndSteel.pdf

Congressional Medal of Honor Society. "Wetzel, Gary George."
http://www.cmohs.org/recipient-detail/3440/wetzel-gary-
george.php

Associated Press. "Saddam's Chemical Belt: Report." 1 Mar.
2003.
http://www.freerepublic.com/ focus/f-news/854171/posts

Chap. 4
Kristol, William. "The Defense Secretary We Have," *The Washington Post.* 15 Dec. 2004.
http://www.washingtonpost.com/wp-dyn/articles/A132-
2004Dec14.html

"The Marine Behind American Flag Controversy," *ABC, Good
Morning America.* 10 Apr. 2003.
http://abcnews.go.com/GMA/story?id=125241&page=1

Chap. 5

"Oral History: Norman Schwarzkopf," PBS Frontline.
http://www.pbs.org/wgbh/pages/frontline/gulf/oral/schwarzkopf/
1.html

Giordono, Joseph. "U.S. Troops Revisit Scene of Deadly Gulf
War Barrage," Stars and Stripes. 23 Feb 2003.
http://www.stripes.com/military-life/u-s-troops-revisit-scene-of-
deadly-gulf-war-barrage-1.5305

"Meal, Ready-to-Eat." http://en.wikipedia.org/wiki/MRE

Londoño, Ernesto. "Surviving, but Hardly Thriving," *The Washington Post*. 24 Jul. 2009.
http://www.washingtonpost.com/wpdyn/content/story/2009/07/2
3/ST2009072303928.html?sid=ST2009072303928

"U.S. Casualties in Iraq," GlobalSecurity.org.
http://www.globalsecurity.org/military/ops/iraq_casualties.htm

Ghosh, Bobby. "In Fallujah, Where the Dead Have Become
Martyrs," *TIME*. 8 Oct. 2010
http://
www.time.com/time/world/article/0,8599,2024179,00.html

Chap. 6
Mother Teresa. "Mother Teresa > Quotes > Quotable Quote,"
goodreads. http://www.goodreads.com/quotes/1264-peace-
begins-with-a-smile

"Madeline Albright Defends Mass-Murder of Iraqi Children." 12
May 1996. *60 Minutes*.
http://www.youtube.com/watch?v=ZgrJ8gNFK_g

Stuff Magazine, Issue 41. "Miller Lite Girls." April, 2003.

Truth, War & Consequences. DVD. Produced by Martin Smith
and Marcela Gaviria. *PBS*. 2005.
http://www.pbs.org/wgbh/pages/frontline/shows/truth/

"Commander in Chief Lands on USS Lincoln," *CNN*. 2 May
2003.
http://www.cnn.com/2003/ALLPOLITICS/05/01/bush.carrier.la
nding/

Chap. 7

Frontline. "The Lost Year in Iraq – Key Controversies and Missteps of the Postwar Period," PBS.
http://www.pbs.org/wgbh/pages/frontline/yeariniraq/analysis/fuel.html

Chap. 8
Penhaul, Karl. "Two Iraqis Killed in Firefight With U.S. Troops, *CNN*. 22 May 2003
http://articles.cnn.com/2003-05-22/world/sprj.irq.fallujah.fight_1_firefight-mike-riedmuller-patrol-with-roc
ket-propelled-grenades?_s=PM:WORLD

"Attack Kills Two U.S. Soldiers," *CNN*. 27 May 2003 http://articles.cnn.com/2003-0527/world/s prj.irq.iraq.attack_1_army-soldiers-fallujah-hostile-fir e?_s=PM:WORLD

Mroue, Bassem. "U.S. Armored Vehicle Damaged in Ambush," *Associated Press*. May 23, 2003.
http://news.google.com/newspapers?nid=1891&dat=20030523&id=3V4vAAAAIBAJ&sjid=ytwFAAAABAJ&pg=4906,2234172.

Chap. 9
"General George S. Patton Quotes," *Military Quotes*.
http://www.military-quotes.com/Patton.htm

Chap. 10
"'Bring 'Em On' Fetches Trouble," *CBS News*. 11 Feb. 2009.
http://www.cbsnews.com/2100-500257_162-561567.html

"Wright, Kid Rock Perform at Baghdad Airport," *CMT News*. 20 Jun 2003.
http://www.cmt.com/news/news-in-brief/1473074/wright-kid-rock-perform-at-baghdad-airport.jhtml

Reickhoff, Paul. *Chasing Ghosts*. (New York, New York: NAL Caliber – a division of Penguin Group USA Inc., 2006), 30.

"Army Capt. Joshua T. Byers," *Fallen Heroes of Operation Iraqi Freedom*.
http://www.fallenheroesmemorial.com/oif/profiles/byersjoshuat.html

Chap. 11
"Poem: Fiddler's Green."
http://lewis184.home.mchsi.com/poem_fiddlers_green.htm

Torriero, E.A. "U.S. Gets Iranian Rebels in Iraq to Disarm,"
Chicago Tribune News. 11 May 2003.
http://articles.chicagotribune.com/2003-05-
11/news/0305110457_1_mujahedeen-khalq-rebels-iraq

Borowiec, Andrew. "Iran Leftists Gun Down Two A.F. Officers," *The Washington Post*. 21 May 1975.
http://humintel.blogspot.com/1991_05_01_archive.html

Puri, Kavita; presented by: Jeremy Paxman. "PMOI," *BBC
Newsnight*. 17 Jan 2007.
http://news.bbc.co.uk/2/hi/programmes/newsnight/6272661.stm

"Cult of the Chameleon." A documentary by Maziar Bahari, *Al
Jazeera, Witness*. 17 Oct 2007.
http://www.youtube.com/watch?v=jDlNWErYCGw

Holland, Keating. "Poll: Support for Bush, Iraq War Dropping,
CNN. 22 May 2004.
http://www.cnn.com/2004/ALLPOLITICS/05/14/bush.kerry/ind
ex.html

"The Spies Who Fooled the World," BBC. Documentary. Reporter: Peter Taylor. Producer and Director: Mike Rudin.
http://www.bbc.co.uk/programmes/b01rh8hd

"Full Text of Colin Powell's Speech," *The Guardian*. 5 Feb
2003.
http://www.guardian.co.uk/world/2003/feb/05/iraq.usa

Weisman, Steven R. "Powell Calls His U.N. Speech a Lasting
Blot on His Record," *The New York Times*. 9 September 2005.
http://www.nytimes.com/2005/09/09/politics/09powell.html?_r=
0

Neff, Donald. "U.S. Troops in Baghdad Kill Award-Winning
Palestinian Cameraman Mazen Dana," *Washington Report on
Middle Eastern Affairs*. Pg 13, October 2003.
http://www.wrmea.org/wrmea-archives/254-washington-report-
archives-2000-2005/october-2003/4810-in-memoriam-us-troops-
in-baghdad-kill-award-winning-palestinian-cameraman-mazen-
dana.html

"Cameraman's Death 'Begs Questions,'" *BBC News*. 19 Aug 2003.
http://news.bbc.co.uk/2/hi/middle_east/3162485.stm

Associated Press. "Angry Crowd in Fallujah Buries Iraqi Police Killed By US," *USA Today*. Sep 13, 2003.
http://usatoday30.usatoday.com/news/world/iraq/2003-09-13-iraq_x.htm

Hurst, Steven R of Associated Press. "U.S. Offers Condolences for Friendly Fire Shooting; Tribal Leaders Call for Strike in Fallujah," *The Florida Times-Union*. 13 Sep, 2003.
http://jacksonville.com/apnews/stories/091303/D7THHOH02.shtml

Chap. 12
N/A

Chap. 13
"U.S. Helicopter Shot Down in Iraq," *CNN World*. 2 Nov 2003.
http://articles.cnn.com/2003-11-02/world/sprj.irq.int.main_1_convoy-attack-cnn-s-jane-arraf-grenades-and-small-arms?_s=PM:WORLD

"Remains of Navy Pilot Found 18 Years Later," CNN. 2 Aug, 2009.
http://newsroom.blogs.cnn.com/2009/08/02/remains-of-navy-pilot-found-18-years-later/

"H-3 Airfield, Al Walid Airbase," GlobalSecurity.org.
http://www.globalsecurity.org/military/world/iraq/h-3.htm

Shakir, Faiz. "Smearing of Shinseki," *ThinkProgress*. 16 Apr 2006.
http://thinkprogress.org/report/smearing-of-shinseki/?mobile=nc

Associated Press. "Bush Honors Tenet, Franks, Bremer," CBS News. 11 Feb 2009.
http://www.cbsnews.com/2100-500257_162-660994.html

"Operation Rifles Blitz, Nov 20, 2003," GlobalSecurity.org.
http://www.globalsecurity.org/military/ops/oif-rifles-blitz.htm

"Bring Steve-O to the States," *Fox News*. 17 Aug 2004.
http://www.foxnews.com/story/0,293,129154,00.html

Vogrin, Cary Leider. "Iraqi Boy Informant Rebuilds Life in U.S.," The Gazette. 21 Jul 2006. http://www.utsandiego.com/uniontrib/20060721/news_1n21stev eo.html

Paulson, Steven K. "Jasim Mohammed Hassin Ramdon, Iraqi Hero Who Aided U.S. Military, Charged in Colorado Sexual Assault," *Huffington Post.* 15 Aug 2012. http://www.huffingtonpost.com/2012/08/15/jasim-mohammed-hassin-ramdon-colorado-sex-assault_n_1779282.html

Schlussel, Debbie. "Jasim Ramdon: 5 Iraqi Muslim Immigrants Charged in Brutal Gang Rape – My Chilling Connection to the Story," *Debbie Schlussel.* http://www.debbieschlussel.com/53146/5-iraqi-muslim-immigrants-violently-gang-rape-colorado-woman-my-connection-to-the-story/

Powers, Rod. "Oath of Enlistment," About.com. http://usmilitary.about.com/od/joiningthemilitary/a/oathofenlist.htm

Chap. 14
N/A

Chap. 15
Title 10, United States Code, Section 12305(a). http://uscode.house.gov/browse/prelim@title10&edition=prelim

Killers: Beheading Avenges Prison Abuse. (2004, May 12). Retrieved from http://www.chinadaily.com.cn/english/doc/2004-05/12/content_329973.htm

Lycos , T. (2004, May 18). Nick Berg is Number One Search Term With Web Users. Retrieved from http://www.prnewswire.com/news-releases/nick-berg-is-number-one-search-term-with-web-users-iraq-war-and-war-related-terms-dominate-five-of-top-10-searches-on-this-weeks-list-al-qaeda-makes-list-for-first-time-ever-berg-tragedy-causes-renewed-interest-in-daniel-pearl-74086832.html

Gettleman, J. (2004, March 31). Enraged Mob in Falluja Kills 4 American Contractors. *New York Times.* Retrieved from

http://www.nytimes.com/2004/03/31/international/worldspecial/
enraged-mob-in-falluja-kills-4-american.html

Oppel, R., Jr. (2004, December 22). Explosion at Big American
Base in Mosul Kills 22. *New York Times*. Retrieved from http://
www.nytimes.com/2004/12/22/world/middleeast/explosio n-at-
big-american-base-in-mosul-kills-22.html?_r=0Oppel, R., Jr.

Chap. 16
Layard, Austin Henry. *Nineveh and its Remains*, 1867, pages
217-218.

McMaster, H.R., Colonel. "A Message from the 71st Colonel of
the Regiment," *The Mounted Rifleman*. Apr 2005.
"http://www.hood.army.mil/3rd_cr/news/MR/05/mr0504.pdf

"Fallen Heroes of Opearation Iraqi Freedom," Army Pvt. Joseph
L. Knott.
http://www.fallenheroesmemorial.com/oif/profiles/knottjosephl.
html

Hickey, Christopher M., Lieutenant Colonel. MEMORANDUM
FOR THE RECORD. "SUBJECT: 2/3 ACR Actions in During
Operation Iraqi Freedom." 30 Jan 2006. *Department of the Army, Headquarters, 2nd Squadron, 3rd Armored Cavalry Regiment, Forward Operating Base Sykes, Tal'Afar, Iraq, APO AE
09379*, 3

Chap. 17
Damon, Arwa. "Tal Afar: Ghost Town Under Siege," *CNN*. 7 Jun
2005.
http://articles.cnn.com/2005-06-
06/world/iraq.ghost.town_1_mortar-attack-iraqi-army-funeral-
procession?_s=PM:WORLD

Hickey, Christopher M., Lieutenant Colonel. MEMORANDUM
FOR THE RECORD. "SUBJECT: 2/3 ACR Actions in During
Operation Iraqi Freedom." 30 Jan 2006. *Department of the Army, Headquarters, 2nd Squadron, 3rd Armored Cavalry Regiment, Forward Operating Base Sykes, Tal'Afar, Iraq, APO AE
09379*, 9

"Faces of the Fallen," Pfc. Eric P. Woods. *The Washington Post*.
http://apps.washingtonpost.com/national/fallen/1966/eric-woods/

"Fallen Heroes of Operation Iraqi Freedom," Army Spc. Hoby
F. Bradfield, Jr.
http://www.fallenheroesmemorial.com/oif/profiles/bradfieldjrho
byf.html

Ghosh, Bobby. "Inside the Mind of an Iraqi Suicide Bomber,"
TIME. 26 Jun 2005.
http://www.time.com/time/magazine/article/0,9171,1077288,00.
html

Chap. 18
Ware, Michael. "Chasing the Ghosts," *TIME*. 18 Sep 2005.
http://www.time.com/time/magazine/article/0,9171,1106333,00.
html

"Joseph L. Martinez," *CBS News*.
http://www.cbsnews.com/2316-100_162-703027-25.html

"Army 2nd Lt. Charles R. Rubado," *Military Times*.
http://militarytimes.com/valor/army-2nd-lt-charles-r-
rubado/1073171

"Army Chief Warrant Officer 2 Dennis P. Hay," *Military Times*.
http://www.militarytimes.com/valor/soldier/1073162/

"Operation Restoring Rights," *GlobalSecurity.org*.
http://www.globalsecurity.org/military/ops/oif-restoring-
rights.htm

Chap. 19
"Al-Zarqawi Declares War on Iraqi Shia," Al Jazeera. 14 Sep
2005.
http://www.aljazeera.com/archive/2005/09/20084914372769870
9.html

Keller, Polli. "Tall Afar Residents Benefit from Rebuilding,"
Free Republic. 10 Nov 2005.
http://www.freerepublic.com/focus/f-news/1519816/posts

Lasseter, Tom and Nancy A. Youssef. "High Voter Turnout in
Iraq Promises Fully Representative Parliament," *Assyrian International News Agency*. 16 Dec 2005.
http://www.aina.org/news/20051216103630.htm

Hickey, Christopher M., Lieutenant Colonel. MEMORANDUM
FOR THE RECORD. "SUBJECT: 2/3 ACR Actions in During

Operation Iraqi Freedom." 30 Jan 2006. *Department of the Army, Headquarters, 2nd Squadron, 3rd Armored Cavalry Regiment, Forward Operating Base Sykes, Tal'Afar, Iraq, APO AE 09379*, 46

Chap. 20
Damon, Arwa, Enes Dulami, Cal Perry, Aneesh Raman and Mohammed Tawfeeq. "Deal May Boost Iraq Constitution Vote," *CNN*. 11 Nov 2005.
http://www.cnn.com/2005/WORLD/meast/10/11/iraq.main/index.html

Damon, Arwa, Enes Dulami, Cal Perry, Aneesh Raman and Mohammed Tawfeeq. "Progress on Constitution; Attack Kills 30 ," *CNN*. 12 Nov 2005.
http://www.cnn.com/2005/WORLD/meast/10/12/iraq.main/index.html

Wong, Edward. "Iraqi Constitution Vote Split on Ethnic and Sect Lines; Election Panel Reports No Major Fraud," *New York Times*. 23 Oct 2005.
http://www.nytimes.com/2005/10/23/international/middleeast/23iraq.html?_r=0

Lasseter, Tom and Nancy A. Youssef. "High Voter Turnout in Iraq Promises Fully Representative Parliament," *Assyrian International News Agency*. 16 Dec 2005.
http://www.aina.org/news/20051216103630.htm

Visser, Reidar. "Beyond SCIRI and Abd al-Aziz al-Hakim: The Silent Forces of the United Iraqi Alliance," *Historaie.org*. 20 Jan 2006. http://historiae.org/UIA.asp

Tristam, Pierre. "Iraqi Elections: Results, Issues and Backgrounders," About.com.
http://middleeast.about.com/od/iraq/a/iraqi-elections-results-background.htm

While I wouldn't typically cite Wikipedia, the following link provides a thorough and accurate breakdown of the December 15, 2005 parliamentary election results:
"Iraqi Parliamentary Election, December 2005," *Wikipedia*.
http://en.wikipedia.org/wiki/Iraqi_parliamentary_election,_December_2005

Hickey, Christopher M., Lieutenant Colonel. MEMORANDUM FOR THE RECORD. "SUBJECT: 2/3 ACR Actions in During

Operation Iraqi Freedom." 30 Jan 2006. *Department of the Army, Headquarters, 2nd Squadron, 3rd Armored Cavalry Regiment, Forward Operating Base Sykes, Tal'Afar, Iraq, APO AE 09379*, 46

Chap. 21
Congressman Steve King of Iowa. "Letter From Najim Abdullah Abid Al-Jiboui," *Congressional Record*. 28 Feb 2006.

Epilogue
"Army Sgt Jacob M. Simpson," *Military Times*.
http://militarytimes.com/valor/army-sgt-jacob-m-simpson/861756

"Fallen Heroes of Operation Iraqi Freedom," Army Sgt. Tyrone L. Chisholm.
http://www.fallenheroesmemorial.com/oif/profiles/chisholmtyronel.html

Worth, Robert F. "Blast Destroys Shrine in Iraq, Setting Off Sectarian Fury," *The New York Times*. 22 Feb 2006.
http://www.nytimes.com/2006/02/22/international/middleeast/22cnd-iraq.html?hp&ex=1140670800&en=1077baccd068bf6b&ei=5094&partner=homepage

"The Toll of War – U.S. Troop Fatalities in Iraq Since March 2003," *NPR*.
http://www.npr.org/news/specials/tollofwar/tollofwarmain.html

"Iraqi Refugees," *The New York Times*. 2 Feb 2013.
http://topics.nytimes.com/top/news/international/countriesandterritories/iraq/iraqi_refugees/index.html

Cave, Damien and James Glanz. "Toll In Iraq Bombing Is Raised to More Than 500," *The New York Times*. 22 Aug 2007.
http://www.nytimes.com/2007/08/22/world/middleeast/22iraq-top.html?_r=2&hp&oref=login&